Mass Media in China:
The History and the Future

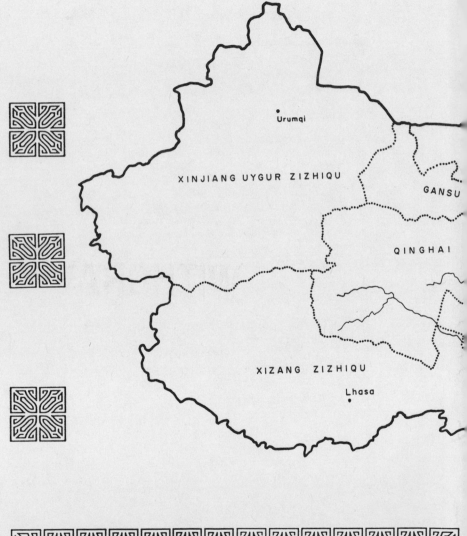

Urumqi

XINJIANG UYGUR ZIZHIQU

GANSU

QINGHAI

XIZANG ZIZHIQU

Lhasa

HEILONGJIANG

• Harbin

• Changchun

JILIN

• Shenyang

LIAONING

NEI MONGOL ZIZHIQU

Hohhot •

Beijing ◉

• Tianjin

Huang He
(Yellow R.)

HEBEI

SHANXI

Qingdao •

• Jinan

SHANDONG

JIANGSU

Yen'an •

Lanzhou •

SHAANXI

HENAN

ANHUI

• Nanjing   Shanghai •

Xi'an •

HUBEI

Hangzhou •

• Wuhan

ZHEJIANG

Chang Jiang   *(Yangtze R.)*

SICHUAN

• Chengdu

Nanchang •

JIANGXI

Chongqing •

Changsha •

HUNAN

Fuzhou •

FUJIAN

GUIZHOU

Guiyang •

GUANGDONG

YUNNAN

Xi Jiang
(Pearl R.)

• Guangzhou

Kunming •

GUANGXI
ZHUANG A.R.

• Hong Kong

Nanning •

Mass Media in China

The History and the Future

Won Ho Chang

Iowa State University Press / Ames

Dr. Won Ho Chang received his Ph.D. in mass communication from the University of Iowa and has been a professor at the University of Missouri School of Journalism for the past 17 years. A Fulbright Scholar, Dr. Chang is former director of the Journalism Computer Center and the director of the International Journalism Graduate Program at Missouri.

© 1989 Iowa State University Press, Ames, Iowa 50010
All rights reserved

Manufactured in the United States of America

First edition, 1989

Library of Congress Cataloging-in-Publication Data
Chang, Won Ho.
    Mass media in China : the history and the future / Won Ho Chang.—1st ed.
        p. cm.
    Bibliography: p.
    Includes index.
    ISBN 0-8138-0272-5
    1. Mass media—China.   I. Title.
P92.C5C48   1989
001.51.'0951—dc19   88-34694
                                                                          CIP

Contents

 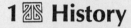

Introduction

The People's Republic of China is now undertaking drastic economic reforms while following an open-door policy in foreign relations. After enduring the turmoil of the 1966–76 Cultural Revolution, Chinese leader Deng Xiaoping and his supporters began systematic criticism of the ultraleftist ideology and practices of Mao Zedong at the Third Plenary Session of the Eleventh Communist Party Central Committee at the end of 1978. The session, in which Deng consolidated his leadership and drove his opponents out of power, is regarded as a milestone in contemporary Chinese history. This change in leadership ushered in a new era of development in all aspects in China, including the mass media and journalism.

Journalism in this changing China bears particular importance, because the Chinese people need more information about themselves and about other nations in their ambitious modernization program, while people outside China need to know more about this once mysterious and often misunderstood nation.

The mass media system in China has been expanding rapidly. The latest statistics show that this country has more than 2,191 newspapers, of which 1,240, or more than half, were founded in the 1980s. In other words, China in the 1980s has founded a newspaper every 36 hours. The total newspaper circulation exceeded 200 million in 1985, an increase of 200 percent over 1978. There were 202 newspapers for every thousand Chinese readers in 1985. China also publishes more than 2,200 periodicals with a total circulation of 138 million.

The trend toward expansion is also evident in the broadcasting system. By 1984 China had 161 broadcasting stations that were on the air a total of 2,767 hours a day. The country also had 595 radio transmission or relay stations and 104 television stations. There were 466 television transmission or relay stations with power exceeding one kilowatt. The China Central Television Station aired 454 TV dramas in 1984.

The Chinese mass media in 1983 had 259,940 employees. Among them 48,531 were reporters, editors, anchor persons, and translators. The rest were management personnel, administrative officials, technicians, printing workers, and service workers.

The function of the mass media in China since 1949 has been slowly changing. Originally it was neither the Fourth Estate nor the watchdog of government. Instead it served to inform and educate the public and to reflect the people's desires and demands. Its task was to promote stability, unite the people for the modernization drive, and contribute to the advancement of socialism in China.

Today the Chinese mass media have expanded to include paid advertisements and increased coverage of entertainment and social news — especially stories about crime and corruption in government. This is a marked change from their original role as the mouthpiece of the Party or government.

The primary purpose of this book is to present an up-to-date description and analysis of the mass media system in a country whose population exceeds one billion people. It is hoped that this book will show the changing trends in the Chinese media and promote the spirit of international communication and cooperation among Western readers, scholars, and students, as well as professional journalists. It is further hoped that this book will furnish a basis and stimulus for further research, while providing a context for comparing the Chinese media with other media systems.

This book consists of three parts: Part I describes the historical development of the Chinese media. Part II deals with the structure and function of major media organizations and includes content analyses of recent programs and publications. And finally, Part III discusses journalism education and the role perception of the Chinese mass media.

Over the years that I have been working on this book, I have been the beneficiary of assistance offered by colleagues and students, especially Edgar Snow Fellows. Since 1980, when the University of Missouri School of Journalism began its Edgar Snow Fellowship Program, about 10 journalists each year have come to the United States from the Chinese media (Xinhua News Agency, Radio Beijing, *China Daily, Beijing Review,* and *China Reconstructs*) to pursue their graduate work at the University of Missouri School of Journalism. As the director of the international graduate journalism program and the instructor of the seminar course "Theory of International Communication," I have constantly discussed the different aspects of this project with various Snow

Fellows, and I have accumulated the products of these discussions.

Some important topics were assigned to Edgar Snow Fellows as their master's theses under my supervision. I address several of these topics in my book, including Historical Development from the thesis of He Shouzhi of the Xinhua News Agency, Journalism Education from Qin Xinmin of the Xinhua News Agency, the Central Public Broadcasting Station from Yu Xuejian of Radio Beijing, and the Role Perception: A Pragmatic Approach from the dissertation of William Mulligan, an associate professor at the California State University at Long Beach. I would like to take this opportunity to express my gratitude to the Edgar Snow Fellows and colleagues who contributed their time and expertise in preparing this book.

This book uses the official romanized Chinese spelling system, known as *pinyin,* in names of persons, places, and publications. The few exceptions are the names of such well known persons as Chiang Kai-shek. Pinyin is used in names of lesser known historical figures, with their old spellings in brackets at the first reference.

Pinyin, though difficult for Americans and other English-speaking people with the frequent use of *q, x,* and *z,* is more accurate and closer to the Chinese pronunciation. The spelling system used on China's mainland before 1979 and still used in Hong Kong and Taiwan was developed by Americans a century ago.

The documents, articles, and letters were translated by the author. Because of the large number of translations, repeated indications of the author's translation were eliminated. Some of the articles and books in the Chinese language are not available anymore, and the notes and bibliographical explanations for these materials are not complete.

1  History

1 Historical Development

Introduction

China, one of the earliest civilizations in the world with a recorded history of about 3,600 years, was among the first nations to print newspapers. China's earliest newspaper, *Di Bao* (*Court Gazette*), which later became *Jing Bao* (*Beijing Gazette*), originated in the first half of the 8th century and continued in various forms until the 20th century.

But journalism in China, like the feudal society that lasted several thousand years, remained largely undeveloped until the late 19th century. With the invasion of China by colonial powers in the mid-1800s, Western missionaries and businessmen began to arrive. In the 50 years after the Opium War of 1840, foreign businessmen and missionaries founded nearly three hundred newspapers, most of them in Chinese. The most notable was *Shen Bao* (*Shanghai Gazette*) founded in 1872.

When China lost the war against the Japanese in the late 19th century, many intellectuals, angered by the corruption of the Qing government, began newspapers to promote their stand on reform so China would be strong enough to resist foreign aggression.[1] To advocate revolution and seize power, *Zhongguo Ribao* (*China Daily*) was founded in Hong Kong in 1900. The China Revolutionary League established as its organ *Min Bao* (*People's Journal*) at its founding in Tokyo, Japan, in 1905, and copies of the journal were smuggled into China. Many other newspapers followed suit, mushrooming throughout the country to call upon the nation to overthrow the feudal rule of the Qing Dynasty.[2]

Numerous progressive newspapers and magazines then emerged throughout the country during the famous May Fourth Movement of 1919, a political and cultural movement calling for democracy and science in China. These journals spread Marxist ideas and paved the way

---

This chapter was written with the assistance of He Shouzhi of the Xinhua News Agency in Beijing, and is based in part on his M.A. thesis (1985), "Journalism in China: A Study of Its Historical Development," University of Missouri, Columbia.

ideologically for the Communist Party of China.[3] After its creation, the Chinese Communist Party set up its own journals, which played an active role in the course of the Chinese revolution.

Before the founding of the People's Republic of China in 1949, journalism was complicated. There were newspapers, news agencies, and radio stations in large cities, owned by political parties, individuals, or foreigners; but for the most part Chinese journalism was under the control of the Kuomintang, or the Nationalists. Under the People's Republic changes occurred in the socioeconomic system, and the general tasks of Chinese newspapers became defined as "serving the cause of socialism and the people; propagating the principles, policies, decrees, and instructions of the Party and the government; reflecting the desires and demands of the people, and telling them what is happening at home and abroad; spreading knowledge on science and culture; and enriching the cultural life of the people."[4] But the development of journalism underwent serious setbacks during the Cultural Revolution of 1966–76. It wasn't until the overthrow of the Jiang Qing clique in 1976 and the convocation of the Third Plenary Session of the Eleventh Central Committee of the Party in 1978 that journalism regained respect and purpose.

Early Period (to 1840)

The Chinese press in its organized form began during the Han Dynasty, 206 B.C. to A.D. 220. Three kinds of monthlies appeared in this period: *Monthly Review* carried articles of commentary and criticism on the character and achievement of contemporary scholars and statesmen; *Monthly Dial* published the important political issues of the month; and *Monthly Bulletin* recorded the current events of the month.[5]

China's earliest newspaper, *Di Bao,* began during the reign of the Tang emperor Xuanzong (712–56), and was published until the 20th century. *Di Bao* was distributed by an office of the local government in the capital and devoted its space to official items such as imperial edicts and memorials to the throne and reports on the political situation. Early in the 12th century during the Song Dynasty (960–1279) a hand-copied newspaper called *Xiao Bao* (*Small Paper*) was published. Near the end of the Ming Dynasty (1368–1644) and the beginning of the Qing Dynasty (1644–1911), the name was changed to *Jing Bao* and it became a commercial enterprise, a daily publication in the form of a small pamphlet. The printing was done from a clay plate that was coated with a mixture of coal dust and water, so the print was not always clear. During the late

Qing Dynasty, both wooden and metal movable type were used in printing.

Jing Bao appeared in two forms, both in manuscript. The larger one, a daily, contained about 40 pages; the smaller one, with 7 to 10 pages, was issued every two days. The larger one was designed solely for high officials such as governors and lieutenant governors. The expurgated edition was designed for inferior officials throughout the province. This edition of *Jing Bao* was sold to the public at a high price. "The original design of the *Gazette* (*Jing Bao*) seems to be entirely for the officers of the government; and its publication to the people is merely connivance contrary to law, like the publication of Parliamentary speeches in England," said the *Chinese Repository* for April 1833.[6]

The rest of the press in China was silent on the affairs of government, but *Jing Bao* contained much important and curious information, which circulated far beyond its intended time and place. Through it the world became acquainted with the feelings, wishes, and desires of an emperor and his advisers, as well as with general occurrences among the people of China and of China's external possessions.[7]

Di Bao, or *Jing Bao,* was the only newspaper that existed for more than a thousand years in China, but it was hampered by the economic and political system of China's feudal era. The feudal landlord state was the basis of power protecting a system of exploitation. The feudal ruling class was composed of those who owned the most land—the landlords, the nobility, and the emperor—while the peasants owned little or no land at all. The emperor reigned supreme in the feudal state, appointing officials in charge of the armed forces, the judicial courts, the treasury, and the state granaries in all parts of the country and relying on the landed gentry as the mainstay of the entire system of feudal rule.

Analyzing the feudal society in China, Mao Zedong said, "It was under such feudal economic exploitation and political oppression that the Chinese peasants lived like slaves, in poverty and suffering, through the ages."[8] Under the bondage of feudalism they had no personal freedom and no political rights whatsoever. Journalism in the form of *Di Bao* or *Jing Bao* in feudal China served only the landlords, the nobility, and the emperor, who accounted for only a tiny minority of the population. They were the only ones who could afford education and who had access to the official newspaper of that time.

"The extreme poverty and backwardness of the peasants," Mao Zedong said, "resulting from ruthless landlord exploitation and oppression is the basic reason why Chinese society remained at the same stage of socio-economic development for several thousand years."[9] And so did Chinese journalism.

1840–1919

During the period from 1840, when the Opium War began, to 1919, when the May Fourth Movement started, the Qing Dynasty ended and the Republic of China began. It was a period when imperialism from abroad and feudalism at home changed China to semicolonial and semi-feudal status. It was also a period when the Chinese people waged a heroic struggle against the imperialists and their proxies in China.

Before 1840 Britain was the most highly developed capitalist country in the world. After gaining control of India, Britain immediately targeted China as its next prey. China was then a feudal isolationist society, with small-scale agriculture and handicraft industries as the major methods of production. The Chinese produced most of what they needed for food, clothing, and other daily necessities. Because cotton textiles and woolens produced in Britain were not well received in China, the British had to ship a vast amount of silver to China in exchange for tea, silk, and other products.

Covetous of China's wealth, the British also smuggled large quantities of opium into China. The number of opium smokers increased substantially, officials became more and more corrupt, and the army began to lose its fighting ability. Afraid that his position might be eroded, the emperor sent Lin Zexu as imperial commissioner to Guangzhou (Canton) to ban smuggling.

Lin ordered all opium confiscated and publicly burned. He then ordered that Sino-British trade be restored only on the condition that British merchants cease smuggling opium. To protect its merchants, Britain dispatched warships in June 1840 to attack the coastal areas of Guangdong. The Opium War had begun.

Threatened by British guns, the Qing government dismissed Lin and sent another official to negotiate peace with the British army. In January 1841 the draft Convention of Chuanbi was signed, whereby China would cede Hong Kong to Britain and open Guangzhou as a trading port. Unhappy with these terms, the British sent more ships to force more concessions. In August 1842 the Qing government signed a humiliating document known as the Sino-British Treaty of Nanjing.

This treaty, the first unequal treaty China had signed with a foreign aggressor, stipulated that China open five ports for trade, cede Hong Kong to the British, and pay an indemnity of 21 million silver dollars; the tariff on British goods also would be subject to negotiations between the two countries. The next year the British forced the Qing government to sign two supplementary documents stipulating that the Chinese tariff on British goods be limited to 5 percent, and that the British be given the right to rent land and build houses in the five ports. The British also acquired the right of consular jurisdiction and most-favored-nation treatment.

In 1844 the United States and France forced the Qing government to sign the Sino-American Treaty of Wangxia and the Sino-French Treaty of Huangpu. Through these two treaties, the United States and France acquired all the privileges provided to Britain in the Treaty of Nanjing and its supplementary documents. In addition the Americans gained a special privilege allowing them to send warships to Chinese ports for the protection of the commerce of their country and to build churches and hospitals in the five ports of trade. These treaties deprived China of its sovereignty.

After the Second Opium War in 1857, China lost not only more territories but also more sovereignty to Britain, France, Russia, and the United States. The aggressive influence of foreign countries spread from the coast to the interior, and the Qing government was subjected to more and more control by foreign powers. Along with the plunder, Western missionaries and businessmen continued coming to China. A number of them published newspapers, and so there is some dispute about the origin of the first modern newspaper in China. The *Culture* volume of the *China Handbook Series* claims that the first modern newspaper was established as early as 1815, but does not mention whether the paper was a Chinese-language or foreign-language publication.[10] John C. Merrill in his *Global Journalism* claims that the first modern newspaper in China was the Chinese-language *Eastern Western Monthly Magazine,* founded by a British missionary and published in 1833 in Guangzhou.[11] But Qian Xinbo of the Journalism Institute of the Chinese Social Sciences Academy suggests that the first Chinese-language newspaper was founded by a German missionary in Guangzhou in 1866. He describes this publication as the beginning of the history of China's modern journalism.[12]

In the 50 years after the 1840 Opium War, foreigners established more than three hundred newspapers, most of them in Chinese and most published in Shanghai. They included *Shanghai Xinbao* (*Shanghai News*), *Wanguo Gongbao* (*International Review*), *Shen Bao, Xinwen Bao* (*News Gazette*), and *Min Bao* (*People's Journal*). The longest-running paper was *Shen Bao* (30 April 1872 to May 1949), and the most important paper in the business world was *Xinwen Bao* (17 February 1893 to May 1949). Both were founded by foreign businessmen and later taken over by Chinese capitalists.

The earliest newspapers founded by the Chinese in modern times were *Zhaowen Xin Bao* (*Clarity News*), published in Hankou in 1873, and *Xun Huan Ribao* (*Cycle Daily*), published in Hong Kong in 1874.

The Sino-Japanese War of 1894–95 was an epoch-making event in China's modern history and also a turning point in the course of national awakening in modern China.[13] China had been defeated by Britain in the Opium War, by Britain and France in the Second Opium War, and by France in the Sino-French War in 1885. These countries were formidable Western powers; but in 1895 China was defeated by the small island country of Japan in the Orient. The Treaty of Shimonoseki at the end of this war created a grave national crisis in China and foreshadowed the partitioning of China by the imperialist powers. The resistance to the treaty throughout the nation pushed forward a reform movement already in existence.

Reform had been advocated during the 19th century by a number of intellectuals who were influenced by bourgeois ideas and witness to the intensity of foreign aggression and the inability of a corrupt government to cope with it. In the 1890s, when the problem of national salvation became even more serious, the idea of reform slowly acquired a new meaning and became a political movement with the support of the masses. Kang Youwei (1858–1927), Liang Qichao (1873–1929), Tan Sitong (1865–98), and Yan Fu (1853–1921) represented this position. They believed that the salvation of the country depended upon reform and that China must learn not only science and technology from the West, but also the structure of political institutions. They advocated adoption of a constitutional monarchy.

When news of the signing of the Treaty of Shimonoseki arrived, Kang Youwei was in Beijing taking the metropolitan examination, one of the major civil service examinations during the Qing Dynasty. He sent Emperor Guangxu a petition with the signatures of 1,300 exam candidates to indicate opposition to the treaty, and he requested the institution of reforms. From 1888 to 1898 he presented seven petitions to the emperor. Intellectuals such as Kang published newspapers, opened schools, and organized academic societies, all for the purpose of impressing the public with the seriousness of the national crisis and the need for reform. A number of intellectuals, angered by the corruption of the Qing government, began newspapers to disseminate their position on reform so China would be strong enough to resist foreign aggression. Among them were Liang Qichao and Tan Sitong.[14]

Liang Qichao started *Chinese Progress,* a magazine published every 10 days in Shanghai. The magazine criticized the government and proposed to abolish the old examination system and establish modern schools as ways of remedying the national crisis. Previously Tan Sitong and others had established a Reform Association of China for group discussions and had founded the *Hunan Daily* and the *Hunan Journal.*[15]

The reform movement of 1898, whose leading spirits were Kang Youwei, Liang Qichao, and Tan Sitong, represented the interests of the liberal bourgeoisie and the enlightened landlords.[16] The movement was favored and supported by Emperor Guangxu, but had no mass basis. Yuan Shikai, who had an army behind him, betrayed the reformers to Empress Dowager Cixi, the leader of the diehards. The empress dowager seized power and had Emperor Guangxu imprisoned and Tan Sitong and five others beheaded, thus defeating the movement.

Sent into exile, Liang went first to Japan and then to America. Hearing of a planned uprising in Hankou, he hurried back to China, but the uprising had already failed when he reached Shanghai. From then on he devoted himself solely to the task of propaganda. In Shanghai he published *New People's Periodical, New Works of Fiction,* and other magazines to explain his ideas and objectives. His countrymen vied eagerly to read them. Even a strict prohibition by the Qing government could not prevent them from spreading.[17]

As the Sino-Japanese War pushed the reform movement to a climax, it also led bourgeois revolutionaries to the political stage of Chinese society.[18] While the war was still in progress, Dr. Sun Yat-sen (1866–1925), the pioneer of the Chinese democratic revolution, set up the first bourgeois revolutionary organization—the China Revival Society—in Honolulu. After the Treaty of Shimonoseki was signed, he began to prepare for an uprising to overthrow the Qing government. Early in 1895 Sun Yat-sen established the headquarters of the China Revival Society in Hong Kong and planned for an armed uprising in Guangzhou. In October the plan was discovered, the scheduled uprising aborted, and Sun forced to seek refuge in foreign countries. But he continued to spread revolutionary ideas and prepare his organization for another armed uprising.

Meanwhile, other revolutionary intellectuals took action. In November 1903 Huang Xing (1874–1916), Chen Tianhua (1875–1905), and Song Jiaoren (1882–1913) founded the Society for Revival of the Chinese Nation in Changsha. That year Cai Yuanpei (1868–1940), Zhang Binglin (1869–1936), and others established the Restoration Society in Shanghai. Both societies staged organized armed uprisings, but they did not succeed.

In 1905 Sun Yat-sen left Europe for Japan, where he incorporated the China Revival Society, the Society for Revival of the Chinese Nation, the Restoration Society, and a similar organization, the Daily Knowledge Society, into the China Revolutionary League. The principles of nationalism, democracy, and people's livelihood were defined as the ideological guide for the revolution led by Sun Yat-sen.

In 1911, less than two months after the 10 October Wuchang Uprising, 15 provinces declared independence from the Qing government. In December Sun Yat-sen returned to China from abroad. Toward the end of the month delegates from the provinces gathered in Nanjing to organize a provisional central government and elect Sun as the provisional president. On New Year's Day, 1912, Sun Yat-sen was sworn in, and the establishment of the Republic of China was formally announced.

In the course of the revolution, the bourgeois revolutionaries spread their ideas by running newspapers and other journals. The first newspaper run by Chinese bourgeois revolutionaries under the leadership of Sun Yat-sen was *Zhongguo Ribao,* founded in Hong Kong in January 1900. One of the most influential papers was *Min Bao,* founded in Tokyo in 1905 by the China Revolutionary League.[19]

In June 1905 Song Jiaoren and Huang Xing founded the magazine *Ershi Shiji Zhi China* (*China of the 20th Century*) to promote revolutionary ideas among the Chinese students. Five months later the magazine was renamed *Min Bao* as the official organ of the China Revolutionary League.

In his articles Zhang Binglin, the chief editor, condemned Kang Youwei and Liang Qichao for still advocating constitutional monarchy and slandering the revolution. He lauded the bourgeois democratic revolution that was taking shape.[20] Chen Tianhua, the manager and main writer, wrote in the first issue that China should not adopt Japan's constitutional monarchy. The best and most suitable political system for China would be a republic, he said, but to establish a republic, revolution was necessary. He also denounced the savage rule of the Qing government and the tyranny of the empress dowager.[21] Copies of the journal were smuggled into China, and newspapers throughout the country called on the nation to rise and overthrow the Qing government.[22] In 1908 the Japanese government closed down *Min Bao.*

Another influential paper was *Zhongguo Nu Bao* (*Chinese Women's Paper*), founded in Shanghai in 1907 by the famous revolutionary Qiu Jin. She advocated the close integration of women's liberation with the liberation of the entire society. Women, like men, should concern themselves with affairs of the state and regard as their duty the liberation of society, she wrote.[23] To overthrow the Qing rulers, save the country from its crisis, and achieve national liberation was not merely the responsibility of men but also of women. She called for women's self-reliance and equality with men.

In 1915, Yuan Shikai, head of the northern warlords, who held the military power of the Quing government, forced the emperor to abdicate and declared himself the Emperor of China. Condemned by the whole nation, Yuan relinquished his crown and died in despair. Duan Qirui took over from Yuan in 1916 and abolished both the constitution and the parliament. In 1917 Sun Yat-sen went to Guangzhou where he organized an anti-Duan military government. Lacking mass support, however, and pushed aside by the warlords in south China, Sun's campaign failed.

While in power the northern warlords pursued the policy of returning to ancient ways and worshipping Confucius. The radical democrats, represented by Chen Duxiu (1880–1942), Li Dazhao (1889–1927), and Lu Xun (1881–1936), did their best to promote a bourgeois culture and fought fiercely against all feudal ideas. This struggle became the basis of the New Culture Movement.[24]

In September 1915 Chen Duxiu published the magazine *Qingnian Zazhi* (*Youth*), which became *Xin Qingnian* (*New Youth*), in the autumn of 1916 with Li Dazhao and Lu Xun as major contributors. This journal served as the main organ of the New Culture Movement, which advocated democracy, science, new literature, vernacular Chinese, and new ethics, while opposing feudal autocracy, superstition, old literature, classical Chinese, and old ethics. It concentrated its attack on Confucianism, the ideological bulwark of the feudal system. Aimed at the emancipation of the mind, the New Culture Movement encouraged the people to pursue democracy and science and seek a way to save the nation and its people.

Since the Opium War of 1840, the Chinese people had been looking to the West for ways to save China, but without success. The success of the October Revolution in Russia in 1917 brought Marxism-Leninism to China, and a number of radical democrats gradually acquired rudimentary Communist ideas. In November 1918 Li Dazhao published in *Xin Qingnian* two articles: "The Victory of the Common People" and "The Victory of Bolshevism." In these articles he praised Russia's socialist revolution and then boldly pointed out: "The world of the future will be the world of the Red Flag!"[25]

The New Culture Movement of this period still functioned within the framework of the old bourgeois democracy, but the progressive elements of China had already begun to use Marxism as a spiritual weapon in their effort to educate and organize the revolutionaries. This paved the way for the Chinese revolution to be transformed from the old-democratic revolution into the new-democratic revolution.[26]

1919–1949

Between 1919 and 1949 China remained a semicolonial and semifeudal society. Led by the Chinese Communist Party, the struggle against imperialism, feudalism, and bureaucrat-capitalism constituted the central issue of this period. The controversy fell within the framework of a bourgeois democratic revolution; however, because the struggle itself was led by the proletariat, and because its vanguard was the Chinese Communist Party, it is referred to as the new-democratic revolution to distinguish it from the old-democratic revolution led by the bourgeoisie.

The May Fourth Movement in 1919 was a nationwide student movement that protested the Paris Peace Conference, which had rejected China's demand to terminate the special privileges of foreign countries in China, to abolish the Twenty-One Demands that the northern warlord regime had signed with Japan, and to return to China the rights in Shandong that Japan had seized from Germany during World War I.

The May Fourth Movement helped the New Culture Movement by elevating it to a higher stage. From then on more and more progressive periodicals were published, and the spread of Marxism became the central thrust of the New Culture Movement. Among the most famous periodicals were *Xiangjiang Pinglun* (*Xiang River Review*) in Changsha, edited by Mao Zedong, and *Tianjin Xuesheng Lianhehui Bao* (*Bulletin of the Tianjin Students' Federation*) in Tianjin, edited by Zhou Enlai, in addition to *Xin Qingnian* and *Meizhou Pinglun* (*Weekly Review*) in Beijing.

Others included the weekly *Laodongjie* (*Labor Circles*) and the monthly *Gongchandang* (*Communist Party*), both founded by the Shanghai Party Group; the weekly *Laodong Yin* (*Voice of Labor*), founded by the Beijing Party Group; and the weekly *Laodongzhe* (*The Worker*), founded by the Guangzhou Party Group. These magazines helped integrate Marxism-Leninism with the labor movement in China and promote the new-democratic revolution in the country.

Meanwhile, many progressive newspapers appeared. Some of the newspaper supplements in particular played an important role in spreading bourgeois learning and culture as part of the New Culture Movement. The four known as supplements of the New Culture Movement were those of *Chen Bao* (*Morning Post*); *Juewu* (*Awakening*), a supplement of *Minguo Ribao* (*Republic Daily*); *Xue Deng* (*Academic Lamp*), the supplement of *Shishi Xinbao* (*China Times*); and the supplement of *Jing Bao* (*Capital Daily*).

After Russia's October Revolution, Li Dazhao gradually but decidedly took the stance of a Marxist, becoming the earliest Marxist Communist in China. In 1918 he worked on the editorial board of *Xin Qingnian* and founded *Meizhou Pinglun* with Chen Duxiu. Both were later founders of the Communist Party of China. Li supervised the publication of the supplement of *Chen Bao* in 1919 and, at the same time, assisted Beijing University students in publishing *Guomin* (*Nation*) and *Xinchao* (*New Trend*).

Also in 1919 Mao Zedong was in Beijing on behalf of the Hunan Students' Association to seek public support for its struggle against the local warlord Zhang Jingyao. Mao founded the Civilians' News Agency, issuing 150 news bulletins every day to be sent to Beijing, Tianjin, Shanghai, and Hankou to expose Zhang Jingyao's crimes.

From its beginning the Communist Party of China paid great attention to the role of newspapers in the revolutionary cause. Soon after its founding in July 1921, the Party set up newspapers in Beijing, Shanghai, Wuhan, Jinan, Guangzhou, and other locations. The most influential were *Laodong Zhoukan* (*Labor Weekly*) in Shanghai and *Gongren Zhoukan* (*Workers' Weekly*) in Beijing. *Laodong Zhoukan* was an organ of the Chinese Labor Union Secretariat and the first national newspaper for workers. It began publication in the summer of 1921 and was banned on 9 June 1922 by the Shanghai Municipal Council in the international settlement because of the "crimes" of publishing extremist opinions and advocating labor revolution. *Gongren Zhoukan* was published in the name of the Workers' Weekly Society by the Communist Party in Beijing beginning in July 1921. In May 1922 the Chinese Labor Union Secretariat moved to Beijing from Shanghai, and not long after *Gongren Zhoukan* replaced *Laodong Zhoukan* as the organ of the secretariat. In 1924 it became the journal of the Chinese National Federation of Railway Unions. It ceased publication in December 1925 after 133 issues.

Chinese Communist Party periodicals included *Xiangdao Zhoukan* (*Guide Weekly*), its first central organ, published from September 1922 to July 1927; *Qianfeng Zhoukan* (*Vanguard Weekly*), a quarterly published in Guangzhou from July 1923 to February 1924; and the quarterly *Xin Qingnian* (*New Youth*), published from June 1923 to July 1926.

The Chinese Socialist Youth League (the predecessor of the Chinese Communist Youth League), which was created in 1920 before the founding of the Communist Party of China, made ideological and organizational preparations for the founding of the Party. From 1920 to 1927 the Youth League had a great influence among the Chinese people, especially among students and young intellectuals.[27] In January 1922 the Youth League set up its official newspaper *Xianqu* (*Pioneer*) in Beijing to promote Marxism and the views of the Communist Party and to report the work of the Youth League and the youth movement, as well as the conditions and experiences of other youth organizations around the world. It ceased publication in August 1923.

Two months later the weekly *Zhongguo Qingnian* (*Chinese Youth*) emerged as the central organ of the Youth League. Its role was to publicize the position of the Youth League as well as the viewpoints and opinions of young people on all political issues, and to promote Marxist and Communist ideas and theories and fight imperialism and warlords.[28]

Famous early Communists Yun Daiying, Xiao Chunu, and Deng Zhongxia worked with, or ran, the weekly, and Mao Zedong and Zhu De wrote articles for it.

In 1919–20 some 1,600 young people left China for Europe to study while working. Supported by Li Dazhao, Chen Duxiu, and Mao Zedong, these people went to the West to seek ways of remolding China. Chinese students in France launched three patriotic movements in 1921. Two of them reported back to China through Zhou Enlai, who was also studying there; reports carried in Chinese papers won the sympathy and support of the nation.

The year after Zhou Enlai's report from Paris on the Chinese students' movement against a government decision to borrow money from France on unfavorable terms, details of the Sino-French negotiations about war reparations appeared on the front page of *Jing Bao* in Beijing. The reporter turned out to be the noted journalist Shao Piaoping, whose career began after the founding of the Chinese Republic in 1912. During that time he ran newspapers and agencies and worked as a publisher, editor, reporter, and teacher of journalism. "He was really a versatile newsman, hard to come by in the early years of the Chinese Republic," said Fang Hanqi, a professor of journalism at the Chinese People's University in Beijing.[29]

Yet the high point of Shao's career did not come until 1916, the beginning of his most prolific decade. During that period he worked as a special correspondent in Beijing for a Shanghai newspaper, and then in 1918 started *Jing Bao* where he worked for nine years as the publisher and chief editor. Shao also opened a news agency in Beijing in 1916, one of the earliest and most prestigious. He regretted that foreign agencies had monopolized the news service in China.

Shao Piaoping has been considered a pioneer in China's journalism, not only because of his long tenure as a journalist but because of his strong sense of responsibility. This motto hung in his office: "Iron Shoulders and Poignant Hand," to show his determination to uphold justice. Warlords and politicians tried to influence Shao with financial and other favors in an attempt to buy his support and manipulate the press, but Shao saw through their tricks and never hid his contempt for them. He once resisted a donation of three hundred thousand yuan (Chinese currency) from warlord Zhang Zuolin and continued to expose the evils of his forces. "The mission of a journalist," Shao wrote in an article, "must be based on ethics and integrity, guided by justice and courage, and promoted by a strong sense of responsibility."[30]

He expressed his support for the policies of the revolutionary government under Dr. Sun Yat-sen, and hailed the victory of the October

Revolution in Russia. When diplomatic relations between China and the Soviet Union were established in 1924, Shao devoted several full pages to the occasion, and a special supplement was devoted to the 105th anniversary of Marx's birthday in 1923.

Despite Shao's denial, some historians argued that he was one of the early members of the Chinese Communist Party. "Perhaps he kept his membership secret deliberately to go on working as a public figure," said Fang Hanqi. "We have enough evidence."[31] Nevertheless, Shao kept close contract with party leaders in the North and helped them to train personnel, offered information, and printed books. He wrote several books to publicize socialism—for example, A Study of New Russia. Shao was imprisoned four times and was considered by the warlords a thorn in their flesh. When Zhang Zuolin's forces occupied Beijing in 1926, friends warned Shao that he was in danger and urged him to leave. But he preferred to walk to his death rather than flee his duty. On 22 April he was arrested. Two days later he was executed on charges of being a Communist.

Shao's experience shaped his code of ethics. He believed in a free and independent press, with public interest as its highest consideration. He argued that a reporter should act as "a king without crown" or "a fair-minded judge" who took no sides. "Truthfulness is the backbone of news, while human interest serves as flesh and blood," he wrote.[32] His theories proved successful and earned his paper, Jing Bao, a circulation of six thousand, a large number at that time.

To spread his ideas Shao taught in several universities and wrote two textbooks. He also invited some friends to set up a journalism association in 1918, the first of its kind in China. Mao Zedong belonged to the association for six months. Later, while talking to Edgar Snow in the 1930s, Mao praised Shao as "a liberal with fervent idealism and excellent qualities."[33]

After the failure of the 1911 Revolution, Sun Yat-sen continued his struggle for democratic revolution but failed each time. The Chinese Communist Party admired Sun's dauntless spirit and sent Li Dazhao and Lin Boqu, another veteran member, to provide him with direct aid. Meanwhile, the Soviet Union also suggested to Sun that a party uniting the workers and peasants be established and a military academy and a revolutionary armed force be organized also. Sun welcomed the assistance of the Chinese Communist Party and the Soviet Union and began to reorganize his Kuomintang.[34] (The China Revolutionary League was renamed Kuomintang after the Revolution of 1911.)

To achieve Kuomintang-Communist cooperation as early as possible, the Communist Party criticized some of Sun's erroneous ideas through its central organ, *Xiangdao Zhoukan,* and other journals. Sun was criticized for uniting some warlords to oppose other warlords and for trying to resolve the contradictions among them through disarmament to achieve peaceful unification. He was also accused of attempting to cooperate with imperialism and paying greater attention to military activity than to propaganda and organization among the people. This criticism and advice, which caught the attention of Sun, played a positive role in the Kuomintang-Communist cooperation.[35] A number of Communists soon joined the Kuomingtang. Several prominent Communist leaders, including Li Dazhao, Mao Zedong, Lin Boqu, and Qu Qiubai, participated in the leadership work of the Kuomintang's First National Congress and were later elected as members or alternate members of the Kuomintang's Central Executive Committee.

While Mao was acting director of propaganda of the Kuomintang, he also worked as the chief editor of its central organ, *Zhengzhi Zhoukan (Political Weekly)*, which began publication in December 1925. Because the organ carried documents of the party, reports of its meetings, and articles by noted Kuomintang figures, it played a significant role in fighting the rightists within the party and had a wide influence on the expedition against the northern warlords. Mao wrote many articles to refute the attacks of Kuomintang rightists on Sun's policies of alliance with Russia, alliance with the Communist Party, and aid to peasants and workers. He stressed that the primary goal of the Chinese revolution was to overthrow the rule of imperialists and warlords. The Kuomintang rightists had, in fact, become the tools of imperialism and the defenders of warlords, he wrote.[36]

The weekly played a most important role in isolating and attacking the rightists and leading public opinion toward support for the Kuomintang's Central Executive Committee in Guangzhou and ultimately for the Chinese revolution. Following the death of Sun, Chiang Kai-shek gradually usurped the power of the Kuomintang and of the army. In 1926 he forced the Communists out of the Kuomintang. Mao resigned and the weekly, *Zhengzhi Zhoukan,* ceased publication.

While the northern expeditionary army was in its victorious march and the worker and peasant movement was developing, Chiang Kai-shek staged a coup in Shanghai on 12 April 1927, killing many workers and Communists. After the First Revolutionary Civil War (1924–27) failed, the Kuomintang of Chiang Kai-shek replaced the northern warlords with a nationwide regime that represented the interests of the big landlord class, the bourgeoisie, and imperialism.[37] From then on the Chinese

Communists decided to stage a revolution of their own, opposing the new regime set up by Chiang Kai-shek. This launched the Second Revolutionary Civil War (1927–37).

The Nanchang Uprising on 1 August 1927 marked the beginning of an armed struggle independently led by the Chinese Communist Party. October of the same year saw the establishment of the first revolutionary base in the rural area of China. From 1927 to 1930 the Red Army and revolutionary bases across the country underwent a process of gradual expansion. In 1930 the central revolutionary base was set up in Ruijin, Jiangxi Province, south China. The following year witnessed the birth of a news agency of the first Communist regime in China. On 7 November, the day when the First National Congress of Chinese Soviet Zones was opened, the Red China News Press was founded. It was the predecessor of today's Xinhua (New China) News Agency.

The News Press released declarations and other documents of the Party Central Committee and the central government, stories on construction in the Soviet areas, communiques on battles fought by the Red Army, and news about struggles carried on by the people in the Kuomintang-ruled areas. These were received by the revolutionary bases in north and south China and by the Party Central Committee bureaus in Shanghai and Tianjin.

In December 1931 the provisional central government of the Chinese Soviet Republic set up its organ, *Hongse Zhonghua* (*Red China News*). Subsequently it became the combined organ of the Chinese Communist Party, the central government, the All-China Federation of Trade Unions, and the Communist Youth League of China. This was the first fairly long-term newspaper printed in letterpress by the Chinese Communist Party in the revolutionary base areas. The newspaper, first published as a weekly and later every three days, was available in all Soviet areas and reported a circulation of 50,000 in 1934.

Another important Communist publication during this period was *Douzheng* (*Struggle*), launched in 1933 as a merger of two official newspapers in the Soviet area, *Shihua* (*Plain Talk*) and *Dangde Jianshe* (*Party Building*). This became the official organ of the Central Bureau of the Soviet Areas of the Communist Party. A third important publication during this period was *Hongxing* (*Red Star*), also launched in 1933 as the official mouthpiece of the General Political Department of the Red Army in the Chinese Soviet Republic in Jiangxi. It lasted until 1934, shortly before the Chinese Communists began their long march from the Jiangxi Soviet bases, where they reportedly published 34 newspapers during the 1930s.

After the failure of the 1924–27 revolution, Xie Juezai, a respected veteran, went secretly to Shanghai to edit the Party's central organ *Hongqi Ribao* (*Red Flag Daily*) and another, *Shanghai Bao* (*Shanghai Paper*). These two papers denounced the Kuomintang for its corruption and other evils, called on the people to overthrow the Kuomintang regime, and reported the activities of the Red Army in the southern provinces. *Hongqi Ribao* began publication on 15 August 1930 and was forced to cease publication in March 1931.

While the Red Army and the rural revolutionary bases expanded, Chiang Kai-shek mobilized large troops to conduct his "encirclement and suppression" campaign against them. As civil war was erupting, Japan occupied Shengyang (Mukden) in northeast China on 18 September 1930. Chiang's order that the northeastern army not resist under any circumstances enabled the enemy to take over the three northeastern provinces in three months.[38]

In 1933 when Japan was launching all-out aggression against China, Chiang Kai-shek mobilized five hundred thousand men for his fourth "encirclement and suppression" campaign against the central revolutionary base. Within the Communist Party a left opportunist line[39] dominated the leadership; as a result, the Communists failed to thwart the campaign and had to leave the base area in a strategic shift. After the Zunyi Conference where the opportunist line was criticized, the correct line with Mao Zedong as its exponent was established,[40] and the Red Army continued the long march all the way to the base area in northern Shaanxi Province. There the Communist Party waged a tenacious fight against the Japanese aggressors.

In 1935 Japan moved many troops south of the Great Wall, threatening Beijing and Tianjin. In June the Kuomintang sent He Yingqin, second only to Chiang Kai-shek, to sign a secret agreement with Umezu, then commander-in-chief of Japan's armed forces in north China. Under the He-Umezu Agreement, China agreed to withdraw its troops from Hebei and ban all anti-Japanese activities.

On 9 December 1935 students in Beijing demonstrated in opposition to Chiang's policy of selling out north China; this was the famous December Ninth Movement. A number of officers and men in the Kuomintang army were deeply influenced by the patriotic movement. The northeastern army led by Zhang Xueliang and the northwestern army led by Yang Hucheng, both of which had been sent by Chiang to northern Shaanxi to attack the Red Army, refused to fight the Communists as the nation faced a common enemy: the Japanese.

Angered and frightened by the changed attitude of Zhang and Yang, Chiang personally went to Xi'an to force them to renew the attack. On 12 December 1936 Zhang and Yang sent troops to arrest him. The pro-

Japanese He Yingqin, who wanted to wrest power from Chiang, tried to use this opportunity to enlarge the civil war and facilitate Japan's aggression against China by sending troops to attack Tongguan east of Xi'an. The Chinese Communist Party resolutely opposed He Yingqin's trick and proposed instead a peaceful solution to the Xi'an Incident. It sent a delegation, headed by Zhou Enlai, to Xi'an to mediate. Before he was freed from captivity, Chiang Kai-shek was forced to accept a number of conditions, including the cessation of the civil war and the formation of an alliance with the Communist Party for resistance against Japan. The peaceful solution of the Xi'an Incident marked the end of 10 years of civil war and the beginning of the second Kuomintang-Communist cooperation in opposing Japanese aggression.

On 7 July 1937 Japan attacked Lugouqiao (Marco Polo Bridge), southwest of Beijing. Known as the Lugouqiao Incident, it marked the beginning of Japan's all-out aggression against China and of China's War of Resistance against Japan (1937–45). To speed up the formal establishment of an anti-Japanese national united front, the Communist Party on 15 July issued a declaration calling for cooperation between the Communists and the Kuomintang and sent Zhou Enlai to Lushan, Jiangxi Province, to talk with Chiang Kai-shek. On 13 August Japanese troops attacked Shanghai and threatened Nanjing, posing a direct menace to Chiang's rule and also to the British and American interests in China. Only then did the Kuomintang government participate in the war against Japan and come to an agreement with the Communist Party on joint resistance. In observance of the agreement, the main force of the Red Army in the northwest was renamed the Eighth Route Army of the National Revolutionary Army. The Red guerrilla forces in the southern provinces were reorganized as the New Fourth Army.

In September the Kuomintang made public a declaration for Kuomintang-Communist cooperation and recognized the legal status of the Communist Party, formally creating the anti-Japanese national united front. But the Kuomintang army was defeated time and again on the battlefield by the Japanese. In less than a month it lost Beijing and then Tianjin. By March 1938 almost all of north China fell into the enemy's hands. In November 1937 Japan occupied Shanghai; in December it captured Nanjing.

In October 1938 Guangzhou and Wuhan also fell. The Kuomintang government moved its capital from Nanjing, first to Wuhan and then to Chongqing. Its major forces also moved to China's southwest and northeast. Meanwhile, the Communist Party mobilized the people of all strata to participate in the War of Resistance. The Eighth Route Army crossed the Huanghe River from Shaanxi and moved eastward until it reached the front of north China. After a victory in which three thousand Japanese were killed at Pingxingguan, Shanxi Province, the Eighth Route Army marched to the enemy-occupied territories where it carried out guerrilla warfare and established anti-Japanese bases. In south China the New Fourth Army moved north and south of the Changjiang River and established anti-Japanese bases in southern Jiangsu and north of the river. Farther to the south the anti-Japanese bases were established in Guangdong.

In 1938 the Eighth Route Army and the New Fourth Army tied up four hundred thousand Japanese troops, more than half of the enemy's total strength in China. These two armies were in fact the main forces in the War of Resistance against Japan. Facing such a savage aggressor, the pro-Japanese clique headed by Wang Jingwei kept insisting that China could be exterminated as a nation if it continued to resist Japan, which was far superior in military strength. On the other hand, the Chiang Kai-shek clique hoped to rely on the strength of Britain and the United States for a quick victory.

On 22 December 1938 Japanese Prime Minister Konoye made the Kuomintang government a tempting offer to surrender, based on three principles: "good-neighbor relations," "joint effort against the Communists," and "economic cooperation." Wang Jingwei left Chongqing, declared his support of Konoye's offer, and set up a puppet regime in Nanjing under Japan's direction. The Chiang clique within the Kuomintang, which served the interests of Britain and the United States, wavered even more. It adopted a policy of actively opposing Communism and passively opposing Japanese imperialism. From the winter of 1939 to the summer of 1943, Chiang launched three anti-Communist onslaughts, which were smashed by the Communists each time.

During the War of Resistance against Japan, the Communists developed their journalistic institutions both in the base areas and in the other parts of the country. In October 1934 the Red China News Press followed the Red Army on its long march. Because of the hard conditions, it suspended news releases to the various revolutionary bases but continued reception of news stories from the Central News Agency of the Kuomintang. In October 1935 the News Press resumed sending news releases after arriving at Yan'an in northern Shaanxi. When Zhou Enlai was in Xi'an in December 1936 to help settle the Xi'an Incident, the News Press set up its Xi'an office to issue to various newspapers in the city news stories and proclamations of the Communist Party.

In January 1937 the Red China News Press changed its name to the

Xinhua News Agency. In the same month *Hongse Zhonghua* resumed publication, changing its title to *Xin Zhonghua Bao* (*New China News*). In May 1941 it merged with *Jinri Xinwen* (*News Today*) to become a paper under the name of *Jiefang Ribao* (*Liberation Daily*). This paper ceased publication in March 1947 when Yan'an was evacuated. Other newspapers set up in liberated areas during the anti-Japanese war included *Jin-Cha-Ji Ribao* (*Shanxi-Chahar-Hebei Daily*), *Jizhong Daobao* (*Central Hebei Guide*), *Dazhong Ribao* (*Popular Daily*), *Ji-Lu-Yu Ribao* (*Hebei-Shandong-Henan Daily*), *Fuxiaobao* (*Daybreak*), *Kangzhan Ribao* (*Resistance Daily*), and *Jianghuai Ribao* (*Central China Daily*).

The Kuomintang-Communist cooperation during the anti-Japanese war permitted the Communists to publish several editions of *Xinhua Ribao* (*New China Daily*) in several Kuomintang-controlled cities. It began publication in January 1938 in Hankou and moved to Chongqing in October of the same year, where it circulated openly until banned by the Kuomintang government in February 1947. The paper was under the direction of Zhou Enlai, who was in charge of the Party's liaison office in Chongqing. *Xinhua Ribao* propagated the line, principles, and policies of the Communist Party, and condemned the Kuomintang for taking a passive attitude toward fighting the Japanese while actively opposing the Communists, suppressing the people, and sabotaging unity. The paper made an outstanding contribution to uniting all patriots as it strove to win the war and build a new China.[41]

The weekly *Jiefang* (*Liberation*), published from April 1937 to the autumn of 1941, was founded in Yan'an as the political and theoretical organ of the Central Committee of the Communist Party. And the weekly *Qunzhong* (*The Masses*), founded in Hankou in December 1937, was considered by the Kuomintang as a legal journal of the Communist Party in the Kuomintang areas.

Beginning in 1938 the Xinhua News Agency established the Jin-Cha-Ji (Shanxi-Chahar-Hebei), North China, Shandong, Northwest Shaanxi, and other offices. Its service areas extended from Yan'an to the liberated areas in the enemy's rear. By 1939 the news agency had become a wire service, providing translation, editing, news releases, and reception of news stories from main news agencies at home and abroad. The Xinhua News Agency disseminated the Party's policies on the united front and reported economic construction in the liberated areas, helping to push the anti-Japanese forces to final victory. As the various base areas were blockaded and separated by the enemy, the agency actually played the role of a national newspaper.

Development of the Chinese Communist broadcast system also had its beginning during this period. In 1940 a broadcasting committee was organized and chaired by Zhou Enlai in Yan'an to make plans for the establishment of a broadcasting station. Within the same year a group of radio workers recruited from all over the country had converted an old automobile engine into a generator with an old assortment of rebuilt or handmade parts and had built the Yan'an Xinhua Broadcasting Station. The Chinese Communists made immediate use of their broadcasting station. In May 1941 Mao, in a directive drafted for the Party Central Committee, asked all liberated areas to receive Yan'an's broadcasts regularly. The Party relied heavily on this channel to keep in touch with liberated areas and, more importantly, with its guerrilla units and armed forces. The Yan'an Xinhua Broadcasting Station, the origin of the Central People's Broadcasting Station today, was inaugurated in September 1945.

One year earlier Xinhua began its English-wire operation, the beginning of the agency's overseas service. The English Service Department of Xinhua consisted of three people—a department director and two editors—who were joined later by an Englishman as an adviser and language polisher. Five or six news stories were released daily in the early days of the service. One of the early editors summed up a few principles to be followed in writing news stories: news stories of the utmost international significance should be given priority; facts should be absolutely accurate without any exaggeration; the language should be easy to understand; and explanations should be made wherever necessary in the interests of foreign readers.[42]

The English service in the early days did draw the attention of foreign readers. Strangely enough, the British Broadcasting Corporation claimed that the Yan'an broadcasts were better received than those released from Nanjing. Some news stories about China that appeared in English newspapers came from Yan'an broadcasts. In November 1945, when the Englishman working with Xinhua's English service left Yan'an for home, he left behind his suggestions about the service. Later he wrote twice from the United States, giving more suggestions. Some dispatches from Xinhua offices lacked objectivity, were fragmentary, and took a one-sided approach to problems, he said, and gave no clear, overall information about the base areas. The reporters were mistaken when they thought they were writing stories for readers who believed everything they wrote, he said. In fact, they were writing for those who knew little about China and had doubts about, or were even hostile to, the Chinese Communists. The Xinhua officials issued to the various offices a circular on his suggestions, with the statement that his views were expressed with honesty and hit the most vulnerable point in Xinhua's overseas service. They asked their offices to discuss these problems to improve the English service.

To understand how Communist journalism worked outside the base areas, we need to go back a decade before these events. The Chinese nation met perhaps its greatest test in 1934. The Japanese invaded northeast and north China, and the Kuomintang went all out to oppose the Communists instead of fighting the Japanese. The left opportunist line within the Communist Party compelled the Red Army to undertake the Long March. Ninety percent of the rural base areas and the Red Army were lost, and nearly all the Party organizations in the cities were destroyed.

The Communists in Shanghai and elsewhere who went underground, however, worked around a cultural commission under the Party Central Committee. They met a great deal of opposition to their work, and some journals they published were quickly banned. Still, a number of them, such as *Dazhong Shenghuo* (*Public Life*), *Dushu Shenghuo* (*Reading Life*), and *Shijie Zhishi* (*World Affairs*), managed to exist for a fairly long time. These journals were run by both Communists and non-Communists.

The monthly *Zhongguo Nongcun* (*China's Rural Area*) was another journal that shed "a ray of light in the long darkness."[43] Basing itself on Marxist theories and Party policies, and on data collected from investigations in the rural area, the monthly endorsed the antiimperialist and antifeudal democratic revolution and the party's policies on the anti-Japanese national united front. In its first two years of publication, the monthly analyzed the relationships among the various classes in the Chinese economy and the influence of imperialist aggression on these classes; it showed how the Chinese rural economy went bankrupt after dual exploitation by the imperialist and feudal forces. It claimed that other theories would lead people astray and harm the revolution.

After the anti-Japanese war broke out, the monthly called on young intellectuals in the cities to go to the countryside and urge the peasants to rise and defend their country. When the Japanese took Shanghai, the monthly moved to the interior, first to Nanchang and then to Changsha and Wuhan. It continued publication in Guilin and Chongqing until it was banned by the Kuomintang in 1943. Even after the ban of the monthly, *Shangwu Ribao* (*Commerce Daily*) in Chongqing published a supplement of the journal in 1945, and *Wen Hui Bao* took over the job in 1946–47.

The semimonthly *Shijie Zhishi* was founded in Shanghai in 1934 to inform readers about the world to which China belonged. "China belongs to the world," was the opening remark of the magazine 50 years ago.[44] In Shanghai, and later in Kunming, the semimonthly brought to readers the latest news about the world and China. Breaking through the blockade of the Kuomintang, it reported how anxious the world's people were about the dark cloud of fascism hovering over their heads, and how the Soviet Red Army fought the German fascists. In addition the magazine acquainted its readers with the latest developments in culture and science, as well as the customs and habits of different people on the globe. It became a best-seller soon after publication.[45]

Under the leadership of the Communist Party, many in Shanghai's cultural circles made use of the special position of foreign concessions to spread anti-Japanese ideas, arouse patriotism, and toughen the fighting will of the people. *Yi Bao* (*Translation Gazette*) and *Dao Bao* (*Guide Gazette*), founded by foreign businessmen, and *Minzu Gonglun* (*National Public Opinion*), *Wenxian* (*Records*), and *Shanghai Zhoubao* (*Shanghai Weekly*) promoted what the Communists advocated. They reported the victories of the Eighth Route Army and the New Fourth Army, denounced crimes committed by the Japanese, and condemned the puppets' betrayal of the nation.

Noted Chinese journalist Yun Yiqun was editor or chief writer with *Yi Bao, Dao Bao,* and other Shanghai newspapers in the 1930s. He began his career as a reporter with the Xinsheng (New Voice) News Agency in the city in 1932 and he was one of the sponsors and organizers of a young journalists' association. As a constant contributor to the evening paper *Damei Wanbao,* he condemned the censorship of the Kuomintang and called for freedom of speech. He met with an agreeable response among his colleagues.[46]

After the Xi'an Incident, Yun wrote two articles for *Li Bao* (*Promptitude Gazette*): "No Spanish Civil War Will Come" and "Possible Peaceful Settlement of the Xi'an Incident." He made a penetrating analysis of the trend of developments and showed that the Communist Party's policy of peacefully settling the incident was based on the fundamental interests of the Chinese people and the assumption of uniting to fight the Japanese. In an editorial dated 13 November 1938 Yun condemned the betrayal of the nation by Wang Jingwei. The editorial, entitled "How Very Extraordinary Wang's Statement Is," was carried in Shanghai's *Dao Bao.*[47]

Dazhong Shenghuo and *Kangzhan* (*Resistance*) were run by Zou Taofen, a great patriot and fighter for democracy who devoted his life to journalism and publishing. Starting in 1922, he edited nationally influential journals including *Jiaoyu Yu Zhiye* (*Education and Profession*), *Shenghuo* (*Life*), *Dazhong Shenghuo,* and *Kangzhan.*[48] Shenghuo Shudian (Life Bookstore), which he founded in 1932, published some 20 magazines before 1948 when it merged with two other bookstores. The bookstore made an indelible contribution by arousing the people to struggle and by denouncing the crimes committed by the Japanese aggressors and the Kuomintang's policies of autocratic rule, betrayal, and surrender.[49]

In Hong Kong a number of journals run by Chinese were under the direct leadership of Liao Chengzhi, son of Sun Yat-sen's close comrade-in-arms Liao Zhongkai, who was sent to Hong Kong by the Communist Party to work for the anti-Japanese national united front. Wu Yuzhang, noted educator and historian, founded the Chinese-language *Jiuguo Shibao* (*Saving-the-Nation Times*) in Paris in 1935 to publicize the Communist Party's policy of the national united front. Copies of the paper were mailed to China, which helped push the formation of the front. Many Communists who had lost contact with their Party organizations in Shanghai and other cities resumed their underground work after learning from the paper about the Party's program on the united front.[50]

During the autumn and winter of 1944, the Japanese marched westward. Tension swept Guizhou. Sichuan was shocked. Students in Chongqing's Fudan University founded a newspaper to call for democracy and resistance to aggression and an end to autocracy and civil war. The paper, called *Zhongguo Xuesheng Daobao* (*Chinese Students' Guide*), reported the anti-Japanese activities of the students and exposed the suppression of progressive teachers and students by the Kuomintang authorities and their agents in schools. It also commented on the political situation and relayed the call of students to resist aggression.[51]

Soon after the surrender of Japan in 1945 and the end of its aggression in China, Mao Zedong and Zhou Enlai instructed that dailies under the Party's leadership and private papers be published as soon as possible in Shanghai, Nanjing, Wuhan, and Hong Kong. This renewal of the propaganda war against the Kuomintang aimed at uniting the country behind the Communists.[52] *Xinhua Ribao, Jianguo Ribao* (*Building-the-Nation Daily*), and *Zhongguo Xuesheng Daobao* were among the many progressive newspapers at that time.

Zhou Enlai, then working in Chongqing, was concerned about *Zhongguo Xuesheng Daobao*. He suggested that the tone of the paper be subdued in order to unite more students and to publish as long as possible. "The anti-Japanese wars have been won, but many difficulties lie ahead," he said. "The paper should strive to exist under the most adverse circumstances."[53]

During the Third Revolutionary Civil War (1945–49), the Xinhua News Agency continued to expand. In addition to its offices in the liberated areas, it set up bureaus in such Kuomintang-ruled areas as Chongqing, Beiping, and Nanjing. It sent reporters to cover the war and set up one office after another on the battlefronts. Military reports in the early days of the liberation war exposed the deployments of Chiang Kai-shek's army for civil war, reflected the resolve of the army and people in the liberated areas to defend themselves, and inspired the nation to overthrow Chiang Kai-shek's rule.[54]

In May 1946 the Xinhua News Agency and *Jiefang Ribao* were designated by the Party Central Committee as its official news agency and official newspaper. In March 1947, when Yan'an was evacuated, the paper stopped publication and the Xinhua News Agency assumed the task of issuing editorials and commentaries. After the evacuation of Yan'an, a small team of Xinhua reporters followed the Party Central Committee into northern Shaanxi. Most of the Xinhua staff crossed the Huanghe River to work in the Taihang Mountain area. While in that area the news agency head office sent its first reporter abroad to work in Prague, Czechoslovakia. The Prague and London bureaus set up in 1948 widened Xinhua's influence abroad.

The Chinese Communists developed radio broadcasting as they developed their news agency and newspaper work. When they formally began their radio broadcasts in 1945, the broadcasting station was in a temple about 19 miles from Yan'an. Equipped with a three-hundred-watt transmitter, this tiny station was on the air only two hours a day. The programs, intended for audiences in Kuomintang territories, disseminated news and commentaries about Communist areas and policies. On its third anniversary the station's daily broadcast was extended to three hours.

A second station, Zhangjiakou (Kalgan) Xinhua Broadcasting Station, began functioning at about the same time. Later, English-language programs were added. By the end of 1948, 16 stations had been established in northeast China, Xinjiang, and northern Jiangsu. The Communists said broadcasting from these stations had a tremendous impact on the morale of Kuomintang officers, and many joined the People's Liberation Army as a result.[55]

In September 1947 the Northern Shaanxi Xinhua Broadcasting Station, set up in April that year in the Taihang Mountain area, began its English-language radio broadcasting, which was the beginning of overseas radio service under the leadership of the Party Central Committee. The programs, lasting 20 minutes every day, informed listeners abroad of the policies of the Chinese Communist Party, the victories of the Chinese Liberation Army, and the construction of the liberated areas.

From June to September 1947 the Liberation Army launched a nationwide offensive, and the main battlefields moved to the Kuomintang-controlled areas. The army captured many heavily defended cities and destroyed much of the enemy's effective strength. In April 1948 the Party Central Committee, led by Mao Zedong, Zhou Enlai, and Ren Bishi, moved to Xibaipo, Hebei Province, to join Liu Shaoqi, who had been leading a working commission of the Central Committee. Xibaipo thus replaced Yan'an as the Communist headquarters. In the following month the Xinhua News Agency head office moved near Xibaipo to join the Xinhua team that had been working with the Central Committee in northern Shaanxi.

After the three 142-day-long campaigns that were unprecedented in the war annals of China and seldom known in the world, all of northeast China, most of north China, and the east and central China areas north of the Changjiang River were liberated. Nearly all of Chiang Kai-shek's best troops were wiped out.

During this period Xinhua developed rapidly, demonstrated by the growing number of words received and released every day, as well as the extent of its publications, personnel, and offices throughout the country. Incomplete figures showed that Xinhua had 53 military and local offices with 33 branches comprising some three thousand people.[56]

In March 1949 Xinhua entered Beiping with the Party Central Committee. The Xinhua Radio Station became independent in June. *Renmin Ribao (People's Daily)*, the organ of the North China Bureau of the Party Central Committee, became the organ of the Central Committee. On 23 April 1949 the People's Liberation Army captured Nanjing, Chiang's headquarters, thus ending the Kuomintang's rule forever. When Chiang was driven to Taiwan, the mainland, except for Tibet, was liberated completely. On 1 October of that year, the People's Republic of China was declared established. Chinese history entered a new phase.

In the course of long years' practice, the Communist Party of China gradually developed its own theories on Party journalism. At a symposium held in Changsha in 1983, the central doctrine of these theories was summarized as "a strong Party spirit." The symposium, sponsored by the Journalism Institute of the Chinese Social Sciences Academy and six other journalistic institutions, developed the following objectives for its theories: whole-hearted service by the people with the scientific approach of seeking truth from facts; truthfulness in news; journalism that follows the Party Central Committee and propagates the Party's guidelines and policies; newspapers run by the Party and the people; a serious attitude toward work; steadfast discipline; and obedience to Party leadership.[57]

These theories on Party journalism formally emerged in Yan'an in

1942–43 when the Communists carried out a rectification campaign. The relationship of journalism to the Party and the people, which had seemed equivocal, was clearly defined during this campaign.

In January 1942 Mao Zedong declared that *Jiefang Ribao* should carry out the Party's lines and policies through its editorials, monographs, news stories, and other contents, and that stereotyped Party writing should be eliminated. On 8 March he wrote the following statement for the paper: "Go deep among the people and don't talk empty words."[58]

On 16 March the Propaganda Department of the Party Central Committee issued a circular on the transformation of Party newspapers, urging Party organizations in various places to investigate and correct the work of newspapers in accordance with Mao's call for "rectifying the three incorrect styles."[59] The circular described the newspaper as "the most powerful instrument of propaganda and agitation." Efficient management of the newspaper was stressed as the center of Party work, as "it connects with and influences tens of thousands of people every day." Debate, criticism, and suggestions by non-Communists were permitted, it said.[60]

As part of the campaign, *Jiefang Ribao* initiated a reform on 1 April 1942, giving greater prominence to events in the liberated areas than to news in the Kuomintang areas and elsewhere in the world. Party policies and the life of the people were also matters of high priority at the Xinhua News Agency.

Mao had already stressed the importance of giving non-Communists opportunities to express their viewpoints in the Party's organ. He said all non-Communists willing to cooperate with the Communist Party had the right to criticize the Party as well as its members and cadres. Party members and organizations at various levels, he said, could disregard malicious attacks, but should listen attentively to all constructive criticism.[61] The Party chairman urged *Xinhua Ribao, Jiefang Ribao,* and all other newspapers and publications in the base areas to invite non-Communists to express their views in the Party's organ and to invite as many non-Communists as possible to take part in the editing board.[62]

Mao also emphasized strengthening the Party spirit in newspapers. In October 1942 he criticized high-level Party organizations for paying little attention to the fact that the news agency and newspapers lacked direction in their work. He called on these organizations to participate in, rather than avoid, discussion about news policies and to exert leadership over news work.[63] In June 1948 Mao again called attention to the responsibility of high-level Party organizations to direct the news agency and newspapers, which he called "extremely important institutions of propaganda." He criticized Party organizations for relinquishing their responsibility for leadership, or at least for failing to take this leadership seriously, and for allowing erroneous ideas to spread unchecked. He urged the leaders of Party organizations to regard the work of propaganda as a serious scientific endeavor.[64]

In a speech to the editorial staff of the daily *Shanxi-Suiyuan Ribao* in April of the same year, Mao summed up the Party's work in journalism. He said that a basic principle of Marxism-Leninism was to enable the masses to recognize their own interests and unite to fight for those interests. Once the masses know the truth and have a common aim, he argued, they will work together with one heart. When the masses are of one heart, everything becomes easy.[65] "The role and power of the newspapers," Mao said, "consists in their ability to bring the Party program, the Party line, the Party's general and specific policies, its tasks and methods of work before the masses in the quickest and most extensive way."[66]

Liu Shaoqi also emphasized the "tremendous significance" of journalism in his talk to the north China press corps in Xibaipo in October 1948. He said that a well-run newspaper can help people unite, progress, and move toward the truth. A poorly run paper is very dangerous to the people, he added, as it can spread backward and erroneous ideas, bring about splits, and create friction.[67] Liu described journalism as "one of the very important channels" and "bridges linking the Party with the masses." But when a newspaper exerts a bad influence by spreading false ideas, thereby stirring up the people's destructive tendencies, it commits a grave error indeed, which can ultimately lead to dangerous situations and to the worst kind of alienation from the masses.

The talks of Mao and Liu, which explained that journalism should serve the people, trust the people, and rely on the people, are considered by Chinese journalists to be two great works on the principle of Party spirit as applied to their work.[68] Seeking truth from facts has been the fundamental approach of journalists throughout the history of Party journalism. "Facts," according to Mao's own interpretation of this philosophy, are all the things that exist objectively, "truth" is the internal relations or laws governing those facts, and "to seek" means "to study."[69]

Around 1945 a serious tendency toward exaggeration and inaccuracy appeared in the press. To stifle this tendency, there was once again a movement to emphasize the principle that news must be absolutely true. A *Jiefang Ribao* editorial published in March of that year stated that journalism should establish a practice of total honesty and full responsibility to society, humankind, the Party, and the people.[70]

In 1947 *Shanxi-Suiyuan Ribao* began a campaign to do away with the phenomenon of *Krikun*, a term taken from the name of a reporter in the Soviet play *The Front* who makes groundless accusations and fabricates lies. *Krikun* in Chinese press circles referred to a kind of news reporting divorced from facts and characterized by fabrication, boasting, exaggeration, and empty talk. The Xinhua News Agency and *Jiefang Ribao* issued a number of editorials and articles around the time of the campaign to correct a tendency toward exaggeration, boasting, distorted facts, irresponsible remarks, and the reporting of only good news and not bad.

In 1948 Zhou Yang, a veteran in charge of cultural affairs, wrote that some reporters depended more on their ears than on their eyes. They seldom went among the masses to make in-depth investigations, he said, and he criticized them for failing to report actual conditions and following certain people who held leading positions.[71] Liu Shaoqi argued that news reports must convey the truth without swagger, sensationalism, or prejudice. Whether the masses opposed, welcomed, or misunderstood the Party, journalists should report what the masses thought and be unafraid to state the truth.[72] He encouraged reporters to examine Party policies and point out any errors or shortcomings. Reporters should not be afraid to report the dark side of things, he added. "The most essential thing in your writing is to be truthful and not to exaggerate, and the second is to be comprehensive and profound."[73]

He described journalists as "the eyes, ears, and voices of the Party and the people." If they could truly, comprehensively, and profoundly report the thoughts and feelings of the people, he said, they would have great effect, for by doing so, "you will have voiced their appeals and given vent to what they dare not or cannot say, or what they desire to say but find no way of expressing."[74] "With our newspapers," Mao said, "we must rely on everybody, on the masses of the people, on the whole Party to run them, not merely on a few persons working behind closed doors."[75] With the Party running newspapers, journalists could work under Party leadership and the supervision of the people. A thorough knowledge of what was happening all over the country could help them determine the direction of propaganda. Knowing what the people wanted, they could decide what to report.[76]

1949–1985

The Chinese Communist Party that came to power in 1949 wanted to build a new China. To do so, it had to eradicate the economic and social consequences of the civil war, undo the damage of a century of foreign domination and unequal treaties, and, at a deeper level, eliminate the injustices and backwardness created by centuries of feudalism.

As new territory was occupied, local Party organizations expropriated existing press facilities. The new regime thus gained considerable experience as well as an already functioning system capable of expansion for the regime's own mass media. The *Central Daily News* and 43 other Kuomintang papers in major cities were the first to be seized and transformed. The policy was to close without exception all periodicals formerly owned by the Kuomintang and to provide conditions that were conducive to the free development of the genuine people's publications. The registration law required all operating papers to furnish information about their past and present political creed, qualifications of their executive personnel, capital, source of income, and a file of the previous year's copies. Newspapers judged to be politically unacceptable were not permitted to be registered. Because Party policy was to guarantee all political rights to citizens of accepted segments of society, including the right to own property, some established nonpolitical newspapers were permitted to continue. Among them were *Xinwen Bao* with emphasis on business news, and *Dagong Bao* (*Impartial Gazette*) with emphasis on finance and economics.

In a 1943 speech, Mao Zedong emphasized the importance of communication in building a new China: "We should go to the masses and learn from them, synthesize their experience into better, articulated principles and methods, then do propaganda among the masses, and call upon them to put these principles and methods into practice so as to solve their problems and help them achieve liberation and happiness."[77] This strategy of organizing and mobilizing the people by communication has been followed since the Yan'an days. By initiating two-way communication, the Party leadership expected to learn from the masses and then reorganize their experiences into new programs of socialist reconstruction. China's mass media have played essential roles in this respect.

Thanks to this policy, the mass media in the early years of the People's Republic grew rapidly. In the 1952–54 period China reported 776 newspapers with a total single press-run newspaper circulation of some 8 million. By 1955 China reported a 408 percent increase over the total number of newspaper subscriptions in 1950, with one source reporting a circulation of some 12 million for 1955. By 1958 the total circulation of all newspapers was 15 million copies per issue, or about five times more than the 3 million copies reported for 1951.[78] There were about half as many monthly and semimonthly magazines in 1952 as there were newspapers, that is, between three and four hundred. The general, popular magazines had the largest circulations, and the more specialized, smaller-circulation periodicals addressed themselves to specific groups. In 1957 China published a total of 600 periodicals, including 130 titles in social science, 230 devoted to natural science, 110 to literature and the arts, and 130 to minority and foreign languages.[79]

In 1958 a group of theoretical magazines appeared, the first of which was the fortnightly journal *Hongqi* (*Red Flag*). Mao and other Party members contributed to this magazine, whose first-issue circulation reportedly numbered almost 2 million copies. Provincial counterparts of the journal were begun by the various provincial Party committees. Because the capital was the communication center of the country, all of the major magazines were published there, though some had branch offices and publishing plants in Shanghai, Tianjin, and Nanjing. The circulation of China's leading national newspaper, *Renmin Ribao,* which was only 30,000 in 1949, increased to 810,000 in 1956.[80] *Renmin Ribao* had become the official newspaper of the Party Central Committee in 1948.

In 1957 there were 19 national newspapers.[81] These, with both general and functional appeals, included *Gongren Ribao* (*Workers' Daily*), the Trade Union Federation organ; *Wen Hui Bao* (*Wen Hui Daily*), the teachers' organ; *Guangming Ribao* (*Enlightenment Daily*), a cultural and educational journal that originally served as the organ of the non-Communist parties; *Dagong Bao,* whose pre-Communist era prestige helped it retain its name, and which had an emphasis on economics and foreign affairs; and *Zhongguo Qingnian Bao* (*Chinese Youth Newspaper*), the organ of the Chinese Socialist Youth League (and later the Chinese Communist Youth League).

Each province, autonomous region, or city had its official newspaper, which served the same function for the territorial and political subdivisions as the national papers for the country. These papers published national and international information in addition to the affairs and problems of their particular areas. In 1957 there were about 341 provincial-level papers, almost all dailies.[82] Town and county papers devoted primary attention to local problems and tasks at hand. One of their major functions was to disseminate information about high-level Party decisions. In 1957 there were more than 936 county papers.[83] Supplementing the printed papers on the local level were wall or blackboard papers serving farms, construction sites, villages, schools, army units, cooperatives, communes, and industrial sites.

In 1957 China had 31 minority-language newspapers. Among the 10 geographical regions that published these papers, the Xinjiang Uighur Autonomous Region published the most — 13 altogether in the Uygur, Mongolian, Kazakh, Sibo, and Khalkhas languages.[84]

The seven leading magazines in 1955 were *Shishi Shouce* (*Current Affairs Pocket Magazine*), *Xuexi* (*Learning*), *Zhengzhi Xuexi* (*Political Study*), *Xin Guancha* (*The New Observer*), *Shijie Zhishi* (*World Affairs*), *Renmin Huabao* (*The People's Pictorial*), and *Lianhuan Huabao* (*The Popular Illustrated*). One-fourth of the total circulation of all magazines was attributed to two youth publications, *Zhongguo Qingnian* (*Chinese Youth*), and *Zhongxuesheng* (*The High School Student*). Some others were *Wenyi Yuebao* (*Literature and Art Monthly*), *Wenyi Bao* (*Literature and Art Semimonthly*), *Yiwen* (*Translation*), *Dazhong Dianying* (*Popular Motion Picture*), and *Zhongguo Gongren* (*Chinese Workers*). There were other publications for groups such as women, children, theatrical workers, and art enthusiasts.

Before 1956 all national dailies published only four pages seven days a week, with occasional supplements devoted to literary reviews, sports, illustrations, education, and other subjects. After 1956 *Renmin Ribao* expanded to eight pages on a regular basis, but cut back to six pages in 1963.

To attract readers, newspapers and Party leaders paid attention to the style of writing. They had long been aware of the tendency to publish dull accounts, of which the classic genre was the printed conference speech. Some Party leaders perceived that few people wanted to read lists of the tasks of organizations, lists of the names of representatives, lists of the names of leaders of standing committees, reports of opening ceremonies, long-winded speeches, and reports of closing ceremonies. To some extent, changes in news presentation and more attractive pages helped. The dailies *Qingdao Ribao* and *Beijing Ribao* in the mid-1950s promised their readers shorter and more informative articles. Brief headlines also became an official policy. After *Renmin Ribao* printed a 61-character dull headline, it published a letter objecting to such practices, claiming that the headline was too long and required too much energy to read.

Problems of credibility were even more basic than problems of format. During the Hundred-Flower era, a flood of letters criticized inconsistencies and inaccuracies in previously published articles. After discovering 80 mistakes in a week, ranging from wrong characters to factual misinformation, *Renmin Ribao* editors promised to strengthen the editing.

The tendency of talking about quantity only and not quality, and about numbers and speed only and not excellence and economy, and the tendency to report only the positive side of an issue all led at times to misrepresentation. National newspapers tried to solve problems of credibility and liveliness by seeking help from local newspapers. In the mid-

1950s *Renmin Ribao* itself resolved to print excerpts from local newspapers. Provincial newspapers such as *Jiangxi Qingnian Bao* (*Jiangxi Youth Report*) promised to carry fewer instructions and more short articles about rural areas. Even the local *Xin Guizhou Ribao* (*New Guizhou Daily*) was encouraged to publish verbatim, from still more local sources, a column entitled "Factory Blackboard Report." When by 1958 it was announced that Bishan County in Sichuan had 113 local mimeographed papers, *Renmin Ribao* hailed this trend: If the articles were about local persons and local happenings, the masses liked to read them. As late as mid-1959, local papers—and particularly evening papers—had extremely large circulations because they were lively and not stereotyped and because they strove to write about events that were storylike. In Shanghai *Xinmin Wanbao* (*New People's Evening News*) completely gave up writing editorials; it substituted instead less directive columns that were generally called articles of "miscellaneous feelings."

At the end of the decade central newspapers were scheduled to arrive on the day of publication in only 50 percent of China's provinces, and province-level newspapers were scheduled to arrive in about 70 percent of the local counties on the same day. But county-level newspapers arrived at over 80 percent of the communes on the publication date. Clearly, one attraction of local papers was their ability to be more up-to-date than papers from higher levels.

Mao Zedong, visiting Nanjing, pointed out that provincial newspapers played a great role in organizing, encouraging, instigating, criticizing, and propelling the work of the provinces and of the people. Liu Shaoqi asked, "Bourgeois newspapers let their reports become interesting; so why can't we make more interesting news?" He told journalists that the primary purpose of their work was to be truthful. "Don't add salt and pepper on purpose," he warned. "And don't use colored spectacles."[85]

The Chinese Communists, after taking power in 1949, also paid attention to the growth of radio broadcasting. When they took over the mainland, 49 government-operated radio stations with a total of 89 transmitters existed. Of these, 17 were newly established, while the others were confiscated Kuomintang stations. In 1950 the number of radio sets was estimated to be about 1 million, half of which were Japanese-made mediumwave receivers. Metropolitan residents and those in industrial areas of northeast and east China were the typical owners, with broadcasting almost nonexistent in rural areas before 1950. To facilitate broadcasting in these areas, loudspeakers were installed for collective listening in the countryside.

With the establishment of the People's Republic, the Communists' first radio station near Yan'an, which had been moved to Beijing, was officially renamed the Central People's Broadcasting Station. It broadcast 15½ hours daily, with 50 percent news, 25 percent public education, and another 25 percent culture and entertainment. In late 1949 the station began a natural-science series featuring lectures by scientists and professors. In January 1950 a social-science series, with emphasis on Marxism-Leninism, was added. A typical entertainment program included revolutionary songs and folk songs, drama, and foreign music, mostly Russian. Choruses and opera troupes from schools, factories, and army units were also invited to present shows. The Central Station's news program covered the editorials of leading national newspapers and news stories provided by Xinhua and its own small number of correspondents.

At provincial, municipal, and local levels, stations transmitted news, commentaries, and other important political programs relayed from the Central Station as well as shows produced to meet the needs of the people, government, and Party units at various levels. In the 1950s one of the most significant programs at many local stations was "Russian Forum," a program designed to teach Russian. Within six months after the establishment of the new regime, 14 local radio stations presented this program with an estimated audience of 40,000.[86]

Despite a shortage of equipment and professional personnel, the development of provincial, municipal, and local stations made steady headway in the 1950s. The number of stations increased from 54 in 1951 to 73 in 1953 and 97 in 1958. By June 1959 China reported 107 stations in operation, with a combined radiating power nearly 33 times that of 1949. By the end of 1959, 122 radio stations existed in the country.[87] To solve the problems of insufficient radio facilities and limited number of radio receivers in the early 1950s, the Chinese began developing the wired broadcasting system. They recognized the importance of radio as an instrument of mass education and propaganda that could obviate the problems of illiteracy and newspaper shortages. The wired broadcasting system was used at the local level for the political and cultural education of the peasants, the dissemination of advanced experiences in agricultural production, and the advancement of cultural life in rural areas.

James C. Y. Chu, professor of mass communication at California State University in Chico, has written: "It is often difficult for Westerners, accustomed to the idea that programs in Communist countries are dull, to realize what brilliant and vivid styles are stressed in mass-communication messages in China."[88] With its deep concern for communication, the Chinese Communist Party placed great emphasis on the style of expression.

Mao Zedong, in one of his major statements concerning the style of literature and art, said, "What we demand is the unity of politics and art, the unity of content and form, the unity of revolutionary political content and the highest possible perfection of artistic form." The literary style advocated by Mao was one that combined brilliancy with vividness.[89] Evidently, many broadcasting programs in the early years of the People's Republic did not measure up to these criteria. In some broadcasting programs many sentences were extraordinarily lengthy, unpolished, and unintelligible. They were partly literary and partly vernacular, with foreign accents and alien intonation, poor vocabulary, inappropriate terminology, excessive use of abbreviations, and generally incomprehensible literary style. Popularization and oralization became the two basic requirements of broadcasting expression in China. The Party urged broadcasters to collect the folkways of the people, to learn their simple, lively speech, and to absorb the spirit of their folk songs. The Central People's Broadcasting Station and 16 local stations introduced special programs aimed at minorities in such languages as Tibetan, Kazakh, Uygur, and Mongolian. Special emphasis was placed on the oppression suffered by minorities in pre-Communist days and on their current happiness.

In 1952, after three years of economic rehabilitation, the Central Committee of the Chinese Communist Party declared that the revolution in China had reached the stage of building a socialist society; in January 1953 the first five-year plan was launched. The Constitution of 1954 called for the socialist transformation of agriculture, handicrafts, and capitalist industry and commerce. By 1956 the Chinese Communists noted with satisfaction that farming had essentially been organized into cooperatives or collectives, that private industry and commerce had been transformed into state or semistate enterprises, that capitalism was definitely on its way out, and that China was entering a new era of socialist construction.

On 14 January Zhou Enlai addressed a Party conference on the matter of intellectuals, with the purpose of strengthening Party leadership and undertaking scientific and cultural work. As a result of the Party policy of uniting and reeducating the intellectuals, Zhou observed, a fundamental change had taken place among Chinese intellectuals in the preceding six years. The overwhelming majority of intellectuals who came from the old society were already part of the working class, he said.[90]

On 5 April *Renmin Ribao* carried an editorial entitled "On the Historical Experience of the Dictatorship of the Proletariat." The editorial warned the leading personnel of the Party and state against the danger of

using the machinery of state to take arbitrary action, alienating themselves from the masses and collective leadership, resorting to autocracy,
and violating Party and state democracy.[91] It also called for the establishment of certain systems to ensure the thorough implementation of
the mass line and collective leadership, to avoid elevation of self and
individual heroism, and to reduce subjectivism and one-sidedness.[92]

On 2 May Mao Zedong announced at the Supreme State Conference the policy of the Chinese Communist Party: "Let a hundred
flowers blossom, and let a hundred schools of thought contend."[93]. On
26 May Lu Dingyi explained this statement by saying that the Communist Party now stood for freedom of independent thinking, of debate,
of creative work. It also supported freedom to criticize and to express,
maintain, and reserve one's opinions on questions of art, literature, or
scientific research.[94] The year 1956 was one of considerable intellectual
activity in China. There was more open criticism then than at any time
since 1949. In forum discussions participants expressed independent
views. The 12-year plan in education and culture had encouraged more
proposals and more publications. New literary magazines made their
appearance.

On 27 February 1957 Mao Zedong made an important address at a
meeting of the Supreme State Conference. He spoke on the general topic
of contradictions in Chinese society during the period of transition to
socialism, and he proposed the formula of "criticism-unity-criticism" as
a means of resolving contradictions. On 27 April the Party Central Committee issued a directive for a nationwide antibureaucratism, antisectar-
ianism, and antisubjectivism rectification campaign, inviting members
of minority parties and non-Party individuals to share their opinions and
suggest ways for improving Party leadership in the period of socialist
reconstruction.

At 11 forums in Beijing from 8 May to 3 June, comprehensive
criticism was heard, which soon spread to other cities, especially
Shanghai and Tianjin. The wave of criticism did not stop at administrative deficiencies; day by day it took on a more fundamental aspect.
Criticism grew steadily sharper, finally concentrating in late May and
early June on a number of substantial demands for changes in the Party
policies. From the start, however, the Communist Party had made it
clear that "blossoming" and "contending" were not to be without limits
and qualifications. At no time did any of the Party leaders suggest that
people would be free to discuss whether or not China should adopt
socialism or whether the Communist Party should yield any part of its
power and authority in the new state. When a handful of people
mounted a wild attack against the Party and the socialist system in an

attempt to replace the leadership of the Communist Party, a resolute counterattack was launched.

Two newspapers, *Guangming Ribao* in Beijing and *Wen Hui Bao* in Shanghai, were charged with falling under the control of rightists and spreading antisocialist views. Both were published under the auspices of the democratic parties that had been in existence since the founding of the People's Republic of China. Compared to other papers in China, these two published more and fuller reports on the activities of the various non-Communist parties and printed more news in the cultural and educational fields. During the "blossoming-contending" season of May and June, they carried full reports of the various forums and helped publicize the bold criticism. Actually, what they printed was not so very different from what could be found in *Renmin Ribao,* and in some instances *Renmin Ribao* printed even stronger criticism. Nevertheless, there were indications of certain significant differences in editorial policy.

The editor in chief of *Guangming Ribao,* Chu Anping, was a member of the Jiu San Society; its managing director, Zhang Bojun, was vice chairman of the Democratic League and chairman of the Peasants' and Workers' Democratic Party; and one of the members of its board, Zhang Naiqi, was vice chairman of the Democratic National Construction Association. Each represented his own party on the paper's board of directors. *Wen Hui Bao* was known as a leftist newspaper and had been popular with radical-minded youth and intellectuals before 1949. After that it followed the Communist line completely but retained its policy of paying special attention to problems of interest to intellectuals.

In May and June the two papers published reports of forums containing bitter attacks on the Communist Party. Now, in the period of the Party's counterattack against rightists, the two papers came under severe reprimand for having adopted an editorial policy of maximizing the faults and minimizing the merits of the new regime. *Renmin Ribao* on 14 June said the two papers were not the only two exhibiting "bourgeois tendencies." Such tendencies were found in other newspapers, in periodicals, and in the journalism departments of some universities. Even *Zhongguo Qingnian Bao* fell under criticism.

In hindsight, a 1981 Party resolution summed up this troubled period by arguing that initiating a rectification campaign throughout the Party in 1957 and urging the masses to offer criticism and suggestions were normal steps in developing socialist democracy;[95] so too was the Party's resolute counterattack justifiable and necessary. But the scope of this counterattack was far too broad, and a number of intellectuals, patriotic people, and Party cadres were unfairly labeled "rightists," with unfortunate consequences.[96] Not only did misfortunes lie ahead for a number of these people, journalists among them, but the normal practice of democracy was destroyed.

Before 1957 there had been brisk discussion in university journalism departments and in mass media journals about such journalistic issues as news values. But after the antirightist campaign, a number of issues about journalistic theories and practice came under attack. The needs of readers and society and the pursuit of knowledge and taste in news coverage were condemned as bourgeois. A discussion of news values was out of the question. As the 1981 Party resolution declared: "1957 was one of the years that saw the best results in economic work since the founding of the People's Republic, owing to the conscientious implementation of the correct line formulated at the Eighth National Congress of the Party."[97]

In 1958 the Second Plenum of the Eighth National Congress of the Party adopted the general line for socialist construction. Mao Zedong and many other leaders, both at the center and in the localities, had become smug about their successes, were impatient for quick results, and overestimated the role of subjective will and effort. Overlooking objective economic laws, they made "leftist" errors, characterized by excessive targets, the issuing of arbitrary directives, boastfulness, and the stirring up of a "communist wind."[98] With the unchecked spread of such errors throughout the country, the coverage of economics in the press also ignored objective economic laws and played a negative role in sabotaging the national economy. From 1958 to 1961, newspapers and newscasts often, though not always, resorted to boasting and exaggeration, and were full of idealistic slogans and unbelievable reports of production outputs. There were even fabricated news photos showing scenes of "bumper harvests."

The year 1958 seemed to be exceptionally good for agriculture—the autumn harvest in particular reached record proportions, at least according to the figures supplied to the state bodies. At the beginning of 1959, however, it became clear that the facts had been greatly exaggerated and that production would fall short of what was needed. The harvest in 1959, which took place during disastrous weather conditions, was worse than mediocre; the food shortage was so acute that the peasants were allowed to suspend their sales to the state.

The situation did not improve in 1960. In part of the country there was an unusually bad drought, while in the south there were catastrophic floods. While only the cities had been affected the year before, scarcity was now widespread. China had to buy foreign grain. The country did not begin to return to normal until 1961, and not fully until 1962.

Industrial production eventually suffered the same fate. Production made definite progress in 1959 and 1960, continuing to extend westward and southward as it had done during the first five-year plan. But the abandonment of small-profit production soon caused a slack that was not overcome until 1963 and 1964. The poor quality of a number of products was equivalent to outright waste, particularly in the case of rural metallurgy products. Even more significant was the wear and tear on machinery and transport equipment everywhere.

In the summer of 1960 the Soviet Union announced that it was withdrawing its technicians from China and ending its assistance. The USSR had originally agreed that during the first three five-year plans it would provide China with 300 industrial installations and technical training; but only 154 installations were completed when it withdrew.

The debate within the Party became more intense during these difficult years and came into the open in August 1959 at Lushan during the Eighth Plenum of the Central Committee when Peng Dehuai, a member of the Political Bureau and minister of defense, was rebuked for his so-called right opportunism. He and his supporters were removed from leadership. The 1981 Party resolution described this struggle as gravely undermining inner-Party democracy from the central level down to the grass-roots level.[99] The resolution concluded that "it was mainly due to the errors of the Great Leap Forward and of the struggle against 'right opportunism' together with a succession of natural calamities and the perfidious scrapping of contracts by the Soviet government that our economy encountered serious difficulties between 1959 and 1961, which caused serious losses to our country and people."[100]

In the winter of 1960, however, the Party set about to rectify its own "leftist" errors in rural work and decided on the principle of readjustment. Liu Shaoqi, Zhou Enlai, Chen Yun, and Deng Xiaoping were in charge of working out policies and measures and putting them into effect. Tendencies to moderate internal policy were accompanied by the attempt of the Party leadership to introduce greater variety into the intellectual life of the country through the revival of the "Hundred Flowers" slogan, especially in philosophy, historical science, and literature.

A group of intellectuals made an appearance as the vanguard of criticism of radical policies in 1958–59. The group was organized around the head of the Propaganda Department of the Beijing Party Committee, Deng Tuo, a veteran journalist; the deputy mayor of Beijing, Wu Han; and the head of the United Front Department of the Beijing Party Committee, Liao Mosha. From this group, particularly from Deng, emanated the satirical essays published in *Beijing Wanbao* (*Beijing Evening News*) and the Beijing fortnightly *Qianxian* (*Frontline*). At the same time

Wu Han wrote his play, *The Dismissal of Hai Rui,* which described the downfall through court intrigue of an honest official who had interceded for the peasants and ended with a demand that the peasants be given back the land—all set in the historical period of the Ming Dynasty. The reader could easily recognize in Hai Rui the Peng Dehuai whose rehabilitation Wu Han had pleaded for in his play. This group of Beijing critics was soon joined by the two leading economic theorists of China, Lo Gengmo and Sun Yefang, who sharply criticized the radical policies in articles carried in *Renmin Ribao* and elsewhere.

In January 1962 the enlarged Central Work Conference attended by seven thousand people made a preliminary summary of the positive and negative experience of the Great Leap Forward. A majority of people who had been unjustly criticized during the campaign against "right opportunism" were rehabilitated before or after the conference. In addition, most of the rightists had their labels removed. The praise of the Great Leap vanished in the print media and was replaced by calls for working step by step, taking into consideration place, time, and the objective conditions systematically, coordinately, persistently, and patiently. With the help of concessions to the peasants and extension of the system of material incentives, the national economy recovered successfully from the middle of 1962 onward.

Nevertheless, these successful policies again came under attack at the Tenth Plenum of the Party Central Committee, where Mao widened and absolutized the class struggle, defending his position that the contradiction between the proletariat and the bourgeoisie remained the principal contradiction in socialist society.[101] He went a step further and claimed that the bourgeoisie would continue to exist and would attempt a comeback to become the source of revisionism inside the Party. This theory later took the form of the contention that members in power taking the capitalist road were the most dangerous force within the Party and should be the main target of attack.[102]

The growth of "leftist" errors in the spheres of politics, ideology, and culture since 1962 was serious, but these ideas had not yet become dominant. In March and April 1964 the Ministry of Education, together with the Department of Education of the Beijing Party Committee, convened the heads of all the secondary schools of Beijing, who decided that pupils would be allowed to spend their holidays according to their own wishes.[103] This call for sufficient leisure time for students appeared in *Renmin Ribao* in the corresponding months.

This trend was further augmented in 1965, when Deng Tuo demanded in *Qianxian* at the end of April that regular courses in all schools should receive priority over political education. On 21 June *Ren-*

min Ribao suggested that workers should receive an opportunity to combine their work with the appropriate leisure.[104] Newspapers like *Guangming Ribao* and *Renmin Ribao* demanded in July and August that all female students and male students who fall ill be relieved of their duty to perform physical labor; the newspaper also criticized political meetings on holidays. *Guangming Ribao* maintained on 5 August that it was the duty of the trade unions to improve the standard of living of the masses. On 7 September *Zhongguo Qingnian Bao* declared that the cadres of student associations were, first, students, and only then cadres.[105]

In the spring of 1965 publications began to upgrade the stature of Liu Shaoqi to such an extent that he frequently appeared to be in a position equal to Mao. The Xinhua News Agency reported on 28 September that at the closing rally of a national sports event on the same day, the Beijing stadium was decorated with two equally large pictures of Mao and Liu placed side by side.[106] At that time ordinary people could hardly expect that in less than two months' time a few articles written by a young Shanghai journalist would be the signal of a forthcoming "cultural revolution," which would cause the most severe setback and the heaviest losses to the Party, the state, and the people since the founding of the People's Republic.

For 10 years the country was thrown into confusion as much at the leadership level as at the base. The speed with which the crisis developed and the shape it took varied according to different social milieus and regions and kept changing as time passed. Because of this, the crisis could not be controlled by the center, and yet the center always had some control over it. At stake in the crisis, when all the country's political structures were challenged, were Mao's theses that a new bourgeoisie had emerged in the Party and socialist institutions had fallen into its hands, and that such power could be recaptured only through a "cultural revolution," which would have to be waged time and again.

And so, on 10 November 1965, the Shanghai paper *Wenhui Bao* directed an attack against the vice mayor of Beijing, Wu Han, describing his play, *The Dismissal of Hai Rui,* as a great poisonous weed that must be eradicated and rooted out.[107] The author of this attack was Yao Wenyuan, a future member of the Gang of Four.

The Party's publications at first refused to reproduce the editorial. Only after it had been published as a pamphlet in Shanghai on 26 November and after *Jiefangjun Bao* (*Liberation Army Daily* under the control of Lin Biao, who replaced Peng Dehuai as minister of defense in 1959) had reproduced it on 29 November, did *Renmin Ribao* at last follow suit on 30 November. However, the newspaper added a footnote labeling the article as a contribution to discussion and calling for a general expression of opinion. Up to early December, only 14 of the more than 35 regional newspapers had reproduced Yao's critique without comment. Aside from *Renmin Ribao,* only two papers, *Guangming Ribao* and *Beijing Ribao,* added comments of interpretation or mitigation. The remaining newspapers did not take any notice of the article at all.

Renmin Ribao itself and the media under the Beijing Party Committee published several articles in December defending Wu Han against Yao's attack. The self-criticism Wu finally published on 30 December in *Renmin Ribao* was equivalent to a defense of his position, and as late as January 1966 the newspaper published a reader's letter condemning criticism of Wu. Subsequently, however, his defenders became quiet, and the demand that workers should combine their work with sufficient leisure was heard for the last time in January.

On 4 and 8 May the *Liberation Army Daily* gave the signal for a general attack on Deng Tuo, Wu Han, and Liao Mosha. They were called "poisonous revisionist weeds" and described as a "black gang of counterrevolutionaries" trying to restore capitalism.[108] The army journal's editorial on 8 May was entitled "Open Fire at the Black Anti-Party and Antisocialist Line." On the same day *Guangming Ribao* contained a similar article: "Heighten Our Vigilance and Distinguish the True from the False." Both papers included a long explanatory text, "Deng Tuo's *Evening Chats at Yanshan* is Anti-Party and Antisocialist Double-Talk."

Hongqi, the Party's theoretical publication, attacked the "bourgeois" position of *Beijing Ribao* and *Qianxian.* In Shanghai an article by Yao Wenyuan, the first critic of Wu Han, appeared on 10 May in *Wen Hui Bao* and *Jiefangjun Bao,* denouncing *Notes from the Three-Family Village,* a series of chronicles written by Deng Tuo, Wu Han, and Liao Mosha in the early 1960s. All newspapers reprinted his article the next day. About a dozen similar attacks followed in other papers, including *Renmin Ribao,* during the month of May.

Actually, the Deng Tuo affair had begun on 16 April, when *Beijing Ribao* and *Qianxian* printed a voluminous, though somewhat empty, criticism of *Notes from the Three-Family Village* and *Evening Chats at Yanshan.* It was accompanied by a self-criticism of the editors, who accused themselves of lacking vigilance and giving in to bourgeois influence instead of taking inspiration from the spirit of the proletariat. The sincerity of this self-criticism, however, was questioned in most of the articles just mentioned.[109]

Criticism of Deng Tuo, Wu Han, and Liao Mosha came from all circles and was repeated over the several months, reappearing throughout the Cultural Revolution and becoming more and more insulting. The darts aimed at the three were actually aimed at the press and cultural circles in the capital and, beyond them, the mayor of Beijing, first secretary of the municipality, and fifth-ranking man in the Political Bureau: Peng Zhen.

The papers and periodicals *Beijing Ribao, Beijing Wanbao, Qianxian,* and *Wenyi Bao* carried on for a few weeks longer, making their self-criticism and seeing their editorial staffs reshuffled, but were eventually suppressed one after another during the months of July and August. Meanwhile, political events quickened, particularly at the end of May when Lin Biao moved up, Peng Zhen and Lu Dingyi disappeared from public, and Zhou Yang, vice minister of culture, was publicly disgraced. At Beijing University the first salvo was fired, openly beginning the Cultural Revolution.

These events were accompanied by a series of editorials and articles intended to fix the general direction of the Cultural Revolution and give its partisans powerful psychological and political support. As a whole, the five articles published by *Renmin Ribao* in the first week of June, each on a clearly defined theme, looked like the first statement of the doctrine of the Cultural Revolution. Wu Lengxi, editor of the paper and head of Xinhua, had just been removed from office with Peng Zhen and the chief office-holders in the Ministry of Culture. Chen Boda, later an important member of the Lin Biao clique, had replaced Wu, bringing with him a team from the *Liberation Army Daily,* and Beijing took over from Shanghai as the center for propaganda.

When the Chinese mass media fell into the hands of people like Yao Wenyuan and Chen Boda, the most unfortunate days came for journalism in China. The publication media joined in a chorus of deifying Mao, lauding ultrademocracy, repudiating the so-called revisionist clique headed by Liu Shaoqi, and humiliating intellectuals. During the decade of tumult from 1966 to 1976, the theory that news must be truthful was discredited, and the fallacy that facts should follow the interest of political line became the guiding principle of journalism. Lies were praised. Facts were distorted. Evidence could be created out of nothing.

Many of Liu Shaoqi's statements were quoted out of context by the mass media and thus became "counterrevolutionary revisionist," "anti-Party, antisocialist, and anti–Mao Zedong thought." His assertions about journalism were severely condemned as "bourgeois" and "reactionary" and therefore "thrown into the garbage heap."

Under the control of the radicals, the mass media spread the idea that spirit decided everything and denounced those who paid close attention to production. Any problems emerging in technical innovations would be described as "a new tendency of class struggle" and "a sabotage activity by the enemy." Any peasants who were better off than others would be labeled "capitalist roaders." The intellectuals were held in contempt because their "four limbs do not toil" and they "do not know the difference between the five grains."

News coverage, which should serve the people, became an instrument with which the Lin Biao and Jiang Qing cliques tried to seize Party and state power. Ignoring or distorting facts, they fostered a kind of writing style characterized by falsification, exaggeration, and empty rhetoric. The newspapers were disliked by readers, who found them to be good material only for wrapping raw meat and fish when shopping. Radio audiences turned off their sets to save electricity.

The Cultural Revolution, which was expected to end in one or two years, dragged on. The Ninth National Party Congress in 1969, seemingly a conclusion of the "revolution," was followed by the disgrace of Chen Boda and, surprisingly, by the downfall of Lin Biao. After the Tenth National Party Congress in 1973, the Jiang Qing clique directed its spearhead at Zhou Enlai and then at Deng Xiaoping, who rose for the second time with the help of Zhou. But it did not take long before the Gang of Four was smashed. This action of 1976 brought the catastrophic Cultural Revolution to an end.

December 1978 marked a crucial turning point in Chinese history. The Party Central Committee began to correct the "leftist" errors of the Cultural Revolution and earlier periods.

Beginning in 1978 there was nationwide discussion in the press on the issue that practice was the only basis for testing truth. The reversal of important unjust verdicts, including the case of Liu Shaoqi, was reported by the newspapers and newscasts. The Tian An Men Incident of 5 April 1976, an incident of national significance during which the people mourned for the late Premier Zhou and opposed the Gang of Four, was given prominence in the press and praised as a "revolutionary movement." This incident indeed laid the groundwork for the subsequent overthrow of the Jiang Qing clique. Mao, who had been treated as God, now was regarded as a man who could make mistakes.

As the focus of Party and government work shifted in 1979 to socialist modernization, centering on economic construction, coverage of economic news became prominent. *Renmin Ribao,* which expanded to eight pages in January 1980, gave increasing coverage to economic news. During that month, of the 29 news stories given primary display on the first page, 21 were economic reports. In January of 1979, only 3 economic stories of 27 occupied the same place. Of the total 312 stories appearing on the front page in January 1980, 173 were economic reports. In January 1979 only 49 economic stories of a total of 151 news reports were carried on page 1.[110] Apart from the first page, nine pages were devoted to economic reporting every week, including the coverage of agriculture, industry, and commerce.

Reports in other fields, including politics, nationality, science, education, literature, and art, also focused to a large extent on economic coverage. The coverage of a stable political situation, economic construction in areas of national minorities, scientific research, personnel training, newly published works of literature, and art all served the interests of economic reporting. Not only economic reforms, but also the changes they brought about, were fully covered.

The Chinese peasants have never been covered in the press as completely as they have been in the 1980s. The peasants are becoming experts, managers, board chairmen, technicians, and even scientists and constitute a generation of strong people who know theory, are good in action, and have full competitive power, according to *Renmin Ribao*. Many farmers have not forgotten those who lagged behind, and this spirit of mutual help has been encouraged by the Chinese press today. The fact that primary emphasis has been placed on economic reporting shows that the old concept of the press as an instrument of class struggle is being challenged. The old concept is one-sided, an experienced Xinhua journalist has said in one of his articles, for the press is an instrument of economic education as well.[111]

In early 1980 *Renmin Ribao* began a special column to discuss how peasants could become rich as quickly as possible. The purpose of this column was to free cadres in rural areas from their fear of encouraging peasants to become wealthier, a fear that had existed since the late 1950s and early 1960s. The discussion also tried to dispel the doubts of farmers about the policy behind helping them to become rich. Four years later the newspaper again organized a discussion, this time to entreat farmers who were the first to acquire some money to help other farmers follow their example. The discussion was well received among the rural people, many of whom wrote letters to the paper, telling the editor they had benefited from the discussion.

Similar discussions appeared on such topics as economic structural reforms in cities (*Renmin Ribao,* June 1984); how to treat intellectuals, including those who had shortcomings and mistakes (*Guangming Ribao,* May 1984); and structural reforms concerning science and technology (*Guangming Ribao,* March 1984). Implementing Party policies toward intellectuals has been another important theme in news reporting in recent years. *Guangming Ribao,* a nationally circulated newspaper with a large readership among intellectuals, paid special attention to the coverage of such news. Apart from news stories, the paper carried in 1984 alone at least two editorials or commentaries a month calling for the improvement of this group's conditions—their political status as well as their working and living conditions.

On 24 February the paper carried a long feature story about a Party secretary in a northeast Chinese factory who, in the early 1970s, supported promoting an engineer who was widely regarded as a "reactionary" to the position of production supervisor. The engineer was later promoted to a position much higher than that of the Party secretary. A commentary in the paper the same day urged all Party cadres at the grass-roots level to follow the Party secretary's example.[112]

A 21 July commentary in *Guangming Ribao* strongly criticized those in power who refused to carry out Party policies concerning intellectuals and urged them to be removed from their posts. The commentary was based on an earlier report that the head and deputy head of a county hydropower bureau in Sichuan persecuted an intellectual alleged to be a rightist.[113]

China Daily, the only English newspaper in China, carried news reports in November 1984 and January 1985 suggesting that more intellectuals should be admitted as Party members. A 20 November *Renmin Ribao* commentary similarly argued that the educational level of present Party members should be raised. Only in this way, it said, could Party leadership be scientific, strong, and effective.[114]

The Chinese press has been taking grave note of the lack of truthfulness in news. In late 1983, when *Renmin Ribao* found a news story to be in error, it carried a commentary with an investigative report and two letters from readers. The commentary, entitled "The Principle of Truthfulness Must Be Maintained in News Coverage," argued that to adhere to such a principle was important for Communists.[115] A national forum on truthfulness in news reporting held in late June and early July 1984 stressed that news reports full of falsehood, exaggeration, and empty rhetoric in this turbulent decade greatly discredited the Party's work in journalism. To maintain truthfulness and eliminate inaccuracy was of major importance in the reform of news coverage.[116]

Critical reports, seldom seen since 1957, began to reappear in the press in 1980. From 22 July to 3 September 1980 *Renmin Ribao* gave full coverage to the sinking of a floating platform offshore. The coverage, which came seven months after the accident, was a breakthrough in economic reporting. The reports consisted of news stories, feature stories, investigative reports, commentaries, editorials, articles, letters from readers, and cartoons. A front-page report on 22 July gave a detailed account of the accident, criticizing the Offshore Oil Exploration Bureau under the Ministry of Petroleum for issuing arbitrary orders that brought about the sinking of the drilling platform.

On the second day *Renmin Ribao* reprinted a *Gongren Ribao* report on the same subject, a clear-cut criticism of those in charge of the bureau, for disregarding scientific law, ignoring safety, and evading responsibility. On 30 July *Renmin Ribao* reprinted a *Guangming Ribao* article that censured certain people in the bureau for trying to shirk responsibility. *Guangming Ribao* described these people as "conceited, stupid, proud, incompetent, and arrogant." "They know little and yet refuse to learn," the article said.[117] In a commentary on 24 August *Renmin Ribao* criticized the petroleum minister. Two days later the paper reported the decision of the State Council to relieve the petroleum minister of his post and to add a serious mistake to a vice premier's record, a decision that had never been reported.[118] A *Renmin Ribao* editorial the next day said the most important lesson to be had from the incident was that no one should become proud. Within six days, beginning 27 August, the paper carried 15 follow-up stories. The sentencing of two people directly responsible for the accident to three- and four-year prison terms showed that the tendency not to act in accordance with objective economic law was a fit theme for reporting.[119]

"There is plenty of scope for newspapers to engage in critical reporting," said a *Renmin Ribao* editorial on 22 October 1983. Critical reporting was indispensable, it said, because it could redeem those who had made mistakes and educate those who had not. The editorial said the power of critical reports lay in their accuracy.[120]

To promote critical reporting, a six-day forum was held in August 1984 in Jinan, Shandong, to discuss how newspapers, radio, and TV stations could present criticism effectively. Those who attended the forum said many good critical reports had brought the Party and the people closer together, enhanced the prestige of the Party, and raised the credibility of newspapers and newscasts among the people.[121] But, they noted, critical reporting often met with resistance from all sides. Some who were criticized tried every means to prevent the reports from being published; others were shielded by their supervisors; still others who had power interceded for their subordinates, brought pressure to bear upon the press, or simply ignored the reports.

Inaccurate, one-sided, or reckless reports are of dubious social worth, they said, and they added that any errors should be corrected, that those who are criticized should be allowed to explain, and that anyone who makes a blunder in reporting should follow up with self-criticism. They called on Party organizations at all levels to remain aware of and to support critical reporting, protecting those who inform reporters of what they know, educating those who are criticized to correct their mistakes, and disciplining those who reject criticism and who willfully make trouble.

According to the Shanghai-based *Wen Hui Bao,* eight reporters from the daily *Hunan Ribao,* a Hunan radio station, and a Hunan TV station had started to probe into the persecution by administration officials of some innocent shop managers in Changsha City and found themselves continually libeled, harassed, and prevented from conducting their investigations.[122] The incident attracted serious attention from the Chinese Journalists' Association and aroused public concern over the protection of the rights of the media, the *Wen Hui Bao* reported. Authorities of the Hunan provincial government took measures to punish those involved in slandering reporters. They criticized themselves and apologized to the reporters, the paper said.[123]

On 25 February 1985 *Renmin Ribao* came out in support of a journalist in Liaoning Province who was illegally detained for 209 days on a false accusation. An accompanying editor's note from the paper reminded readers that a few officials and ignorant people were hostile to journalists and obstructed their work. In some recent cases cameras were snatched and reporters beaten and detained.[124] "All these acts are against the law and must not be allowed," the paper said. It urged Liaoning and Hunan provinces to learn from the Beijing Municipality, which had severely punished a group of people who beat up a photographer and snatched his camera while he was performing his duties.[125]

A signed article from *Renmin Ribao* on 26 March 1985 praised the resurgence in the past few years of penetrating investigative journalism in the Chinese press. Reports that exposed problems and malpractices had influenced public opinion greatly, urged people to make changes, and strengthened the bond between the government and Party on one hand and the masses on the other, the article said.[126] For example, a series of articles in Hunan provincial newspapers in 1983 reported that an engineer in a factory was persecuted and discriminated against by factory leaders, and as a result was unable to do his job properly. The reports, calling for an end to such maltreatment of professionals, drew the attention of local authorities to the problem, and measures were taken to improve the engineer's situation. He was later elected deputy mayor of Hengyang City in the province.[127]

Another engineer's invention—an energy-saving motor—was virtually ignored by his factory leaders, who envied and disliked him. After his story was reported in the press, his case received the attention of the local authorities, and the value of his invention was recognized. Production of the new motors went up from a few hundred to eight thousand per year, bringing the factory big profits. The engineer was elected a model worker and became the director and chief engineer of the factory.[128] The article said that these two cases, and many others like them, demonstrated the positive effect of exposés. Criticism and the uncovering of malpractices forced leaders to improve their work. Most investigative reports were based on hard facts, the article went on to say, because journalists gather firsthand information to substantiate their claims. The article therefore urged government organizations and leaders to take notice of this type of reporting and benefit from it.[129]

From February 1984 *Renmin Ribao* carried a number of critical reports that attracted public attention. A 26 February report said two foreign trade companies in Jiangsu Province, each bickering with and blaming the other, allowed 1,590 tons of potatoes shipped to Hong Kong to rot, resulting in a loss of some $330,000 in U.S. money.[130] A 20 March story reported that the irresponsibility of Beijing foreign trade companies in their work had caused a loss of some $868,000. This serious dereliction of duty was a result of the bureaucratic way of doing things, the report claimed.[131]

The provincial trade department in Henan was said to have many serious problems, according to a 5 April report: bureaucracy, confusion in management, acceptance of bribes, and even smuggling. A work team sent by the central and provincial discipline-inspecting commissions was investigating the various problems, and initial results had been obtained, but arduous work lay ahead, the report said.[132]

The deputy director of a cigarette factory in Guangdong Province, who was bribed into helping a Hong Kong businessman in a tobacco deal, brought a loss of 2.97 million U.S. dollars to the provincial foreign trade company. Dereliction of duty was the crime, the 8 April report said. The factory director was sentenced to death and the malfeasants were sentenced to imprisonment.[133]

On 25 April *Renmin Ribao* claimed to have received many letters from readers who expressed indignation at those who had caused great losses to the state and severely reproached the bureaucrats who handed the wealth of the people over to others. An accompanying commentary advised that the bureaucrats should not be treated lightly.[134] Readers' letters constitute an important part of Chinese newspapers, especially Party papers. *Renmin Ribao* now devotes at least half a page every Thursday and Saturday to such letters. This section also includes investigative reports in response to some of the letters, especially those about Party and government officials. A factory worker in Gansu Province was beaten and, instead of getting help from the Party secretary, was persecuted and those who beat her were shielded. Finding no way out, she wrote a letter to *Renmin Ribao,* which sent reporters to investigate the matter. The provincial Party committee was solving the problem, but the solution, delayed for eight years, was worth pondering, the investigative report said on 26 May 1984 in *Renmin Ribao.*[135]

In 1980 a county post-office worker in Shandong Province wrote a letter to *Renmin Ribao,* saying he was persecuted for revealing that two people from the county Party committee illegally censored letters. The director and deputy director of the post office persecuted the post-office worker under the orders of the head of the county Party committee office, the investigative report said, adding that they were shielded by the provincial and district Party committees. These people, however, had been removed from office, according to the report dated 11 August 1984.[136]

The ultimate fate of readers' letters was revealed to the public by *Renmin Ribao* in a report on 4 August 1984, which explained that apart from a small number of letters that were printed, most of the letters were sent to Party and government departments to be processed for solution.[137] According to a survey conducted by the paper, 22 percent of the letters sent for solutions were well treated, and the problems had been or were being solved. The other letters had different destinies. Some were ignored; others were delayed; the writers of still others were given empty promises.[138] *Renmin Ribao* called for greater attention on the part of Party and government officials, improved coordination among concerned departments, and stronger support from people working at the grass-root levels.[139] To strengthen the socialist legal system, newspapers, news agencies, and radio and TV stations have been encouraged to make every law known to the people. A forum sponsored in April 1984 by Peng Zhen, chairman of the Standing Committee of the National People's Congress, to urge the media to play their part in this respect was immediately followed by a special section on the legal system in *Renmin Ribao.*

The 26 April 1984 issue carried a story about a woman who won a case against her sister's husband for poisoning his wife. An accompanying commentary compared the two sisters. One, poisoned four times before her death, failed to go to court due to her limited knowledge of the law; the other brought the affair before the court in spite of threats by her sister's husband.[140] This issue also carried questions and answers about lodging an appeal, and an introduction to laws in Indonesia, Egypt, Peru, and the United States.

The 11 June 1984 issue reported that the intermediate people's court in Xiamen City, Fujian Province, had sentenced 13 of the more than 40 members of a hooligans' gang and was trying the others. These young-sters all came from families of people who held high positions. The social order in the city had turned for the better, the report noted, and the people were living in peace.[141] The issue also carried an analysis of a case on the succession of property, a story about a legal case in ancient China, and a commentary condemning the idea of feudal privilege, which prevented people from looking into cases where sons and daugh-ters of high officials were involved.[142]

A 4 January 1985 issue of the *Renmin Ribao* legal section surprised readers with a report describing how a chief justice drove an attorney out of a county people's court in Shaanxi Province while the trial was in session. Commentary appearing in the same section attributed such practice to the several-thousand-year-long feudal system in Chinese his-tory. The civilized and progressive attorney system is an important com-ponent of a socialist legal system, the writer said. In the face of a situa-tion where law should be applied to aspects of social life, he demanded that more good lawyers be trained and more relevant laws enacted.[143]

A signed article appearing in *Renmin Ribao* on 25 May 1984 urged cultural laws to be enacted. The Party's policy of "a hundred flowers blossoming and a hundred schools of thought contending" should be manifest in cultural laws, the article said. In order to eliminate the possi-bility of another cultural autocracy such as that during the reign of the Gang of Four, a press law must be enacted. Such a law should ensure the right of free speech and prevent such freedom from being abused, the article said.[144]

The nature and content of broadcasting in China have been closely linked to China's printed press. The Central People's Broadcasting Sta-tion, as the national radio station, has the function of disseminating news, social education, and entertainment. The radio station depends heavily for its news reporting on the Xinhua News Agency and on *Ren-min Ribao*. Complete reliance on news agencies and newspapers, how-ever, dilutes the value of broadcasting, kills the wisdom and creativity of those who work at radio stations, and weakens the role of broadcasters as members of an independent mass media.

To remedy this situation, the central station in 1954 asked 18 local radio stations in Hebei, Shanxi, Shanghai, and other parts of the coun-try to cover local news for its service. Until 1963, 53 local radio stations were doing the job. These local stations had played their part in helping the central station and Radio Beijing (overseas service) improve their work. But this reform could not change the situation completely.

In 1965 the central station set up its own reporters' stations in places other than Beijing to cover local news for both the central station and Radio Beijing. By the end of the year such stations were located in 17 provinces and in autonomous regions, as well as in Shanghai and Tianjin. From 1966 to 1976, however, the central station fell into the hands of the Gang of Four. The newscasts were then nothing but what Xinhua, *Renmin Ribao,* and other journals reported, losing their own unique characteristics. A debate ensued concerning whether the reporters' stations should continue. After the Gang of Four was smashed, however, the reporters' stations continued to grow. In 1981 alone 11 such stations were established; another 4 were established in 1984. By then a network of reporters had spread throughout the country.

Incomplete figures indicated that the reporters' stations provided 16,900 news stories for the central station in 1979–83. In 1983 the central station used 4,526 stories, 3,334 of which were "hard" news. Forty-one percent of the hard news was used for such important programs as nationwide hook-up and press summaries.[145]

Since the end of 1978, these local reporters, together with central station reporters in the capital, have taken part in the coverage of the war of self-defense against Vietnam, the sessions of the Fifth and Sixth National People's congresses, the People's Political Consultative Conference meetings, the National Science Conference, the Party National congresses, the Fourth and Fifth National Sports meets, and the 35th anniversary of the founding of the People's Republic. They also covered important construction projects, major events worth radio criticism, and advanced personalities.

Local spot news is covered by local reporters who work for the central station. From late June to mid-September 1981, when floods hit the upper reaches of the Changjiang and Huanghe rivers, these reporters from Sichuan, Shaanxi, Gansu, Ningxia, Qinghai, and Inner Mongolia rushed to the sites to cover the floods. In two months they wrote over 40 stories describing how people in the affected areas fought the floods and overcame difficulties. After 1979 the local reporters wrote many critical reports, which resulted in significant social changes. The second day after the radio broadcast of a story about a primary school teacher in a Hebei county who was beaten, the provincial Party committee met to discuss measures to solve the problem. The Ministry of Civil Administration, the Ministry of Education, and the Central Committee of the Democratic Alliance also looked into the matter to show their concern.[146]

In 1983 and 1984 the reporters' stations increased the number of stories for overseas service. In 1983 alone Radio Beijing used over three hundred stories written by local reporters, a near 100 percent increase over 1982. But still these reporters could not satisfy the growing need of the service, either in terms of quality or quantity. Radio Beijing now broadcasts 138 hours a day to different regions, in 38 foreign languages as well as in standard Chinese and four local dialects. Apart from the regular programs, every language service produces programs for target audiences or at the request of its listeners. There is much room for improvement in overseas service programs by local reporters.

The content of newscasts improved when the general situation in China changed for the better. Out of the total broadcasting time for the central station, news now accounts for 15 percent. News programs include nationwide hook-up, press summaries, news and commentary, and international affairs. News programs are also provided by local stations. Altogether the central station broadcasts more than 60 programs a day.

Educational programs account for 20 percent of the total broadcasting time. These include study sessions; programs for peasants, youth, children, and soldiers; economics for the masses; reading and literary appreciation; sports; world and national events; tales from history; legal information; science and hygiene; and also radio teaching programs.

Sixty percent of broadcast time is devoted to entertainment programs, which include music, opera, literature, ballad singing, and radio drama. Entertainment programs are especially well received because of their notable absence in the past decade. Service programs, which comprise about 5 percent of total broadcast time, include mailbag, foreign exchange rates, weather forecasts, radio calisthenics, program announcements, and advertisements. These programs can be received with good fidelity in more than 80 percent of the country through MW, SW, and FM transmitters and relay stations. But reception is not good in the remaining 20 percent of the country, which includes mostly remote areas.[147]

Besides the central station, there are 122 local radio stations, with up to 11 stations in every province, municipality, and autonomous region and in some of the other large cities. And there are 516 transmitting and relay stations in the country. Every county has a rediffusion network to relay news programs from the central and the local radio stations.[148]

Television broadcasting began to develop in the late 1950s. In May 1958 the Central People's Broadcasting Station inaugurated television in the People's Republic. By the mid-1960s, 12 stations served the densely populated urban areas, and by 1970, 30 urban stations had been developed. In December 1972 at least one station reached each of China's 29 provinces, autonomous regions, and municipalities under central authority, except Tibet.

TV programs during the Cultural Revolution were dull even to the

Chinese. The opening program was a newscast with stories on topics such as the commemoration of a hero, the work of an educated youth in a remote village, the reception of foreign visitors by the Chinese leadership, and the heroic struggle of the North Vietnamese against the United States. Next came revolutionary ballet and films, usually old Chinese movies about the anti-Japanese war or the war against the Nationalist Chinese. Occasionally North Korean, North Vietnamese, and Albanian movies were shown. The entire program was devoid of any commercial interruption.

Before 1973 China Central Television broadcast only one channel in black and white. In May 1973 it began its experimental color programs on two channels. The first of these is now relayed to 27 provincial capitals and municipalities by microwave. There are 52 TV centers and 385 TV transmitting and relay stations of a thousand watts or more throughout the country. The second channel broadcasts only to the Beijing area. The total transmitting time of the two channels is about 15 hours a day.[149]

At the beginning of 1979 Central Television and the Ministry of Education jointly inaugurated a Television University. Central Television broadcasts TV University programs for about three hours in the morning to the entire country, and there is a rebroadcast for the Beijing area in the afternoon. TV University has a student enrollment of 450,000, which does not include the large number of unenrolled. The university has already graduated 160,000 full-course students and 200,000 single-course students.[150]

Television programs now are more entertaining. Every year TV stations all over the country are capable of producing more than three hundred TV plays and other entertainment programs, live broadcasts of sports events, and synchronized dubbing of foreign TV plays and feature films. A new color TV center is designed to broadcast programs on three channels simultaneously to the entire country and on one channel overseas. Daily broadcasting time will increase by 180 percent, allowing the production of 172.5 hours of programs every week. The broadcasting system will be operated by program control with electronic computers. Modern technology will be used extensively in news gathering and editing.[151]

Conclusion

In the latter part of our discussion about China's journalism, we focused our attention on the Xinhua News Agency, *Renmin Ribao, Guangming Ribao,* the Central People's Broadcasting Station, and

China Central Television. These are among the leading media in China today. All of these media, with the exception of *Guangming Ribao,* have from the beginning worked under the Party's leadership. In the course of more than 35 years of publication, *Guangming Ribao* has become a national newspaper under the Party's direction since 1957. It is a paper focusing its attention on science, education, culture, theory, academic discussion, and the united front.

Party journalism is different from other kinds of newspapers or journals run by the People's Political Consultative Conference and various democratic parties like *Tuanjie Bao* (*Solidarity Paper*), and unlike specialized and technical publications run by cultural, educational, scientific, and other establishments. Party General Secretary Hu Yaobang defined the nature of Party journalism as "serving as an organ of the Party, the government and the people. . . . The function as organ of the Party also includes the function as a link between the Party and the people, and the function of reflecting the voices of the people and satisfying the needs of the people for information," he said at a meeting of the Secretariat of the Party Central Committee on 8 February 1985.[152]

Since 1979 the Communist Party of China has been pursuing a policy of invigorating the domestic economy and opening the country to the outside world. The restructuring of the national economy has been accelerated both in the countryside and in urban areas. As the winds of reform sweep the cities, there are those who suggest that journalistic institutions become independent producers, like industry and other enterprises. The practice of applying current economic reforms to journalism, however, has been discouraged. Hu Yaobang has said that although journalistic institutions are managed as a kind of enterprise, they are above all mass media organizations. "No matter how many reforms are introduced, the nature of the Party's journalism cannot be changed," Hu said.[153]

Yet others have suggested that China needs different voices. Hu has replied that while it is necessary to listen to different viewpoints, the voices are the same on the political orientation and fundamental policies of the Party and government because the Party and government represent the people and share the same interests.[154] But on specific problems, he said, there are indeed different voices. These voices are already published by different newspapers and magazines and have been encouraged by the Party and welcomed by the people. If these are not enough, more will be published, an indication, Hu has promised, of democratic life in China.[155]

China's journalism, or the dominant part of it, is an organ of the

Party, and its political orientation and fundamental policies largely or totally depend on those of the Party. When China is on the right track, the Chinese are allied to their press. When the Party line goes wrong, as it did during the Cultural Revolution, journalism goes in the wrong direction.

The Party general secretary has said that the most fundamental of the basic requirements for the Chinese Party press is to take a clear stand, to uphold the basic viewpoints of Marxism and the Party's policies, and to adopt pragmatic methods of seeking truth from facts. These requirements have been emphasized throughout the Party's history, particularly during the years in Yan'an, in the post–civil war years before 1957, and after the Cultural Revolution. The Chinese Communist Party is correcting the leftist errors committed during the two decades between 1957 and 1976.

The continued development of Chinese journalism along the path charted by the Party depends on whether it will adhere to the present policies of modernization. With China marching swiftly on the road to modernization, the process of urbanization, the literacy of the people, and the growing economic and political participation will accelerate. This process is indeed already in progress. Twenty percent of the rural work force is now surplus labor, and that proportion is expected to rise to 70 percent by the end of the century. Small towns will be designed to absorb more than half this labor, thus easing the population flow into cities.[156]

Chinese peasants, who have historically suffered from illiteracy, have become better off in recent years. Some, though they are still small in number, have been investing in the operation of primary, middle, and technical schools. In Gongxian and Fugou counties, where such schools have been set up, as well as in the Xuchang area, Henan Province, schoolteachers who were once looked down upon are now living treasures. The peasants, who have subscribed to more and more newspapers and magazines for information, are complaining about the limited number of journals published for rural areas. Publication of specialized journals for the countryside has been encouraged, and necessary help and support was promised at a forum attended by representatives of 23 specialized journals for rural areas in Jilin Province in June 1984.[157]

The mass media promote the process of modernization, which in turn helps promote the growth of mass media. Veteran Chinese journalist Hu Qiaomu, a member of the Political Bureau of the Party Central Committee, foresaw this in his letter dated 28 November 1984 to journalists from all over the country attending a three-day conference in

Beijing. He wrote that the introduction of advanced technology in the reporting, editing, and transmitting of information, as well as advanced management methods borrowed from other countries, would allow China's journalism to reach the highest level in the world in content, in form, and in technology.[158]

2 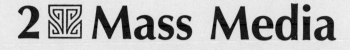 Mass Media

2 ⚏ Xinhua News Agency

History

The state-run wire service of the People's Republic of China, the Xinhua News Agency, was established in 1931. Xinhua, formerly spelled Hsinhua, means "new China" in Chinese. With its head office in Beijing, the Xinhua News Agency is China's biggest news center, with a total staff of five thousand. It has branch offices in 29 provinces, in autonomous regions of minority nationalities, in municipalities under the direct jurisdiction of the central government, and in the People's Liberation Army units. Some of the branches have placed resident correspondents in big cities and industrial enterprises. In addition the agency has a large number of part-time reporters at the grass-roots level. Xinhua also currently has over 160 correspondents in 82 overseas bureaus in foreign countries.

Establishment of the Xinhua News Agency

After 1927, with the development of the Red Army Movement led by the Communist Party of China, revolutionary bases and local revolutionary governments were set up one after another in south China. Against this background the First National Congress of the Workers, Peasants, and Soldiers was held in Ruijin, Jiangxi Province, east China, in November 1931. The congress declared the founding of the Chinese Soviet Republic and organized its Provisional Central Government with Mao Zedong as its chairman. Among the 60 members of the Central Executive Committee were Zhou Enlai, Zhu De, and Liu Shaoqi, who were later to become the Party and state leaders of the People's Republic of China.

On the day of the opening of this congress, 7 November 1931, the Red China News Service was inaugurated and began to release news. It was to be renamed Xinhua News Agency (New China News Agency) in 1937 and become the state news agency of the People's Republic of

China in 1949. In the course of the congress, the agency sent out the declaration of the founding of the Chinese Soviet Republic, its draft constitution, labor decrees, and land decrees of the Provisional Government. In its radio transmission, the agency adopted the call sign of CSR—Chinese Soviet Radio. This call sign continued to be used by the later Xinhua News Agency until September 1956. In addition the agency received news from the Central News Agency of the Kuomintang and printed it as reference news for the six hundred delegates attending the congress.

Although the Red China News Service was poorly equipped and much needed to be improved in its organization, it was the first wire service set up by the Communist Party of China, which used the modern technology of telecommunication. In December 1931 the newspaper *Red China,* organ of the Provisional Government of the Chinese Soviet Republic, started publication. The paper and the Red China News Service then had only one editorial board and staff.

During its initial stage the Red China News Service shared a radio transmitter with the Military Commission of the Provisional Government of the Chinese Soviet Republic. Its daily output totaled two to three thousand words, covering documents of the Central Committee of the Communist Party and the Provisional Government, news about construction of the Red areas, and reports from the Red Army's battlefields. These releases reached the Communist organizations based in the provinces of Hunan, Hubei in central China, Jiangxi Province in east China, Shaanxi Province in northwest China, as well as the then Central Bureau of the Communist Party in Shanghai and the Northern Bureau of the Communist Party in Tianjin.

At that time the Red China News Service relied on a transmitter-receiver belonging to the Red Army for receiving news from outside. It was not until March 1933 that the agency installed its own receiver especially for receiving news released by the Kuomintang-run Central News Agency. Later it also began to receive a small amount of news from some foreign agencies.

In October 1934 the Long March began. It was a major strategic movement of the Chinese Workers' and Peasants' Red Army, by which the army succeeded in reaching the revolutionary base in northern Shaanxi after traversing 11 provinces covering 125,000 kilometers. Because of the extremely difficult conditions in the course of the Long March, the Red China News Service had to stop releasing news; however, it managed to continue to receive news.

By 1936 the Japanese stepped up their invasion of China. In December of the same year Zhang Xueliang and Yang Hucheng, two Kuomintang generals, put Chiang Kai-shek under house arrest in Xi'an, where he was supervising military operations against the Chinese Workers' and Peasants' Red Army. They demanded Chiang cease the civil war and form an alliance with the Communist Party to fight against Japanese invaders. The pro-Japanese forces in the Kuomintang government in Nanjing intended to take power from Chiang Kai-shek and sought a compromise with the Japanese invaders. On learning this, the Chinese Communist Party sent a delegation headed by Zhou Enlai to Xi'an, whose mediation peacefully settled the Xi'an Incident. A national united front against Japanese invasion was formed.

Under these new circumstances, in January 1937 the Central Committee of the Chinese Communist Party of China decided to change the name of the Red China News Service to the New China News Agency, or the Xinhua News Agency. On 25 January 1937 the Xinhua News Agency started releasing news to the entire country in Yan'an, Shaanxi Province, where the Central Committee of the Communist Party was at that time based. At the same time the newspaper *Red China* was renamed *New China Daily*.

After the outbreak of the war against Japan in 1937, branches of the Xinhua News Agency were set up in various anti-Japanese base areas, including Shanxi-Chahar-Hebei, northeast China, Shandong Province, and northwest Shaanxi Province, and exchange between the Xinhua head office and its branches increased. In 1939 the Central Committee of the Communist Party of China made a decision for the Xinhua News Agency to establish its own organization independent of the *New China Daily*. By that time Xinhua already had its own foreign language department, editorial board, and a network of correspondents. It had also installed a transmitter-receiver of its own. Its daily output had increased to around five thousand words, and it was receiving news from more foreign agencies.

In addition the Xinhua News Agency tried to set up a broadcasting station in the spring of 1940 when the Central Committee of the Communist Party formed a broadcasting commission with Zhou Enlai as its chairman. The broadcasting station as part of Xinhua News Agency began to broadcast on a trial basis on 30 December 1940. The transmitter used by the station was brought from the Soviet Union by Zhou Enlai in person.

In May 1941 the Central Committee of the Communist Party of China issued a circular stating that the Xinhua News Agency was to become a unified news center, and that radio stations set up in various areas were to be administered by Xinhua's branch offices, which in turn should accept the leadership of the Xinhua head office in Yan'an. The decision was carried out and by 1942 the Xinhua News Agency had already set up a unified network of news gathering and reporting. Because the liberated areas at that time were severed by enemy blockade, the wire service virtually played the role of a national newspaper.

Owing to the lack of adequate equipment and technicians, the broadcasting station stopped broadcasting in the spring of 1943, but resumed its work on 5 September 1945, when the Chinese people won the final victory of the eight-year-long war against Japanese aggression. The broadcasting station was renamed Yan'an Broadcasting Station and remained part of the Xinhua News Agency until it moved into Beijing (then Peking) on 25 March 1949. After the 1949 founding of the People's Republic of China, it became the Central Broadcasting Station.

Two Prominent Early Leaders of Xinhua

During those years Xinhua had survived severe hardships and many leaders had contributed to its development. Particularly newsworthy are Qu Qiubai and Bo Gu.

Qu Qiubai (1899–1935) was one of the early leaders of the Communist Party of China. He had done a great deal for the promotion of proletarian literature in Shanghai between 1931 and 1933. He left Shanghai for the central Soviet area in 1933 and arrived at Ruijin, Jiangxi Province, on 4 February. At the Second National Congress of the Soviet China he was elected member in charge of education of the Central Democratic Government of the Workers and Peasants as well as director of Red China News Service. In these capacities he made great contributions to China's revolutionary education and mass media.

When the Long March began, he had to stay behind because of illness, though he remained the head of the Propaganda Department of the Central Bureau of the Red Area and the editor in chief of the newspaper *Red China*. In February 1935 he was arrested by Kuomintang troops in Fujian Province, southeast China, and was shot there in June after several months of imprisonment.

Before his execution, a high-ranking Kuomintang officer tried once again to get Qu to capitulate, showing him Chiang Kai-shek's order "to be shot on the spot." Qu said, "Men cherish their own histories more than birds do their wings. Please don't tear my history." On his way to the execution ground, he sang the "International." When he came to a lawn, he looked around and said, "This is a nice place," and then sat down and met his death with composure. He was only 36 years old. In the history of Xinhua Qu was the first to lay down his life. Bo Gu (Qin Bangxian), one of the founders of Chinese Communist journalism, was the first director of the Xinhua News Agency when it adopted the name. A native of Wuxi, Jiangsu Province, he joined the Communist Party of China in 1925. Between 1926 and 1930 he studied in the Soviet Union. In February 1942 he took part in the negotiations with Kuomintang in Chongqing and died in an air crash on his way back to Yan'an together with a number of Communist leading figures.

A Marxist theoretician, Bo Gu held that the Party's press was as good as its eye and mouth and stressed the importance of reporters going among the masses to make in-depth investigations. He also emphasized that news must be entirely true, and propaganda must be supported by irrefutable facts and reasoning.

Xinhua in the Period of the Liberation War

The years following the victory of the Chinese People's War of Resistance against Japan in 1945 saw further development of the Xinhua News Agency. During this period the agency set up a number of new branches in the newly liberated areas. While the peaceful negotiations between the Communist Party and the Kuomintang were under way, it had even established offices in Kuomintang-ruled cities, including Chongqing, Beijing, and Nanjing.

In May 1946 the Xinhua News Agency underwent an overall reform in its organization. Its head office gathered all the journalists in Yan'an and a large number of press people who had just arrived from the Kuomintang-ruled areas, thus greatly strengthening its editorial board.

In June of the same year when the third National Civil War broke out, the Xinhua News Agency set up its first frontier office in the field stationed in Shandong Province, east China. In the meantime, Xinhua's branches in the various localities sent reporters to the major battlefields. Later, Xinhua offices were also set up among the Communist armies stationed in the provinces of Shanxi, Chahar, and Hebei and in northeast China.

On 14 March 1947 the Kuomintang launched large-scale attacks on the central Red base in the Shaanxi-Gansu-Ningxia border area. The Communist Party Central Committee was forced to leave Yan'an. The head office of the Xinhua News Agency then set up a station in Wa-Yao-Bao, a village 50 kilometers to the northeast of the city of Yan'an, where it continued to work even after the Kuomintang troops seized Yan'an.

Part of the staff of the Xinhua head office formed a team that followed the Central Committee of the Communist Party, headed by Mao Zedong and Zhou Enlai, from one place to another. The rest of the staff crossed the Yellow River and set up a provisional head office in the

Taihang Mountains, Shanxi Province. In the course of moving, which lasted more than two months, Xinhua did not for a single day stop its work. Because the newspaper *Liberation Daily,* organ of the Communist Party Central Committee, had stopped publication at the time, Xinhua took upon itself to include in its program the commentaries, or editorials, which were normally the work of the *Liberation Daily.*

It was then that Xinhua sent its first resident correspondent abroad. In 1948 Xinhua set up overseas bureaus in Prague and London.

In May 1948 the provisional head office of Xinhua moved once more to Jianping County, Hebei Province (now Pingshan County), where it joined the Xinhua team that had been following the Communist Party Central Committee. In autumn the Party Central Committee called together key members of Xinhua at the living quarters of the top leaders, who instructed them in ideology, policies, and working style as well as news reporting and editing.

Xinhua has enjoyed the meticulous attention of the leadership of the Communist Party since its founding. The late Communist Party chairman Mao Zedong himself had written quite a number of important articles for the Xinhua News Agency. Liu Shaoqi, late chairman of the People's Republic of China, and Zhou Enlai, late premier, had often polished Xinhua's papers.

With the unfolding of the Liberation War, branches of the Xinhua News Agency in the armies increased rapidly, resulting in a network of military reporting. During the war Xinhua correspondents were active on the major battlefields, and many of them laid down their lives on post. In March 1949, while the war was nearing its end, the Xinhua News Agency moved into Beijing with the Central Committee of the Communist Party. In June the Xinhua Broadcasting Station became independent from Xinhua. In August the *People's Daily,* a former newspaper of the North China Bureau of the Communist Party, became the organ of the Central Committee of the Communist Party of China. Xinhua then had completed its historical mission of integrating the services of broadcasting station and wire service.

Shortly after the founding of the People's Republic of China, the Xinhua News Agency became the country's national news agency, authorized to issue communiqués, statements, and important news on foreign affairs and to provide domestic and international news for newspapers and broadcasting stations across the country. In November 1950 the Xinhua News Agency convened its first national meeting to improve its organization and coordinate the work of its branches in the various provinces. Meanwhile, a photography department and a department of domestic news for overseas service were added.

Xinhua's Organization

Xinhua is governed by an editorial board composed of the director general, the deputy directors general, the department chiefs, and other senior executives. Directly under this editorial board is the general editorial office, which supervises the agency's day-to-day work. Mu Qing, a veteran journalist in his 60s, noted for his feature articles on outstanding figures, is the present director general of the Xinhua News Agency.

The head office of Xinhua in Beijing consists of the following departments:

General Managerial Department, which handles Xinhua's business other than news.

Domestic News Department, which covers domestic news for the media in China and whose Chinese-language service has a general wire and a local wire, serving 36 national newspapers and more than 300 local papers with a total circulation of about 70 million copies a day.

International News Department, which covers news abroad and whose Chinese-language service goes to the media in China and foreign-language services go overseas.

Department of Domestic News for Overseas Service, which covers Chinese news for foreign consumption and whose foreign-language and Chinese services go to media overseas.

Photo Department, which distributes news photos in China and abroad.

Reference News Department, which provides news from foreign media.

Journalism Research Department, whose task is to sum up Xinhua's experience in news practice and study the experience of foreign agencies.

Foreign Affairs Department, which administers Xinhua's overseas bureaus and its foreign affairs in general.

Technology Department, which transmits news and receives news from foreign news agencies and is in charge of improving Xinhua's equipment.

Xinhua has in addition a number of affiliated units as follows:

Journalist Training School, which offers training courses in news reporting and editing as well as in foreign languages, including English and French.

Xinhua Publishing House, which publishes books of various categories with emphasis on politics and journalism.

China Photo Service, which prints news photos for display.

Xinhua's Functions in China's Mass Media

In China, mass media are regarded as a link between the govern-ment, the Communist Party, and the people, and one expected to help advance the socialist cause. Apart from keeping the people informed about what is happening in the world and in China, Xinhua takes it upon itself to publicize the policies of the Communist Party and the People's Government, canvass the people's views about these policies, and report these views or transmit them to the highest leadership through a feedback system. It also holds itself responsible for educating and inspiring the people to make concerted efforts for the prosperity of the country.

In its domestic news for overseas service, Xinhua seeks to reflect all aspects of Chinese life, focusing on the current modernization drive involving the government's streamlining, readjustment of the national economy, more flexible policy in the rural areas, open policy and foreign trade, and the Chinese people's cultural life.

The following are Xinhua's news services:

Chinese-language general wire, which provides both domestic and international news for the major print and electronic media in China— 40,000 to 50,000 words per day.

Chinese-language local wire, which provides both domestic and for-eign news for provincial and regional newspapers, broadcasting stations, and TV stations—30,000 to 40,000 words per day.

Foreign-language overseas service—50,000 to 60,000 words per day, covering both domestic and international news.

Photo service, with dozens of pictures transmitted every day both domestically and internationally.

Overseas feature service, with two to three hundred articles in four foreign languages sent at regular intervals every year to over one hun-dred countries and regions.

Xinhua has a dozen centers in Hong Kong and foreign countries that publish Xinhua news bulletins of various kinds. In addition, the agency now has agreements with 47 foreign news agencies for the ex-change of news and is currently receiving news from 43 foreign news agencies or broadcasting stations, averaging 1.3 to 1.5 million words per day.

Major publications of the Xinhua News Agency include the follow-ing:

Xinhua News Bulletin, available in six languages and published daily.

News Photo, published every Wednesday.

Cankao Xiaoxi (Reference News), a tabloid-form newspaper that carries Chinese translations of foreign-agency dispatches without editing. With a circulation of about 8 million, it is the biggest daily newspaper in the country and is printed in 25 cities across the country.

Two foreign-language reference news bulletins similar to *Cankao Xiaoxi,* one in English and the other in French.

Economic Reference News, a paper published every Monday, Wednesday, and Friday, providing information on economic trends at home and abroad.

Journalism Review, Xinhua's house organ in which members of the staff exchange views about journalism in general and the agency's news reporting in particular; published monthly.

Ban Yue Tan, a twice-monthly popular political review with a total circulation of 1.48 million.

Observation Post, a journalistic monthly designed for government functionaries, intellectuals, and workers with education above secondary level, with a total circulation of 310,000.

Globe, a journal devoted to articles about important and interesting events in politics, economy, military affairs and social life in foreign countries, with a circulation totaling 380,000.

Photography World, a monthly with a circulation of 80,000 introducing world photography.

People who follow Xinhua's domestic news service will find that one of its special characteristics is the relative scarcity of breaking news stories. There is more explanatory and analytical material than hard news, except for stories about important conferences, meetings, visits of foreign dignitaries, completion of major construction projects, economic and scientific achievements, and so on. The domestic news service instead places emphasis on progress and achievements that have been made in China. This does not mean, however, that investigative journalism and criticism of social ills are totally excluded. Party and government officials guilty of corruption, embezzlement, bureaucracy, abuse of power, negligence, malfeasance, or seeking privileges have been openly criticized in Xinhua's reports. Bad social habits or conventions, waste, extravagance, and attempts to acquire luxury goods in short supply through the "backdoor" have also been subject to censure.

In handling news coverage, Xinhua generally follows the principle that most of its space, roughly 70 to 80 percent, is devoted to achievements and successes, and the rest to criticism and exposure of negative phenomena. The reasons for such an approach are that, first, in China achievements and successes really do outweigh corruption, crime, and immorality, and second, Xinhua tries to encourage the people to look forward and work for the good of the country rather than discourage them and undermine the nation's goal of building socialism.

Stories about political affairs and policy matters are, in most cases, roundups or reviews, with the exception of the promulgation of a new law by the National People's Congress, or similar instances. Occurrences like crime, violence, and litigation normally do not get the same amount of coverage as in the Western press. But the trial of the Gang of Four was a notable exception. All media in China gave the trial extensive and prominent coverage, carrying a number of stories every day.

Standard practice for covering a trial that is important enough to be reported is ordinarily the appearance of one story at the beginning of the trial, and another at the end of it. The first story describes the issue, the relevant facts, the scheduled court proceedings, and so on. The second provides the decisions of the bench, a review of the entire case, the root source of the issue, and finally, the lesson to be learned from it all.

Natural disasters are handled in much the same way as court cases, with roundups at various stages. The stories present the facts and the causes along with background information, analyses, final lessons, and measures taken by the government to bring the calamities under control and to minimize damage or loss. Xinhua's philosophy in such matters is that, while the news agency should inform and alert the people of possible danger, it should not spread panic among them. At the same time, it should also inform them how to deal with the situation most effectively.

It is also part of Xinhua's services to report discussions and debates about important issues before the final policy decisions are made by the Communist Party and the Central Government. There have been in recent years, for instance, keen discussions about the use of material incentives to encourage people to work harder and the kinds of reasonable limits appropriate to such incentives, as well as discussion about the enterprises' right to determine their own production plans.

But once a decision or policy is adopted by the Communist Party and the government, everyone in China is expected to abide by it. This is what is described as "the principle of democratic centralism," under which everyone is free to voice an opinion during the stage of discussion, but must abide by the majority vote once a decision is reached. This does not mean that people are absolutely forbidden to dissent even then. They can use a variety of channels to make their views known to the Party leadership while still carrying out the decision. One of these channels is writing letters to the Xinhua News Agency or to other mass media; another is writing memos to the leadership of one's own work unit, who will then refer them to the higher authorities. Views expressed by the people will be seriously considered and if they are found correct and useful, they will be used to revise and improve the policy or decision in question.

As a channel for two-way communication, Xinhua has the obligation to bring the people's views to the attention of the top leadership, namely, the Central Committee of the Communist Party and the State Council, which make up the central government of China. Herein lies one of the major differences between Xinhua and the Western news services. The people of China look upon Xinhua as a mouthpiece of the Communist Party and the government, which is why its reports have much greater impact among the people than the Western news agencies have among their people. The same is true of Xinhua's overseas services because of its status as an official news agency.

The journalistic technique of Xinhua's foreign news service is much the same as that of its domestic news coverage, with more roundup and analytical material than hard news. As one of its special features, it devotes more attention to news from Third-World countries than do most Western media. Xinhua's coverage of Third-World countries also tends to emphasize progress and achievements, although difficulties and problems are not ignored.

In covering the Western world, Xinhua attempts to report news events in a matter-of-fact, objective, and balanced manner. On international affairs, Xinhua tries to present the policies of the Chinese government accurately and the particular situation objectively, while refraining from interfering in other countries' internal affairs. Concerning China's relations (including disputes) with other countries, Xinhua tries to present China's position clearly without antagonizing these countries.

The primary guidelines for Xinhua's foreign news coverage are (1) to uphold China's national independence, territorial integrity, and sovereignty; (2) to support the just struggles of all peoples, particularly the struggles of the Third World for independence, emancipation, social justice, and economic and cultural progress; (3) to publicize the principles of peaceful coexistence and self-determination; (4) to work for understanding and friendship among people; and (5) to contribute to world peace and security.

To meet China's modernization drive, the Xinhua News Agency is currently making efforts to modernize itself. This task will involve the improvement not only of technology and equipment, but also of news quality. Although it may be years before Xinhua becomes a truly modern news agency with substantial international influence, it is nevertheless gradually gaining recognition throughout the world.

The Foreign News Department

The Xinhua News Agency has a Foreign News Department that is exclusively in charge of foreign news services. This department distributes items of foreign news for both domestic and overseas use. It has a staff of more than four hundred, including foreign correspondents in most countries of the world. The domestic staff is divided into two sections: one that handles news items for domestic use, and one that handles news items for overseas use. The latter is itself divided into several sections according to geopolitical regions and languages. For instance, there is a Euro-American section, an East Asian section, a French section, an Arabic section, and so on. In addition, there is an extensive morgue that serves the entire Foreign News Department as well as other departments within the agency.

The main news sources for the Foreign News Department are the 88 foreign branches all over the world. Foreign correspondents send back news in various languages, most commonly English, news about the countries where they are stationed and about important international events. The department also receives information from many foreign news agencies: Associated Press (AP); United Press International (UPI); Reuters; Agence France Presse (AFP); Telegraphnoye Agentstvo Sovyetskovo Soyuza (TASS); Deutsche Presse-Argentur (DPA, West Germany); Agenzia Nationale Stampa Associata (ANSA, Italy); Press Trust of India (PTI); Kyoto; Middle East News Agency (MENA); Tanjug, and others, and uses news items from these agencies on a complimentary basis. Once news items are received by the department, they are delivered to various sections for editing and translation. The staff of the section in charge of foreign news for domestic use translates the news item into Chinese or rewrites it, then distributes it by facsimile to domestic news media.

The staff members who handle dispatches for overseas use first translate them into English and then edit them. The edited foreign news items are sent abroad by teletype. After receiving these items, foreign branches copy and deliver them to clients in the concerned countries. At present clients of Xinhua news bulletins are mainly in Africa and South America; few are in Western countries. On the average, the Foreign News Department releases nearly one hundred news items a day. Compared to other news agencies, especially Western news agencies, Xinhua attaches more importance to coverage of the Third-World countries.

The working system of the Foreign News Department involves four major steps: news gathering, news selection, news translation, and news release. Each stage engages its own unique process of news handling.

1. News gathering: Xinhua foreign correspondents all over the world cover the important events in countries where they are stationed. They also gather news from official bulletins, newspapers, news magazines, and television in the countries in which they are stationed and send them back for home use. At the same time, the Foreign News Department also receives information distributed by foreign news agencies. The junior editors discard a large part of the news they deem not newsworthy and give the remainder to editors in charge of various regions.

2. News selection: All news items sent back by Xinhua correspondents and picked up from foreign news agencies are given to the editors who decide what to publish. The news items the editors use most frequently are those from the Western Big Four: AP, UPI, Reuters, and AFP.

3. News translation: News items selected by editors are translated from foreign languages into Chinese for domestic use. If news items selected for distribution abroad, whether sent back by Xinhua correspondents or picked up from foreign news agencies, are in a language other than English, they must be translated first into Chinese and then into English.

4. News release: The translated news items are then released to the domestic news media through facsimile, and news items for overseas use are sent by teletype to Xinhua foreign branches all over the world. The Xinhua branches then deliver them to the concerned countries.

Gathering the News

In the initial step of news selection, Xinhua foreign correspondents go to press conferences, interview officials and other news sources, read newspapers and newsmagazines, and watch TV news reports. They write or rewrite news items about events they consider important and send them back home. There, editors tear the roll of the newsprint at regular brief intervals to check the news that comes from the foreign agencies. Usually junior editors, who are rarely qualified at this stage to make more than the simplest selection decisions, perform this job. Only when the news gatherers are confident that a piece of raw news is not newsworthy can they discard that news. Any item whose news value is uncertain would be turned over to the next step.

Certain criteria, or "gatekeeping factors," exist in this initial step that govern which news items, correspondents, as well as junior editors, will select as newsworthy. For a Xinhua correspondent, the primary determinant is the importance of the event that occurs in the country where he or she is stationed and the relevance of the background information.

For those at home, several determinants govern the selection process. The first determinant is precedent. When news gatherers are not sure if they should pick up a news item, they follow precedent, checking the day's or the past day's news-article book. Junior editors with little experience often refer repeatedly to precedent in picking up news. If they confirm that a news item has been issued before, news gatherers will not discard that news.

The second determinant is instruction. When Xinhua is watching a particular event, the junior editors are instructed not to miss any related or follow-up news stories. When a war breaks out, for instance, the editors in charge of that region are instructed to follow the news, and if the war is important enough, editors in charge of other regions will pick up responses toward the war.

The third determinant covers specially classified news. Some kinds of foreign news, such as sports news, science news, and economic news, require special knowledge. News gatherers do not discard such news solely on their own judgment, as they are rarely able to discern the news value. These kinds of items are instead forwarded to the sections or persons with the appropriate expertise.

The fourth determinant governs China-related news. News gatherers make it a rule to pass all such news on to the editors and to keep up with news about other countries' actions and reactions towards China.

Selecting the News

All news items not discarded are given to the editor in charge of various regions. These editors are the true news selectors, the most influential foreign news controllers at Xinhua. Not surprisingly, there are a great many gatekeeping elements effective at this step.

The first determinant that affects the selection process is Xinhua's foreign news policy, which emphasizes getting as much Xinhua foreign news as possible published or broadcast by its client news media. The rate of publication by client media is used as an index of success in news management. The rate of reporting Xinhua foreign news by the local news media is high, but the competition from the *People's Daily,* which is sending out more and more foreign correspondents of its own, is increasing.

The second determinant at this stage is the agency's committee of editors. Editors of the Foreign News Department participate every evening in a newsroom meeting and sometimes are notified by the government about what kinds of foreign news to select or to emphasize. Decisions by the head of the agency or the committee of editors are conveyed downward on a daily basis to other editing members.

The third determinant is the nature of the agency itself. Xinhua is an official news agency whose policy of foreign news reporting serves China's foreign policy. It is worth noting, however, that Xinhua grows more and more objective by the day in its foreign news reporting.

The fourth determinant is consensus among editors. At times the editors will have section meetings to discuss news selection. The purpose of these meetings is to decide which of the day's events are newsworthy, and how each item should be played. When defining and evaluating the news differs significantly among editors, they may take a group consensus.

Translating the News

One of the main tasks of the section in charge of foreign news for domestic use is to translate raw news items written in English, or in other foreign languages, into Chinese. These editors not only select and translate news, but sometimes rewrite it.

The most important gatekeeping element in translation is determining the differences in literacy and newswriting styles between English and Chinese. In the Chinese-written news of Xinhua, most of the articles are arranged in the conventional inverted pyramid pattern. Editors pick up news factors, such as who, what, when, where, and so on, that are scattered in the raw news articles and assemble them into a new, Chinese-written article.

The second determinant at this stage is the news source. Usually editors will group together articles on the same news events, read them all at once, and write one translated news article. They sometimes pick up news aspects from different world news agencies. For instance, editors may pick up a basic news outline from AP and add to it an angle from UPI. Different original news stories thus become mixed in this translation process. Although the end result may be a news item close to "perfect," it is nobody's news story. It reflects the opinion of the Xinhua News Agency.

The third determinant is the credibility of the news source. Although Xinhua receives copy from many foreign news agencies, each agency's unique news-covering characteristics result in different degrees of credibility. When the same news event is reported differently, the editors of Xinhua are sometimes faced with the problem of not knowing which source—for example, AP or AFP—is more credible. A Xinhua editor will typically trust AP, UPI, Reuters, and AFP, in that order, but does not lose sight of the fact that the credibility of a particular world news agency varies according to the nature of the news event. For example, AFP would be regarded as the most credible news source for a news event that occurred in France.

Releasing the News

News items translated into Chinese for domestic use are released through two channels: the wire service and the publication service. These two channels operate on different systems; the wire service runs 24 hours a day, while the news bulletin is issued once a day. The foreign news for overseas use is released by teletype to Xinhua foreign branches all over the world. The wire service, using facsimile, distributes the news to domestic news media in just a few seconds. High speed is the advantage of this service.

Role of the Press

The director of the Department of Domestic News for Foreign Services, Chen Lung, who studied first journalism and then economics at Yenching University at the time Edgar Snow was teaching journalism there, started working with the Xinhua News Agency in 1938 in the caves of Yunan. In a 27 April 1983 interview in his home in Beijing, where he was recovering from a stroke he suffered in December 1981, Chen Lung, speaking in English, provided his personal views of the Chinese press's role:

> The starting point for the press is different in China. The mass media have a grave responsibility to people and society in China. Formerly China was controlled by foreign countries and by feudalism. If we want to overthrow these two yokes, we have to rely on people. So our primary task is to awaken the people so that they will understand the overthrow of imperialism and feudalism, that it is of common interest, so that they will fight for it. The primary role of the news is to educate and awaken the people. And

you see the same thing now. We want to modernize China. It is a very gigantic task. And you have to awaken the whole people to work hard for it.[1]

Chen Lung went on to say that news is not a commodity or an enterprise for making profit but an instrument for educating the people. Because news is regarded as enterprise in the West, journalists must win readers. Sometimes in the West journalists write very interesting stories to win readers, but they lack a sense of social obligation. The result is sensationalism—crime, sex, and violence—which may appeal to the basic instincts of the people, but which is of dubious social value, Chen said. In the West, furthermore, some newspapers do not want to offend people for fear they may lose advertising. The Chinese understanding of the function of the press is different.[2]

As an agency of the government, the Chinese press is responsible for serving the nation's modernization program and for promoting the welfare of the people. Such responsibility plays a direct role in the news content of the Xinhua News Agency, the nation's papers, and broadcasting stations. Chen Lung said that the Department of Domestic News issues stories that explain the policies of the Party and government to the people and the best way to implement these policies, while the Foreign Services Department of Domestic News issues news of important events that will attract the attention of Chinese leaders. He said that, despite many difficulties, Xinhua has presented a genuine picture of China to the world, and the greatest challenge faced by Xinhua is its goal of becoming a world news agency.

Another Xinhua News Agency leader, Wang Renlin, a deputy director of the Department of Domestic News for Foreign Services, explained in English his personal view of the criteria for choosing news in the People's Republic:

First of all you must have some news value—that, I think, is common to all news agencies and to all newspapers. If it has no news value then it is useless. But one important difference between the Western press and Chinese press is that the Chinese believe the press should further the progress of their country. Sometimes I read Chinese papers published in Hong Kong—rape cases, murder cases. I wonder, What is the function of the press there? Is the press helping to increase the crime rate in that city?

We know in our country that life has unsatisfactory aspects. I don't think we need to cover them up. But the press—as a mass medium—has a day-to-day influence, a very strong influence on the public. And I think the press must play a positive role in furthering the progress of our country.

I don't think it is as simple as good news or bad news. Sometimes we also have to report bad news to show bureaucratic evils. This also has a positive function—to mobilize the people, to awaken them to these things and to find solutions.

And I think this is my view. Of course we have to tell the truth. During the Gang of Four, the Cultural Revolution, the fake stories and all were not true. But the Western press now says, "You're a Communist press and you're just propaganda." But why does the Western press print one story and not another? As a journalist, I want to work for the good of my country, or otherwise I can simply leave my job and do something else that will be of benefit to my country. This is my general view.[3]

Wang Renlin went on to say that stories from the Department of Domestic News for Foreign Services must be of some interest, which is difficult to determine, to foreign audiences. Generally, he said, Xinhua tries to report on China's progress, the problems the nation faces, and plans to solve those problems. With the Chinese audience, the Department of Domestic News takes into consideration the different sectors of the population, such as young people, workers, intellectuals, and cadres, he said. Some people read the *Beijing Wanbao* for its human interest stories while others read the *Renmin Ribao* to learn about the Communist Party's policy.[4]

Another Xinhua News Agency official, Huang Zumin, deputy director of the International Department, said in a 29 April 1983 interview that the criteria for choosing news are very similar to those of Western agencies, including the latest happenings, important events, and stories of interest to readers. He said that his department's international coverage is too narrow, with an overemphasis on political coverage and Chinese sports and not enough emphasis on economic and cultural events.[5]

With regard to the freedom of the press in China, Chen Lung said that he is free to report everything he wishes as long as he carries out his responsibilities as a journalist to present a correct picture about China and present it expertly. Chen Lung said that department should cover both good and bad news, such as news of landslides, earthquakes, floods, and plane crashes:

Events with human beings cannot avoid being reported, but we must consider the consequences of such reporting. We try to report that we have done everything to alleviate the distress of the people so as not to increase their despondency or suffering.[6]

Wang Renlin said that press freedom is based on the underlying principle of progress and that all news agencies have their criteria for what can and cannot be reported.

> We should cover such things as disasters. Why not? If we haven't covered them, we haven't fulfilled our responsibility. If it is a major disaster, we should let the people know. And we do cover them, although maybe not adequately. That's another question. The Tang Shan earthquake [Hebei Province, 28 July 1976] during the Cultural Revolution wasn't covered in a timely fashion. Most people in Xinhua think that's wrong, which shows the progress of the Chinese press in the last few years. We don't want to frustrate the people, making them feel things are hopeless.[7]

Huang Zumin said that the policy in the International Department is to cover disaster. He said that the West has a misunderstanding about the selection of news in China.

> Yes, of course I feel free to report anything I wish at Xinhua. We can decide about 90 percent of what we report in our department; a few are decided by the editorial board of our news agency. I think there's a misunderstanding among Western agencies. We decide most commentaries and most news.[8]

In 1957, on the 20th anniversary of the Xinhua News Agency, the director of the Chinese Communist Party's Department of Propaganda said that the role of Xinhua is as important to society as the roles of other organizations such as the Party, the government, the court, and the army.[9] But according to a 1956 *Journalism Quarterly* article, the Chinese press, including wall and blackboard newspapers and other outlets, serves as a political medium for propaganda, agitation (Marxism, Leninism, and Mao Zedong thought as well as production and economic development), public information, and public control.[10]

As early as 1957 the Xinhua News Agency had said, at its 20th anniversary meeting, that it was on its way to becoming a world news agency.[11] In a 22 April 1983 briefing of foreign polishers working at the Xinhua News Agency, Vice Director Chen Bojian outlined the agency's four-stage reform plan for becoming a world news service center in China. First, through a series of world regional conferences in Mexico City (November 1982), Beijing (January 1983), Prague (March 1983), Cairo (March 1983), Beijing (March 1983), Harare (April 1983), and Bonn (April 1983), preparations for branch offices in the reform movement were discussed. Second, the agency planned to concentrate on reform news work at the Beijing headquarters in the last half of 1983. Third, Chen Bojian said, the government had allocated funds for new equipment. The agency also planned to build a new office building in Beijing.[12] Speaking through translator Liu Qizhong, the vice director said:

> To improve the timeliness of our news coverage, we will make some necessary changes on the structure, the solid work, and our system. . . . When . . . stories come into this room, they will be handled by responsible editors and approved by the authorities in the same room. That means the working system will have to be changed. At present we have a two-shift working system. During the later part of the night, we don't have any editors working in the news offices. This does not suit the work of a world news agency. It is possible that we'll change it into a working system on a 24-hour basis.
>
> Changes will be made, of course, in the process of handling these stories. A news story will go first to an editor who can approve that story. If he believes that it's all right and doesn't need any changes, that story will be passed on immediately. If he thinks it needs editing he will send it to some other editors for that job. We think that this will quicken the tempo of our work. Apart from these changes in timeliness and structure, we will make other fundamental changes, too. For instance, concerning concepts of news coverage, we will consider readers inside and outside China. Content of news stories will be different, too.
>
> We'll try in many ways to train our personnel—reporters and editors—to raise their standards to levels that are suitable for a big news agency. In this respect, huge efforts have already been made. We've asked the State Planning Commission to give us more graduates from the universities and colleges. We have also trained some of the first graduates in the School of Journalism under the Social Sciences Academy of China. I was one of those graduates. We'll try to send more students to study journalism abroad. We have just set up an institute to train reporters and editors that will give them in-service education. They will study journalism; they will study English in several classes. Other more advanced classes will train English-speaking and French-speaking reporters. Those who haven't achieved higher education will attend classes in which they'll learn Chinese and other subjects so that after three to five years they will have reached the level of graduates of higher universities and colleges.[13]

At the briefing Chen Bojian also listed Xinhua's shortcomings. He said that news coverage was not timely, that reports were not specific, that coverage was too narrow, that stories were not vivid and therefore lacked interest for foreign readers, and that stories were limited in number. He also said the agency had problems with bureaucratic editing procedures, personnel matters, and outdated equipment. Chen Bojian said that unlike the AP and AFP, many Xinhua articles are not issued in the native language.[14]

At the end of 1984 a new computer system had been installed at the Xinhua News Agency in Beijing as part of the effort to modernize and make Xinhua a world news agency. The agency had 91 foreign bureaus, most of which were in Third-World countries at the time. "Before, we were following the leftist line, presenting all these things as true," Director of Foreign Affairs Ding Yangyan said. "But now we stick to the facts. So far as the news is concerned, we're more balanced." He said there is no censorship of the press in China, but editors are expected to carry out government policy as outlined in briefings conducted by Mu Qing, who holds the ministerial position of Xinhua Director General.[15]

Writing for UPI, Ron Redmond reported from Beijing:

> In place of the bombast and Maoist rhetoric, the state news agency now churns out 150,000 words daily on topics ranging from the latest foreign exchange quotations to pig farming to commentaries on space law.
>
> There's still a smattering of leftist jargon, but nothing like the old days.[16]

Topics in the News

A content study was conducted to determine the Western press's use of dispatches from the Department of Domestic Services of the Xinhua News Agency. The publications that were reviewed were the *South China Morning Post* from Hong Kong and *News from Foreign Agencies and Press* (called the *Blue News* in reference to the color used for the title), a daily English-language bulletin from the Xinhua News Agency that permits major news stories from the foreign news agencies and from foreign publication. In addition, the daily Foreign Reaction File of the Department of Domestic News for Foreign Services was studied. This is a file of foreign press-agency wire dispatches that cite Xinhua News Agency as a source—including AFP, AP, Kyoto, Reuters, and UPI. The two publications were reviewed for a one-year period from 14 February 1982 through 13 February 1983. The Foreign Reaction File was reviewed for the same period, but no foreign-service dispatches were placed into the file 12–18 April 1982 and the file was not available 13–20 August 1982 and 2–14 December 1982.[17]

The daily English-language *Xinhua News Agency News Bulletin* (also called *Red News* in reference to the color of the title's ink), which contains dispatches from the Department of Domestic News for Foreign Services and the International Department, was used to verify that the source of the domestic articles cited by the foreign press was the Xinhua News Agency.[18]

Both the number and the types of news articles were noted. Each article was identified by major content and placed into one of 18 categories: Agriculture, Airlines, Culture, Disasters, Economics, Education, Energy, Environment, Journalism, Law, Politics, Population, Religion, Rights, Science and Health, Social Ethics, Sports, and Television.

Several of the major categories were subdivided into additional categories. These subcategories include the following: under Airlines — Hijacking, Others; under Culture — Film, Literature, Photography, Publishing, Others; under Disasters — Floods, Quakes; under Politics — Constitution (national), Communist Party of China, Hong Kong, Japanese Textbook Issue, Leaders, National People's Congress, People's Liberation Army, Taiwan/Kuomintang, United States, Soviet Union, Others; under Rights — Women's, Others; under Science and Health — Computers, Others. The "Leaders" category under "Politics" was further subdivided into Deng Xiaoping, Mao Zedong, Song Chingling (Honorary Chairman of the People's Republic of China), and Premier Zhao Ziyang. Although few in number, stories about *Renmin Ribao* editorials, analyses, and commentaries were included in these categories, but separately identified.

The study revealed that between 14 February 1982 and 13 February 1983 the Department of Domestic News for Foreign Services issued a total of 6,713 stories, of which 1,368, or 20.37 percent, were cited as a source by the foreign press. For the sake of accuracy, it must be noted that of the 6,713 stories issued by the Department, seven of these were actually government documents:

Communique on Fulfilment [sic] of China's 1981 National Economic Plan, by the State Statistical Bureau, 29 April 1982, which was cited as a source by Reuters, 6 May 1982, in the *South China Morning Post* business section.[19]

Create a New Situation in All Fields of Socialist Modernization — Report to the Twelfth National Congress of the Communist Party of China, by Hu Yaobang, which was delivered 1 September 1982 and issued by the Xinhua News Agency on 7 September 1982.

Constitution of the Communist Party of China, adopted by the Twelfth National Congress of the Communist Party of China on 6 September 1982 and issued by Xinhua on 8 September 1982.

Constitution of the People's Republic of China, adopted by the Fifth National People's Congress of the People's Republic of China at its fifth session on 4 December 1982.

Report on the Draft of the Revised Constitution of the People's Republic of China, delivered by Peng Zhen, vice chairman of the Committee for Revision of the Constitution on 26 November 1982 at the Fifth Session of the Fifth National People's Congress and issued by Xinhua on 5 December 1982.

Report on the Sixth Five-Year Plan, delivered by Zhao Ziyang, premier of the State Council, at the Fifth Session of the Fifth National People's Congress on 30 November 1982 and issued by Xinhua on 13 December 1982.

Report on the Implementation of the State Budget for 1982 and the Draft State Budget for 1983, delivered by Minister of Finance Wang Bingqian at the Fifth Session of the Fifth National People's Congress on 10 December 1982, and cited as a source by AFP in a *South China Morning Post* news article on 16 December 1982 and by the Associated Press on 19 December 1982.[20]

Table 2.1 summarizes the findings of the study. The largest percentage of domestic Xinhua stories cited as sources by the foreign press for any given month occurred during March 1982 with 152 of 448 foreign press stories cited — almost 34 percent. September 1982 had the largest monthly total of stories — 655 (including two documents) of which 136 foreign press stories, or 20.76 percent of Chinese domestic wire, cited Xinhua as the source. The lowest monthly percentage of stories used by the foreign press was 14.17 percent in October 1982 when the department issued 628 stories of which only 89 foreign press news stories listed Xinhua as the source.

TABLE 2.1. Foreign Press Usage of Xinhua News Agency Stories

Year	Month	Number of Stories Issued[a]	Foreign Press Usage	
			Number	Percent
1982	Feb. 14–28	194	63	32.47
	March	448	152	33.92
	April	621	131	21.09
	May	625	108	17.28
	June	584	100	17.12
	July	512	96	18.75
	August	565	117	20.70
	September	655	136	20.76
	October	628	89	14.17
	November	544	127	23.34
	December	607	107	17.62
1983	January	480	109	22.70
	Feb. 1–13	250	33	13.20
Total		6,713	1,368	20.37

[a]During the period of this study, the Xinhua News Agency issued seven documents, each of which is counted as one story.

The content of these stories is broken down in Table 2.2 and identified by the Western press agencies that carried them. These agencies include the following: AFP, AP, Reuters, UPI, Xinhua News Agency (stories published in the *South China Morning Post* from the Xinhua wire), and others including All Agencies, Kyoto, *South China Morning Post* staff, New York Times News Service, and the *Financial Times* of London.

As indicated in Table 2.2, a total of 881 foreign press stories, or 45.69 percent of the 1,928 accounts that listed Xinhua News Agency as the source, were about Chinese policies.[21] The breakdown by news topics in the "Politics" category included Premier Zhao Ziyang, 88 stories, or 4.56 percent of the 1,928 total; the Communist Party of China National Congress, 78 stories, or 4.04 percent; Vice Premier Deng Xiaoping, 69 stories, or 3.57 percent; National People's Congress, 60 stories, or 3.11 percent; United States and China, 35 stories, or 1.81 percent; Taiwan/ Kuomintang, 33 stories, or 1.71 percent; People's Liberation Army, 30 stories, or 1.55 percent; Soviet Union and China, 24 stories, or 1.24 percent; national Constitution, 21 stories, or 1.08 percent; the Japanese Textbook Issue (this issue concerns the controversy over allowing historical facts about the Japanese war against China to be published in Japanese textbooks), 19 stories, or .98 percent; and Hong Kong, 12 stories, or .62 percent. Four foreign-press stories, or .20 percent, were about Mao Zedong while three stories, or .15 percent, were about Song Chingling, who had died in May 1981. Foreign news stories in the "Others" subcategory of Politics totaled 405 stories, or 21 percent.

These stories included the topics of international relations (with 19 stories on Vietnam fighting and prisoner release), Communist Party (other than the National Congress) Youth League activities, and state policy.

Ranking second to Politics was the "Economics" category which included 318 stories, or 16.49 percent, of stories that cited Xinhua News Agency as the source. In this category were news accounts on construction, production (including soft drinks and beer), tourism, and trade. The "Culture" category ranked third with 143, or 7.41 percent. Subcategories in the Culture division were Film, 11 articles, or .57 percent; Literature, 13 articles, or .67 percent; Photography, 1 article, or .05 percent; Publishing, 7 articles, or .36 percent; and Others, 111 articles, or 5.75 percent.

The "Energy" category ranked fourth with 86 stories, or 4.46 percent, and Law (including police and judicial affairs) was fifth with 69 accounts, or 3.57 percent. Science and Health was sixth with 6 reports,

or .31 percent, on computers and 60 reports, or 3.11 percent, in the
"Other" category, which included medicine, health, safety, technology,
telephone communications, missiles, space technology, and Antarctic research.

The remaining categories in descending order were as follows: Environment, 51 stories, or 2.64 percent; Religion, 43 stories, or 2.23 percent; Education, 42 stories, or 2.17 percent; Airlines, 16 stories, or .82
percent in the "Hijacking" category and 24 stories, or 1.24 percent in
"Others"; Agriculture, 39 stories, or 2.02 percent; Population (including
the 1982 census that reported a population of one billion in China), 35
stories, or 1.81 percent; Disasters, 20 stories, or 1.03 percent in the
"Floods" category and 14 stories, or .72 percent, in the "Quakes" category; Sports (including foreign mountain climbers in China), 32 stories,
or 1.65 percent; Rights, 2 stories, or .10 percent, in the "Women's"
category and 18, or .93 percent, in the "Others" category (including
minorities and overseas Chinese); Social Ethics, 15 stories, or .77 percent; Journalism, 8 stories, or .41 percent; Television, 6 stories (including TV set production, satellite transmission, and TV programs), or .31
percent.

During the period studied, the foreign press carried four reports
about *Renmin Ribao* editorials. The four editorials in question were the
traditional New Year's report (included in the "Others" category of "Politics"); an article on Chinese law; a report on the newspaper's comments
on the national Constitution as well as an article on problems with the
"iron rice bowl" method of payment; and equal pay for unequal work
(included in the "Economics" category). The foreign press also cited
Xinhua News Agency commentaries as the source for four stories (under
the "Politics" category), which included one report on India, one article
on Sino-Soviet relations, and two reports on Sino-American affairs.

Of the 1,928 foreign-agency domestic Chinese news stories that cited the Xinhua News Agency as the source, 693 articles, or 35.94 percent,
were carried by AP; 483 articles, or 25.05 percent, by AFP; 400 articles,
or 20.74 percent, by Reuters; 142 articles, or 7.36 percent, by UPI; 87
articles, or 4.51 percent, by the Xinhua News Agency (that is, stories in
the *South China Morning Post* with the Xinhua wire as carrier); and 123
articles, or 6.37 percent, by other news organizations (see Table 2.3).

Table 2.4 shows that the *News from Foreign Agencies and Press*
bulletin cited 85 stories, or 1.27 percent, of the 6,713 news accounts
issued from the Xinhua News Agency's Department of Domestic News
for Foreign Services. The *South China Morning Post* published 662 reports, 34 percent of Xinhua's foreign service wire.

TABLE 2.2. Content of Foreign News Stories Citing Xinhua News Agency as Source

Content	AFP	AP	Reuters	UPI	Xinhua	Others[a]	Totals
Agriculture	8	15	11	2	1	2	39
Airlines							40
Hijacking	2	6	5	2		1	16
Others	3	7	5	4	2	3	24
Culture							143
Film	4	2	2	1	1	1	11
Literature	7	4		1		1	13
Photo		1					1
Publishing	1	2	2		1	1	7
Others	25	42	20	9	12	3	111
Disasters							34
Floods	2	7	6	1	4		20
Quakes	2	7	3	1	1[b]		14
Economics	78	116	78	16	10	20	318
Education	11	17	5	3	5	1	42
Energy	15	38	19	5	1	8	86
Environment	8	20	13	4	5	1	51
Journalism	4	3				1	8
Law	15	23	22	7	1	1	69
Politics							
Constitution	2	9	3	1	1	5	21
CPC	16	31	19	6	1	5	78
Hong Kong	3	4	2	1		2	12
Japanese Texts	4	5	5	2		3	19
Leaders							
Deng	21	23	14	6		5	69
Mao	1	2	1				4
Song	1	1	1				3
Zhao	21	28	27	7	2	3	88
NPC	7	17	7	4	9	16	60
PLA	8	7	5	5	1	4	30
Taiwan/GMT	7	15	5	3		3	33
USA	9	14	7	5			35

TABLE 2.2. *(Continued)*

Content	AFP	AP	Reuters	UPI	Xinhua	Others[a]	Totals
USSR	5	8	5	3		3	24
Others	137	144	66	19	15	24	405
Population	8	13		12	2		35
Religion	9	18	12	2	2		43
Rights							
Women's	1	1					2
Others	4	5	2	3	3	1	20
Science & Health							
Computer	1	1	2		1	1	6
Others	16	18	15	5	4	2	66
Social Ethics	7	4	1	1	1	2	15
Sports	7	13	9			1	32
TV	3	2	1	1			6
Total	483	693	400	142	87	123	1,928

The number of stories in this table include duplications by agencies in which two or more foreign agencies used the same Xinhua News Agency domestic story as a source for their news accounts.

[a] This category includes news stories in the *South China Morning Post* from a news organization with a byline or dateline listing the news carrier as: All Agencies (8 stories); Kyota (47 stories); SCMP Staff (54 stories); and others including the New York Times News service (1 story); *Financial Times* of London (1 story); and agencies identified as DC (7 stories), MTN (1 story); and PH (1 story) as well as stories without an identified news organization (3 stories).

[b] The *South China Morning Post* carried two Xinhua News Agency photographs with one of the quakes stories.

TABLE 2.3. Domestic News Stories in Foreign Press Citing Xinhua News Agency as Source

Agency	Number of Stories	Percent
Agence France Press (AFC)	483	25.05
Associated Press (AP)	693	35.94
Reuters	400	20.74
United Press International (UPI)	142	7.36
Xinhua News Agency (NCNA)	87	4.51
Others[a]	123	6.37
Total	1,928	100.00

The number of stories in this table include duplications by agencies in which two or more foreign agencies used the same Xinhua News Agency domestic story as a source for their accounts.

[a]This category includes stories in the *South China Morning Post* from a news organization with a byline or dateline listing the carrier as: All Agencies (8 stories, .41 percent); Kyoto (47 stories, 2.43 percent); SCMP Staff (54 stories, 2.80 percent); or others including New York Times News Service, *Financial Times* of London, and agencies identified as DC, MTN, and PH as well as stories without an identified agency (14 stories, .72 percent).

In the *South China Morning Post,* stories in the "Politics" category ranked first with 309 stories, 46.67 percent of its Chinese domestic reports citing the Xinhua wire as a source. In this category, the newspaper carried 41 stories, 6.19 percent of its domestic coverage, on the Communist Party of China National Congress; 37 stories, 5.58 percent, on the National People's Congress; 24 stories, 3.62 percent, on Zhao Ziyang; 20 stories, 3.02 percent on Deng Xiaoping; 12 stories, 1.81 percent, on the People's Liberation Army; 10 stories, 1.51 percent, each on the United States and the Soviet Union; 4 stories, .60 percent, on Mao Zedong; 3 stories, .45 percent, each on Hong Kong and the Japanese textbook issue; 1 story, .15 percent, on the national Constitution; and 136 stories, 20.54 percent in the Other subcategory.

In the "Politics" category, 74 articles, or 87.05 percent, of the *Blue News'* 85 stories were subdivided into the following categories: 15 reports, 17.64 percent, on the Communist Party's Congress; 12 stories, 14.11 percent on Zhao Ziyang; 7 stories, 8.23 percent, on Deng Xiaoping; 6 stories, 7.05 percent, on the United States; 6 stories, 7.05 percent, on the Soviet Union; 2 stories, 2.35 percent, on Hong Kong; 2 stories, 2.35 percent, on the Japanese Textbook Issue; 2 stories, 2.35 percent, on the National People's Congress; and 22 stories, 25.88 percent, in the Other subcategory.

Again, the "Economics" category ranked second in *South China Morning Post* domestic Chinese coverage with 82 articles, 12.38 percent of the *Post's* total 662 stories. Culture was third with 64 stories, 9.66 percent (which included the subcategories of Literature, 5 stories, .75 percent; Film, 4 stories, .60 percent; Publishing, 3 stories, .45 percent; and Others, 52 stories, 7.85 percent); Law, fourth with 25 stories, 3.77 percent; Education and Energy, each ranked fifth with 22 stories, 3.32 percent; Science and Health, sixth with 21 reports, 3.17 percent (Computers, 3 stories, .45 percent, and Others, 18 stories, 2.71 percent); Religion, also sixth with 21 stories, 3.17 percent; Disasters, also sixth with 21 reports, 3.17 percent (Floods, 15 stories, 2.26 percent, and Earthquakes, 6 stories, .90 percent); Population, seventh with 16 stories, 2.41 percent; Sports, eighth with 14 stories, 2.11 percent; Airlines, ninth with 12 stories, 1.81 percent (Hijacks, 7 stories, 1.05 percent, and Others, 5 stories, .75 percent); Agriculture, tenth with 11 stories, 1.66 percent; Social Ethics, eleventh with 8 stories, 1.20 percent; Rights, also eleventh with 8 stories, 1.20 percent (Women's, 1 story, .15 percent, and Others, 7 stories, 1.05 percent); Journalism, twelfth with 4 stories, .60 percent; and Television, thirteenth with 2 stories, .30 percent.

In *News from Foreign Agencies and Press,* the Other subcategory of Science and Health ranked second to Politics with 4 stories, 4.70 percent; Law was third with 2 stories, 2.35 percent; and Population, Religion, Rights, Social Ethics, and Sports were in the fifth spot with 1 story, 1.17 percent, each.

In summary, the Xinhua News Agency's Department of Domestic News for Foreign Services increased production of news stories during the 12-month period from 14 February 1982 through 13 February 1983. During this same period, usage of Xinhua News Agency reports by the Western press also increased. The foreign news agencies, led by the AP, cited political stories from the Department of Domestic News for Foreign Services the most often, followed by news about China's economy, while news about Chinese culture ranked third. The *South China Morning Post* reflected the same pattern in its usage of domestic Chinese news released from the Xinhua News Agency, while Xinhua's bulletin *News from Foreign Agencies and Press* considered science and health, and then law, most important after politics. All of these developments took place over a period of time when the Xinhua News Agency's Department of Domestic News for Foreign Services was becoming increasingly aware of the requirements of the foreign press, when Xinhua launched its campaign to become an international agency, and when Xinhua's role became established as the government press service involved in the campaign to modernize the People's Republic.

TABLE 2.4. Content of Stories in News from Foreign Agencies and Press and *South China Morning Post* Citing Xinhua News Agency as Source

Content	NFA&P	% Total NFA&P	SCMP	% Total SCMP	Totals
Agriculture			11	1.66	11
Airlines				1.81	12
Hijacking			7		7
Others			5		5
Culture				9.66	64
Film			4		4
Literature			5		5
Publishing			3		3
Others			52		52
Disasters				3.17	21
Floods			15		15
Quakes			6		6
Economics			82	12.38	82
Education			22	3.32	22
Energy			22	3.32	22
Journalism			4	.60	4
Law	2	2.35	25	3.77	27
Politics		87.05		46.67	
CPC	15		41		56
Constitution			1		1
Hong Kong	2		3		5
Japanese Texts	2		3		5
Leaders					
Deng	7		20		27
Mao			4		4
Zhao	12		24		36
NPC	2		37		39
PLA			10		10
Taiwan/GMT			12		12

TABLE 2.4. (*Continued*)

Content	NFA&P	% Total NFA&P	SCMP	% Total SCMP	Totals
USA	6		9		15
USSR	6		9		15
Others	22		136		158
					383
Population	1	1.17	16	2.41	17
Religion	1	1.17	21	3.17	22
Rights					9
Women's			1		1
Others	1	1.17	7	1.20	8
Science & Health					25
Computer			3		3
Others	4	4.70	18	3.17	22
Social Ethics	1	1.17	8	1.20	9
Sports	1	1.17	14	2.11	15
TV			2	0.30	2
Total	85	100	662	100	767

91

3 ▦ People's Daily
(Renmin Ribao)

People's Daily, or *Renmin Ribao* in Chinese, is an official, serious, and quality newspaper in China that boasts the world's largest readership. The paper sells 5 million copies, the second largest among China's 1,776 papers, next only to *Children's News,* whose circulation is 8 million copies. However, the circulation figure of *People's Daily* belies actual readership. Issues of the paper are posted at most city intersections and read in political sessions of such institutions as the People's Liberation Army. Its editorials and commentaries are often relayed by Xinhua, China's official news agency, radio stations, TV stations, and local papers. Therefore, it is no exaggeration to say that the paper has the world's largest audience.

People's Daily is headquartered in a huge complex in the eastern part of Beijing, China's capital, about half an hour's drive from the city proper. The paper has a total staff of 600, with over 30 correspondents stationed in the major Chinese cities and 25 stationed in foreign metropolises such as Washington, New York, Mexico City, Tokyo, Pyongyang, London, Paris, Cairo, Algiers, Rawalpindi, and Bangkok. *People's Daily* produces several other publications, which include two tabloids and one magazine. It also owns a publishing house that prints the papers, the magazine, and books of various kinds. The paper started an overseas edition on 1 July 1985 for the entire Chinese-reading public: overseas Chinese, foreigners of Chinese origin, foreigners who read Chinese, and Chinese who work or study outside China.

China's First Paper

People's Daily has been known as China's most influential paper since its establishment on 15 June 1948. Though its large circulation

This chapter was written with the assistance of Zhang Qianxiang, former editor of *Renmin Ribao* and Liu Qizhong, managing editor of *China Features.*

figure helps in this connection, many people credit its influence to the fact that it is the organ of the Central Committee of the Communist Party of China. The Communist Party, the ruling party of the country, has more than 40 million members, the largest of such parties in the world. The status of the Party determines the importance of the paper.

As the organ of the Party, the *People's Daily* has an official duty to propagate the Party's political line, policies, and tasks among the one billion Chinese. The paper plays the role of a liaison officer between the Party and the people, telling people what the Party expects them to do and reporting their views and wishes to the Party leadership. In other words, *People's Daily* is the voice of the Party as well as the voice of the people.

The paper has a long revolutionary history. As early as China's Second Revolutionary War period (1927–37), the Communist Party started two newspapers in the liberated areas in the south: *Red Flag Daily,* printed in Shanghai, and *Red China Daily,* published in Ruijin, Jiangxi Province. During the War of Resistance against Japan (1937–45), the Party ran two other papers, *New China Daily* and *Liberation Daily,* in the base areas in northwest China. The *Liberation Daily* was closed in mid-1947 when the Communists evacuated Yan'an, capital of the base areas, to avoid direct attacks by troops of Chiang Kai-shek. In early 1948, as the Communist forces grew, the Party decided to set up a North China Bureau, which later started its organ, called *People's Daily,* in Xibaipo Village, Pingshan County, Hebei Province. The paper moved to Beijing when the city was liberated in January 1949. In August of that year the daily was upgraded to become the official organ of the CPC Central Committee. The paper has an editorial board, which makes all the major decisions about editorial policies and administrative matters.

Why is a Party paper named the *People's Daily?* "Because," an editor of the paper wrote in the early 1950s, "the paper is of the people, by the people, and for the people." Being such a paper, the editor said, the *People's Daily* propagates the Party's policies and advocations, reports major happenings in and outside China, explains and discusses theoretical and ideological problems, and helps exchange experiences in administrative work and economic construction.

The paper is prepared and edited at its headquarters in Beijing and printed in 23 major Chinese cities, which are Beijing, Shanghai, Wuhan, Shenyang, Jinan, Harbin, Nanjing, Changsha, Changchun, Xi'an, Guangzhou, Nanchang, Chengdu, Chongqing, Nanning, Lanzhou, Kunming, Urumqi, Haikou, Lhasa, Guiyang, Hangzhou, and Fuzhou. Such a printing network ensures that people all over the country can read the paper the same day it is printed. *People's Daily* is also printed in

Hong Kong, Tokyo, and San Francisco for deliveries to 123 countries and regions in the world.

The paper's present director is Qian Liren, a member of the CPC Central Committee and at one time a departmental chief of that committee. Its editor in chief is Tan Wenrui, a veteran newsman and an expert on international affairs. Tan is currently assisted by three deputies.

The paper has several editorial departments: the Editor in Chief's Desk, the Theoretical Department, the Commentary Department, the Department of Domestic Politics, the Department of Industry and Commerce, the Department of Rural Affairs, the Department of Science and Education, the Department of Literature and Art, and the Department of Correspondents.

This organizational structure is based on two principles—editorial requirements and the division of labor in Chinese society. The Editor in Chief's Desk, for example, is responsible for drafting the paper's editorial policies and general planning; the Department of Correspondents undertakes special assignments; and the editors and correspondents in other departments look after the coverage of news for specific pages, such as the industrial page, the business page, or the cultural page.

Each issue has eight pages. The first page is usually devoted to editorials, commentaries, and major events, both domestic and international. The second page is for economic news; the third page for news on culture, education, and sports; the fourth page for news on domestic politics and legal matters; the fifth page for theories on literature and for letters to the editor; the sixth and seventh pages for international news; and the eighth page for supplements, photos, and cartoons. Each day the paper prints 75,000 Chinese characters in its news items and articles. On the fifth, seventh, and eighth pages, it usually runs advertisements that occupy one full page. These ads promote products ranging from consumer goods to books and magazines.

The paper carries its news and articles under 50 to 60 different columns, including "Editorials," "Commentaries," "My View on China's Economic Reform," "Major News in Today's Press," "Sports," "Letters from Abroad," "International News," "Cultural Life," "Book Review," and "Theater Review." Some of these columns appear on specific days of the week, while others are printed every day.

The *People's Daily* also publishes several small publications. One of them is *Market,* a tabloid devoted to the coverage of production and consumption. This weekly, started in 1978, is the first of its kind in China to be printed in color. It has 80 pages an issue, with a circulation of five hundred thousand. Its readers range from consumers and manufacturers to managers and agents. Providing both domestic and international market news, the paper promotes communications and understanding between market managers and consumers as well as between Chinese and foreign business executives.

The weekly contains dozens of columns, which include "Major News on Domestic and International Markets," "Hong Kong and Macao Markets," "Tourism," "Family Consultant," "Voice of the Reader," "Legal Cases of Economic Disputes," "Customers' Corner," "How to Become a Good Manager," "Home Cooked Dishes," "Antique Market," and "Shelves of New Books."

The *People's Daily* also produces a cartoon section called "Satire and Humor." Started in 1979 and edited by the paper's Department of Literature and Art, the tabloid appears three times a month and sells some eight hundred thousand copies an issue. The small paper uses cartoons, humorous pictures, satirical poems, and essays and humor, as well as biographies, life stories, and anecdotes of Chinese and foreign cartoonists to praise the fine qualities and actions of hegemonism, feudalism, and hedonism. Over the years the paper has achieved fame and loyalty of millions, both young and old.

Journalism Front, another *People's Daily* product, is a monthly for professional journalists, freelancers, stringers, and all those interested in journalism. The publication carries studies on both theory and practice of the Chinese press, discussions on newswriting, news photos, news cartoons, life stories of renowned correspondents and editors, and major events in the Chinese and foreign press. The magazine features many special columns, which range from "Theoretical Studies," "Analysis on Good Reporting," "Studies on Newspapers," "Notes of Editors," "Clinic for Newspaper Languages," to such titles as "Fledgling Reporters," "Promising Correspondents," and "Latest Events in the Foreign Press."

The *People's Daily* overseas edition is targeted at the Chinese reading public outside China, whose interests and habits are different from those on the mainland. The purpose of the overseas edition is to relay the major editorials and reports of the *People's Daily* to overseas readers, transmit the most important policies of the Communist Party and the Chinese government, and inform the readers of what is happening in China. The paper also provides readers with advice on exchange rates of Chinese money and major foreign currencies, procedures of investment in China, formalities for remitting money to people on the mainland, ways to purchase real estate in China, and even how to locate lost relatives and friends, or how to find a spouse in one's native home.

The eight-page paper devotes its front page to major domestic and foreign events; its second page to commentaries, features, and special articles; its third page to economic news; and its fourth page to politics, law, education, science, technology, and sports. The fifth page to reports on Hong Kong, Macao, and Taiwan as well as Chinese people scattered all over the world; the sixth page reports on international news; the seventh page on literature and art; and the eighth page provides excerpts from the major reports in the Chinese press. These articles are arranged under different columns, which include "Editorials," "Random Discussions," "Interesting Events on the Vast Land," "Famous Chinese Dishes," "Sports," "Reports from Taiwan," "Latest Information from Hong Kong and Macao," "In the Native Places of Overseas Chinese," "Famous Words by Famous People," "Roundups on International Events," "Flashes from Abroad," "Literary Creations," and "Excerpts from the Chinese Press."

To facilitate reading, the new edition uses the old-style Chinese characters, instead of the simplified version that has been in use on the mainland since 1964. The paper also differs from its domestic edition in page design. It prints more and larger photos, more attractive headlines, and presents a style of writing that suits the reading habits of overseas readers. This edition is prepared and printed in Beijing and the pages are then transmitted via satellite to San Francisco, New York, Tokyo, Paris, and Hong Kong for reprinting and distribution in surrounding areas.

The affiliated publishing house of the *People's Daily* prints papers, periodicals, and books. It turns out several dozen titles each year, mainly books on journalism, politics, history, education, literature, science, and technology. Among its latest publications are *Press Laws in the World* and *Famous Economic Essays*.

To train more competent reporters and editors, the *People's Daily* set up a Wisdom Development Center in early 1984, which started a training program in April that year. Currently in training at the one-year program are 40,000 young professionals in the 29 provinces, autonomous regions, and municipalities on the mainland. The program uses textbooks prepared by veteran *People's Daily* correspondents and editors, including such titles as *Topics in Journalism, Basics of Journalism,* and *Readings for Beginners*. These books, totaling 3.2 million words, along with reference readings totaling 2 million words, are provided to trainees free of charge. The center has a full-time staff of 26 plus 357 visiting professors and instructors. To provide on-the-spot individual consultancy, the training center has set up 30 coaching stations scattered in almost all China's provincial capitals.

People's Daily has a readership that is broad and varied. According to a 1983 survey, the details of which are printed in the *Chinese Press Yearbook — 1983,* the paper's readers consist of 80.6 percent of all Chinese scientists and technicians, 79.4 percent of Chinese government employees, 52.4 percent of Chinese professors and teachers, 42.1 percent of Chinese workers, 36.4 percent of Chinese students, 16.1 percent of Chinese retirees, and 12.6 percent of Chinese peasants. The paper's total readership can be divided into similar categories:

Workers	32.9 percent
Government employees	22.0 percent
Scientists and technicians	11.9 percent
Peasants	9.0 percent
Students	8.1 percent
Employees in business	7.3 percent
Professors and teachers	6.1 percent
Retirees	2.0 percent
Others	0.7 percent

The survey also reveals that 65.3 percent of the paper's readers are male and 34.7 female; 90 percent live in cities and towns and 10 percent in the country; 25.3 percent have a college education and above, 66.6 percent have a high school education, and 8.1 percent have an education lower than primary schooling.

The majority of the readers, according to the survey, are workers, government employees, intellectuals, and students. Most are interested in reading international news, reports on domestic political events, news on education, science, technology, sports, literature and art, and letters to the editor.

Among the paper's six hundred staff, about one hundred are correspondents. Of these most are in their early 40s or older, and over 60 percent are college graduates. Many veteran staff members joined the revolution when they were young, having little chance to get more education. They acquired skill in reporting and editing in the depth of wars. Today, many have retired, and few of those in the older-age and lower-education bracket are still active at responsible positions on the paper. Each year several dozen college and M.A. graduates join the paper, bringing the average age of the staff down and its academic record up.

Over the years the *People's Daily* has produced many famous journalists, of whom Deng Tuo definitely ranks first. Deng Tuo, a native of Fujian Province, south China, and director and editor in chief of the paper in the 1950s and early 1960s, was a professor of history who went to the liberated areas in northwest China in 1937. In April of that year he started a Party paper called *Resistance Daily,* which later changed its name to *Shanxi-Chahar-Hebei Daily* to meet the needs of the growing readership. In the fierce fighting against Japanese aggressors at that time, Deng worked out a quality paper for the resistance movement at the enemy rear under extremely difficult conditions. To escape from the repeated Japanese mop-up campaigns, he had to move all his machines and office facilities with horses. Many a time he drafted editorials on horseback. As soon as he arrived at the day's destination he would start writing on his knees under the dim light of an oil lamp. After the nationwide liberation, Deng Tuo became the director and editor in chief of the paper. In that post he wrote many editorials and important articles.

His contributions can be found in many other fields. He originated the motto, "The decisive battle is won out of the editorial room," meaning that the best news stories can be found only in society. He sent reporters to the depths of society, building close relationships with people and writing about them with solid information. As the editor in chief, he personally answered letters from readers and questions from young reporters and stringers, while asking the rest of the staff to do the same. In this way the paper gradually built its reputation among the Chinese readers.

Deng Tuo paid great attention to writing editorials and commentaries. "These are articles," he said, "that can best explain the Party's political line and policies to the readers."[1] Over the years, as an editorial writer, he had worked out his own theory and style in work and in writing. On the skills of writing, Deng stressed the following principles: try to write them on a higher theoretical plane and give the major arguments a penetrating edge; always use solid and convincing information and eloquent logic; try to use relevant anecdotes and historical stories to illustrate the point; and write with simple language and a lively style.

Deng Tuo's success is a result of his devotion to the Party's cause and to the Chinese press, as well as to his diligence in learning, thinking, writing, and rewriting. Between 1938 and 1958, when he was with the press, he wrote and edited numerous articles, commentaries, and editorials. These practices prepared him to be an extremely skillful correspondent, editor, writer, and commentator. His talent, wide interests, and studies won him a reputation as a noted historian, essay writer, poet, calligrapher, and cultural relic expert. Never for a moment in his life did he lay down his pen, even when he had to handle a considerable administrative burden in his later years. He fought tirelessly as a journalist at the forefront of the Chinese press corps. His contributions to the Party's cause and to the Chinese press made him a fine example for the entire staff of the *People's Daily* and for all China's journalists to follow. Deng Tuo was framed and put to death by the Gang of Four during the Cultural Revolution, but his ideas on journalism, his style of work, and his creative writings have become an invaluable heritage of the *People's Daily* and of the Chinese media in general.

Also outstanding among *People's Daily* veterans is Hu Jiwei, director and editor in chief of the paper in the late 1970s and early 1980s. Born in Sichuan Province, southwest China, in 1916, Hu majored in economics at the State University of Sichuan in the early 1930s. After graduation, he founded several progressive publications, which were forced to close down one after another by the reactionary regime at that time. In 1937 he went to Yan'an, capital of the liberated areas in the war years, and started *Yan'an People's News,* and later, when the paper was expanded to be renamed *Northwestern People's Daily,* he became its director. During the 30 years between 1952 and 1982, he was with *People's Daily* in Beijing, first as a deputy editor in chief, then as editor in chief, and finally as director. His present post is deputy chairman of the Committee of Education, Science, and Culture of the Standing Committee of China's National People's Congress, and he is concurrently chairman of the Federation of China's Journalistic Societies.

The paper's current editor in chief is Tan Wenrui, a 64-year-old veteran newspaperman from Guangdong Province, south China. Tan graduated in 1945 from the Journalism Department of Yanjing University, a department founded in the early 1920s with the help of Walter Williams, founder of the School of Journalism at the University of Missouri. Before China's nationwide liberation in 1949, Tan was an editor with *Ta Kun Bao,* a renowned paper in Shanghai. Since liberation, he has been with *People's Daily,* serving as an editor, executive editor of the paper's international section, chief of the paper's International Department, and editor of the paper's overseas edition. He was promoted to his present post in April 1986.

Among other famous Chinese newsmen and newswomen are several dozen *People's Daily* correspondents and editors. They include Li Zhuang, editor in chief of the paper in the early 1980s; Wang Ruoshui, outstanding philosopher and deputy editor in chief in the late 1970s and the early 1980s; Tian Liu, executive editor of the paper's feature section; Liu Binyan, renowned investigative reporter; and Ai Feng and Meng Xiaoyun, promising correspondents whose investigative pieces and stirring articles have won them honor.

All for Reforms

Sweeping China today is another revolution—the reform. So, the major task of *People's Daily* is to report and promote the reform. Opening the paper on any day, one will find that it has devoted a large percentage of its space to the coverage of the reform. Such treatment of the event, according to an editor of the paper, aims at mobilizing the masses of the people to focus their attention on reform and urge them to work even harder for the realization of China's modernization program.

People's Daily's coverage of the reform focuses first on theoretical and ideological aspects and current policies. In this connection, the paper emphasizes the policy of "letting a hundred flowers blossom and a hundred schools of thought contend," a policy set forth by the Party in the late 1950s to promote the progress of art and science and the development of a flourishing socialist culture.

A ready example to show the work *People's Daily* has done in this regard is the paper's editorial carried on 2 May 1986. Entitled the "Two Hundred Policy—The Only Way to a Developed Science," the editorial said that 30 years ago, when copying "Soviet experiences" was in vogue, China set up Michurin's theory on genetics, represented by Lysenko, as the only orthodox school, while rejecting the modern genetics represented by Thomas Morgan that had already been recognized internationally for about half a century. Such arbitrary "setting-up" of one school of thought while negating others buried free discussion and abolished the freedom of academic studies. The result put political labels on those who held different views and deprived many scientists of their right to study and to publish their research results, hindering the development of science and theory. The editorial reminded people of this historical lesson and called on them to guard against its reoccurrence.

Though the subject of this editorial was genetics, the same idea applies to all scientific research. Such open discussion of past mistakes benefits theoretical study and promotes current reform.

In a recent editorial arguing that theoretical studies in China lag behind practices, the paper strongly advocated free debate and discussion among those with different views. Only in this way, the editorial said, could China experience a rapid development of theories. It was obvious, the editorial contended, that by publishing different views, by allowing the expression of both pros and cons, and by giving equal treatment to criticism and countercriticism, the *People's Daily* was encouraging China's theoreticians to become bolder in their research and render better service to China's reforms with their theories.

The *People's Daily* places great emphasis on coverage of policy matters. For example, the paper has taken a very active stance in reporting rural reform ever since its introduction to the countryside in 1979. Whenever the Party makes a new move or the peasants achieve new progress, the paper will report it and give it full support.

While reporting reforms, *People's Daily* is trying to reform its own reporting. In 1983 the paper drafted a reform plan with the following points:

1. Write a variety of penetrating editorials and commentaries.

2. In news reporting, change the old style of writing, which is characterized by long and tedious narration, to short but interesting reports.

3. In writing theoretical articles, try to improve the quality and make each article answer one or more questions closely related to what readers care about.

4. In writing economic stories, try to include those involved in the events: what they thought, said, and did, and how they were affected by the events.

5. In international reporting, print more stories on the latest happenings outside China, including those in literature, art, science, and technology.

To help make the plan a success, the *People's Daily* has created the slogan, "Reform the press through reforming newswriting." As an editor of the paper once said, "news is the major element of the newspaper, or how can it truthfully be called a newspaper?" This truth, however, became clouded during the Cultural Revolution. At that time, news was reduced to a secondary place in the paper.

Reforming the press also has been a demand of readers. They have longed for a press that carries more information with better quality; otherwise, they believe, a paper is not worth reading. And the subject matter in the Chinese press has indicated a need for reform. For years the *People's Daily* failed to give sufficient coverage to economic affairs, legal matters, and progress in education, science, and technology. Much still needs to be done to make the coverage commensurate with the great changes that are taking place in China.

The reform of the *People's Daily*, the most influential paper in China, will automatically affect the reform of all other newspapers in the country. In fact, similar reforms have been going on quietly but quickly in other papers. These reforms are something that will raise the quality of the Chinese press to a much higher level. And the improvement of the press will in turn help promote economic and political reform in China.

In short, "all for reforms" has become the guideline in Chinese society. It is under this guideline that *People's Daily* is operating: helping to promote China's overall reform while reforming itself.

Criticism in the Paper

Carrying criticisms — running articles or letters to the editor, or exposing the wrongdoing, errors, or shortcomings of government officials and business executives in the hope of getting them corrected — has been a fine tradition of the *People's Daily*. To the editors of *Renmin Ribao,* criticism is as important to the paper as sunshine and water are to human life. Criticism can help the paper grow. Past experience has shown that a paper is livelier and more attractive when it prints criticism. Otherwise, it is flat and tired, and stirs few people.

On 22 July 1980 the paper exposed and criticized the capsizing of oil rig Bohai Number 2, which caused many casualties and great material damage. Along with the news report, the paper ran a commentary, saying that for a long time leaders of the China Ocean Oil Exploration Bureau, whose job was to guide the oil exploration on the East Sea, ran risks in its production, paying little attention to the safety of its employees. More serious yet was their attempt to hide mistakes when the rig capsized.

Starting on the day the breaking news was carried in the paper, *People's Daily* published a series of follow-ups, commentary, and letters to the editor, all dealing with the serious nature of the accident. As the situation developed, the paper carried a wrap-up entitled "Work Style of Petroleum Ministry Leaders as Viewed from the Oil Rig Accident," which sharply criticized the bureaucracy and mistakes of the leaders of the Ministry, especially those of Minister Zhou Zhenmin. In due course, China's State Council made a decision about the accident: to punish Vice Premier Kang Shi'en by giving him a serious demerit, and to punish Minister Zhou Zhenmin by removing him from office. Other people who were directly responsible for the accident were given either prison terms according to law or administrative disciplinary punishment according to government regulations. The paper printed the decision and responses from the readers and ran two more commentaries, as well as self-criticism from the minister. For a month the paper never failed to give sufficient coverage to the event, running several dozen detailed reports and sharp commentaries.

The coverage of the accident exerted great influence on the readers and received very positive reaction. Editors of the paper believed that this was due not only to the fact that the paper criticized a minister, but also to the earnest efforts the paper made to investigate the hidden details. Commenting on the coverage, one reader wrote: "By learning all this, I now have more faith in the government and in your paper, and I'll work even better in my own field."

The *People's Daily* not only directs its criticism against erroneous tendencies in political and economic fields, but also against harmful ideas and practices in society. Items about problems like the following are often printed in the paper: poor service in shops, rude treatment of policemen toward citizens, poor quality vegetables in state-owned gro-ceries, dirty surroundings in living quarters of big cities, noise pollution of various kinds in downtown areas, government officials making sight-seeing trips with public money, and so on. Shortly after these items appear in the paper, responses usually will come in. Those criticized will either make a self-criticism, report what has been done to correct the mistakes, or explain why they cannot take immediate measures to over-come the shortcomings or redress the wrongdoing. Most of these re-sponses will be printed in a column called "Responses to Criticisms."

The *People's Daily* began this practice in the early 1950s. On 19 April 1950 the CPC Central Committee made a decision "Concerning Conducting Criticisms and Self-Criticisms in Newspapers," which was carried in the paper on 22 April. Part of the decision reads:

> Today, it has become all the more important to draw the masses of the people to openly criticize in newspapers the errors and shortcomings in our work and educate our Party members, especially those in leading posts, to make self-criticisms in newspapers. This is because the war on the mainland has come to an end, and our Party has become one in power, leading the whole nation. Thus, errors and shortcomings in our work are liable to harm the interests of the broad masses of the people. At the same time, the leading position of many of our Party members and their grow-ing prestige are apt to engender arrogance, which tends to make them refuse criticisms from within and outside the Party, or even suppress them. Under these circumstances, if we do not openly conduct criticism and self-criticism before the broad masses of the people against the shortcomings and errors committed in the Party, in the government, and in economic institutions and mass organizations, we will be seriously poisoned by bu-reaucracy, thus being unable to fulfill our tasks of building up New China. Considering this, the Central Committee of the Communist Party of China decided to conduct criticism and self-criticism against the shortcom-ings and errors committed in all our work on all public occasions, among the masses of the people, especially in newspapers and the other media.[2]

The *People's Daily* staff welcomed, studied, and implemented the decision seriously. They realized that conducting criticism and self-criti-cism in newspapers is an event of the utmost importance, and, as the most powerful weapon of the Party, newspapers are obliged to do so. At the same time, they believed, criticism and self-criticism could help in-vigorate the paper, raise its prestige, and promote its status in the Chinese media.

In conducting criticisms and self-criticisms, the paper has followed some guidelines. On this point, Liu Shaoqi, late vice chairman of the

Party, once said that criticisms should follow three principles: (1) they must be run in newspapers; (2) they must be accurate; (3) their publication must be conducted under the leadership of the Party. Under these guiding principles the *People's Daily* has been conducting these activities for more than 30 years and has won tremendous success in the process.

In 1979 Hu Jiwei, then director of the paper, explained the significance of such practice in his discussion of the relationship between "hitting flies" and "hitting tigers." In China people like to refer to criticism of big issues or important figures as "hitting tigers," while criticism of minor events or less important people is "hitting flies." Some would complain that the paper has hit far fewer tigers than flies. Hu Jiwei responds,

> It is true that we have hit more flies than tigers. This is because flies exist in large numbers. We should not belittle those flies, for they stand on the head of the people, riding roughshod. When we hit a fly in one place, people in the whole area as well as those in other places will be happy. Sometimes, when a fly is hit, a tiger feels the pain. There are cases in which we aim at a fly but direct our arrow to a tiger. Our paper often exhorts the tiger by hitting the fly, warning him to rein in at the brink of the precipice. If he refuses to mend his ways, our criticisms will make him blush with shame and feel uneasy, even bringing him before the law or discipline.[3]

These remarks are a vivid description of what the *People's Daily* has done in conducting criticism. The paper has carried out serious criticism against both major and minor events and people, thus exerting great influence on its readers.

In conducting criticism, some people have taken a skeptical or opposing attitude. They say criticism is throwing mud at people, making them suffer, or needlessly raking up their faults. In their view, China's social system is already perfect, brooking no criticism. They say that criticism in the papers will make socialism lose its brilliance. *People's Daily* has refuted this view in several of its commentaries. In an article entitled "Criticisms in Papers are a Spur," which appeared on 22 December 1985, the paper said that "conducting criticism and self-criticism has played a positive role in improving our work, the style of work of the Party, and the general mood of society. This point has been realized by more and more people nowadays."

The commentary cited several examples in this regard. *Shekou Bulletin,* a paper printed in Shekou Town, Shenzhen City, Guangdong Province, carried an article in May 1984 criticizing Yuan Geng, mayor of the town, and found among the people full agreement and support of Yuan. He said that the article would help bring a fresh mood of renewed society to the town.

Gao Qingying, mayor of Hengshui City, Hebei Province, wrote in 1985 to *Hengshui Daily,* proposing that the paper devote a special corner to criticism and suggestions on city management. The day after the letter was printed, one reader sent in a letter criticizing the city government for its failure in managing a major market. The city council took immediate measures to improve the situation and achieved successes in a matter of days.

In another example, a paper in Luliang Prefecture, Shanxi Province, carried a letter from a reader saying that the local Party decision on improving the conditions of intellectuals was something resembling the old practice of "eating from the same big pot." After reading this, the Party secretary of the prefecture located the writer of the letter and sincerely solicited his suggestions. The Party committee then amended the decision, making it more favorable to intellectuals.

So, a *People's Daily* editor said, conducting criticism in the papers is not throwing mud at people, but helping to remove the dirt from their faces; it is not making people suffer, but helping them get rid of disease and grow healthier; it is not raking up people's faults, but helping them correct their mistakes and overcome their weaknesses.

Criticism in newspapers plays a unique role in helping society, too, the paper said. Today, there are still people who are afraid of being exposed in the papers. One such person has said that "I would rather have a two-year term in prison than be criticized in newspapers." Fearing criticism in the papers is in fact fearing public opinion, fearing the people. These people know that once exposed in the papers, they will lose face and can no longer use the protection of those in higher position.

In conducting criticism, editors of the *People's Daily* learned that it must place strict demands on itself and set a good example. Only by having the courage to accept criticism can it have the courage to criticize others. No newspaper can be free from making mistakes, and once it makes one, the only correct thing to do is accept criticism and try to correct the error right away. In the face of criticism, all people are equal, be they editors or readers.

There have been cases in which criticism carried in the paper was inaccurate or the facts exaggerated. When this occurs, the *People's Daily* is willing to accept countercriticisms and make self-criticisms in due time. On 18 August 1982 in a commentary entitled "Correctly Use the Weapon of Literary Critique," the paper said that "the shortcomings we have pointed out above also exist in this paper's literary critique. . . . We are determined to do our utmost to correct them." In the commentary "Criticisms in Papers are a Spur," quoted previously, the paper expressed the same sincerity. It said that "in carrying out criticism and self-criticism, this paper has also made mistakes. We are willing to do our best to correct the mistakes and overcome the shortcomings, and are ready to cooperate with all the other newspapers in a concerted effort to improve this practice and help bring about a change for the better in the style of work of the Party and in the general mood of society."

All this shows that the *People's Daily,* while conducting criticism, also engages in serious self-criticism. In this way the paper has, in the past 30 years or more, made steady progress and promoted its prestige and influence among the readers.

Letters to the Editor

A unique feature of the *People's Daily* is its way of handling letters to the editor. In 1980, for example, the paper received 780,000 such letters, averaging 2,135 a day. It then devoted a total of 48 pages plus 44 special columns to print more than 1,300 of them. In addition, the paper relayed many of them to relevant government departments, enterprises and institutions, requesting them to give a responsible answer. Over the years the pages that carry these letters have become the most interesting sections of the paper and have been widely read.

The practice started in March 1950 when the paper opened up a "Readers' Corner" in its supplement for printing letters from the readers. These were letters that contained criticism and suggestions. In November of the same year, the supplement was renamed "Special Page for Letters to the Editor," which consisted of a dozen columns. These columns included "Voices of the People," which prints criticism against government leaders and suggestions for correcting wrongdoings; "List of People and Units Criticized," which publishes criticism against anyone who has made serious mistakes; and "Readers' Forum," which carries views of the readers on all social issues. On days when the special page does not appear, the paper prints some of these letters on its second page. In 1953 alone the paper ran a total of 218 such special pages, which carried 1,241 letters to the editor. In the past 30 years and more, the paper has never stopped this practice.

In recent years, the "Special Page for Letters to the Editor" has become richer and more colorful and has been honored as "a page one must read." Under the column "Suggestions and Demands" of that page, many valuable views and suggestions have been printed. On 8 December 1984 the paper published a letter from a middle-school teacher in Anshan City, northeast China, proposing to set a day aside for the teachers in the country. This letter got enthusiastic response from readers and came to the attention of national leaders. In the following year, the National People's Congress decided to set 10 September each year as China's Teachers' Day.

People's Daily pays great attention to letters exposing bureaucracy and unhealthy tendencies in society. In July 1984, the paper received a letter from Liu Yanmin, an employee on a state farm in Xinjiang, northwest China. The letter revealed that leaders of his farm refused to make good the terms laid down in a contract between the farm leadership and the employees. The leaders instead framed Liu and put him into custody for 40 days. Upon receiving the letter, the editor sent a reporter to Xinjiang to investigate the case. The result was an investigative story entitled "Who Is in Power on This Remote Farm?" The report exposed those who tried to obstruct the proper settlement of the dispute. The event soon won nationwide attention and concern, which helped bring an end to the case in favor of the farm workers.

The *People's Daily* is very much concerned about the problems in the daily life of the ordinary people and has done its utmost to help them. Under the column "Never Forgetting to Serve the People," the paper often prints letters criticizing the service trade's callous disregard for the interests of consumers. In another column, "Questions and Answers," the editor avails himself of the opportunity to give prompt reply to any questions readers may ask.

The *People's Daily* forwards a large member of the letters to relevant government departments or organizations and sees to it that they are all handled properly. In April 1984, the paper sent an editor to Fuyang and Liu'an prefectures in Anhui Province for interviews with local government officials to see what had happened to the 49 letters the paper had sent to the localities earlier. The editor found that some of those criticized had paid little attention to the letters. On 4 August the paper produced a report on "What Happened to the Forty-nine Letters We Had Relayed to Them." The article sharply criticized those grassroots leaders who cared little about the criticism. This shocked the leaders there, as well as those in other places, and helped them change their bureaucratic practices.

The paper has also tried its best to help those people who are besieged by problems. There had been a young girl, named Shi Yuan, in Shanxi Province, northwest China, who was partially paralyzed in a traffic accident. The girl, a former announcer with a county radio station, told the editor of the paper in a letter that she had wanted to end her life on several occasions in the past two years. A *People's Daily* story, which had mentioned a hospital in northeast China that could treat cases like hers, fanned her hopes. As a last resort, she asked the editor to help her find the hospital. Upon receiving the letter, the editor wrote to the hospital. When he found out that the hospital had been disbanded, the editor consulted many doctors in Beijing. He then sent her in a letter all the advice he had gathered. He said that "many paralyzed people like you in the capital are brimming over with hope for a new life. Some are learning English, preparing themselves to become translators; some are practicing embroidery to enrich their lives while earning money for their families; others are. . . . Why cannot you do the same?"

The letter worked. Shi Yuan began to learn story-writing while seeing her doctor regularly. Later when two *People's Daily* reporters went to Shanxi on business, they made a detour to see the girl and encouraged her to persist in what she was doing. All this helped to change her. Today she has become the author of a novel and some short stories and poems. In a recent letter to the editor, she wrote: "You have comforted my wounded soul and helped me relieve my spiritual pains. You are a true doctor."

The desk that looks after letters to the editor, called the Mass Work Department, was set up in early 1953. Working in the department today are 55 editors, among whom are veteran newspapermen and M.A. and B.A. graduates. These people have a common belief that letters to the editor are a treasure of the paper and a huge bridge that links the editor with the readers. Through these letters they can learn about all sorts of social problems and produce many story ideas. They also regard these letters as the voice of the people. As long as the paper listens to the people, allows them to express their views, and serves their interests, it can remain a good paper.

These letters have attracted the interest of people abroad. The China Study Center of Japan, for example, has compiled more than two thousand such letters in a book entitled *Letters to the Editor of "People's Daily."* The editor of the book has added commentaries and explanations to more than one hundred of the letters. These letters, he has explained, reveal the major problems that most concern readers, as well as government leaders, in China. They are very useful tools in helping foreigners understand today's China.

Editorials and Commentaries

In February 1985 Hu Yaobang, Secretary-General of the CPC Central Committee, published his article "On the Journalistic Work of the Party." In the article Hu said that "the real nature of the Chinese press is the organ of the Party, the government, and the people." If this is so, the *People's Daily* is the most important organ of the Party, the government, and the people. In the 40 years since its establishment in 1948 (excluding the 10 years of the Cultural Revolution), *People's Daily* has enjoyed very high prestige among the Chinese people. It is in fact a mirror and voice of China.

Editorials of the *People's Daily* have always been interpreted as voicing the official viewpoint of the Communist Party and the Chinese government. Over the years they have become more authoritative and more influential. The paper pays great attention to writing good editorials. The work is looked after by an editorial board, which meets regularly to discuss the topics of editorials. Specific writing is under the direct supervision of the editor in chief, who usually writes the most important editorials himself. The story about Deng Tuo, the paper's editor in chief in the 1950s and early 1960s, is a fine example.

Deng Tuo is famous for his skill in writing. In the 20 years that he served as the editor in chief, he devoted much of his time and energy to organizing the writing of editorials and commentaries. He edited, rewrote, and finalized large numbers of editorials and he wrote many himself. As an editorial writer, he had resolutely opposed stereotyped writing. In his article "On Writing Newspaper Editorials," he said that

> today's fashion in writing editorials is to begin with a few paragraphs on the present situation in the country and cite one or two good examples followed by one or two bad ones. Then the writer points out the subjective reasons to show why that is good and why this is bad and throws out some points as experiences or lessons. He then gives some suggestions for improvement which are nothing but repetitions of previous writers. Finally, he shouts some slogans such as "Under the leadership of the Party, this task will surely be accomplished." To tell you the truth, this formula makes me vomit.[4]

Deng Tuo's editorials are entirely different. His are written on a very high theoretical plane coupled with a deep political insight. He always tried to use solid facts and sharp language sealed with eloquent logic. His formula: whole-hearted devotion to the Party, to the people, and to the press; hard work and wide reading; thinking, writing, and rewriting diligently. These ideals have in fact become a motto for all the staff writers of *People's Daily* today.

The paper's staff writers regard commentary writing as part of editorial writing. Over the years they have established the following guidelines for their work: Everyone on the editorial board writes commentaries, long ones as well as short ones. If each and every one plays a part in writing commentaries, they believe, production will be much higher and the variety of styles greater. Persistence in following this practice will produce a large contingent of commentary writers.

Long articles usually comment on important events, and short ones on minor issues. These commentaries, especially the shorter ones, are often written by a variety of different people, even by stringers and readers. In 1981, under the column "Today's Topics" on page 1, the paper carried 272 commentaries in 131 days. Usually such commentaries are short, lively, sharp, and directly related to the topics most people are concerned about.

Today, still fresh in the readers' minds from late 1985, is the short commentary "It Is Time to Give Them a 'Time-Out.'" The commentary was written after the return of the Chinese women's volleyball team from the world-cup competition in Japan. Excited by the women's victory, people of various organizations in the country flooded them with letters, inviting them to welcoming parties, dinners, and lectures, and asking them to write articles or do TV or radio programs. Seeing that such invitations seriously interfered with the players' rest and left them little time for personally assessing their recent experiences, the *People's Daily* printed a short commentary requesting the readers to give them a time-out. This short piece, using many sports terms, provided timely criticism and advice, thus helping the women volleyballers considerably.

The impact of the paper's editorials and commentaries lies in penetrating analysis, choice of the proper target, solid information, and sharp language. A good example is the commentary entitled "The Cultural Revolution Must Be Negated Thoroughly," which was carried in the paper on 28 April 1984. The commentary maintained that "the curtain of the farce of the 'Cultural Revolution' has fallen for years. However, in the corners here and there in the country, some people, though small in number, are still making repercussions of the revolution." The so-called Cultural Revolution, the commentary said, must be negated thoroughly; otherwise, there can never be a situation in which an atmosphere of unity, stability, and vigorous development prevails.

This statement was one that few people dared to utter at that time, one that needed political courage and deep political insight to make. The statement aroused great attention in the country and was widely and quickly accepted. It resulted in a sweeping repudiation of the "leftist" ideas that had been in vogue in China for years and greatly inspired the nation in its effort to carry out reforms in various fields.

On the Way to Modernization

To run a big newspaper such as the *People's Daily* well, in a country with a billion people and 9.6 million square kilometers of land, it is absolutely necessary to have up-to-date communications and production facilities. As early as the early 1950s, the paper began to use rotary presses, which were highly advanced at that time. However, the typesetting and makeup, coupled with the rotary presses, still had to be operated manually, and the characters still had to be picked out one by one from the six thousand to seven thousand types. This situation could not meet the fast-production demand of newspapers today. In the late 1950s the paper switched to typing-type composing machines, which, however, were still based on manual operation. In the early 1980s the paper began to use more advanced technologies, such as offset presses and electronic color scanners. In 1985, when the paper's overseas edition was started, electronic photo typesetters were introduced to the paper's printing shop.

For the future, the *People's Daily* plans to import the most advanced technologies of the 1980s to upgrade newswriting, news editing, and newspaper production so that by the end of 1987 the paper will be able to replace all its old equipment with advanced electronic facilities. At that time writing, editing, typesetting, printing, and distribution, as well as data processing, will all be computerized. The modernization of the *People's Daily* will herald the modernization of all newspapers in China.

4  *China Daily*

Introduction and Background

China Daily is the first and only English daily newspaper published in China since the founding of the People's Republic. It was launched to meet the needs of China's open policy and to serve the increasing number of foreigners in China, including foreign tourists and foreign business-men as well as Chinese who understand English. Under the supervision of the Information Department, *China Daily* has its own editorial poli-cies, which define the paper's principal goals as objectively presenting China and China's news to its unique group of readers and providing services and entertainment specially suited to those readers, such as eco-nomic information for foreign businessmen, sports news, TV programs, movie schedules, bridge and crossword puzzles, and so on.

Technologically, *China Daily* is a showcase for the nation's newspa-pers — its production process is completely computerized. *China Daily* is striving to be lively and timely, and it pays special attention to graphics, often neglected in other Chinese newspapers. In many respects *China Daily* is a trailblazer among Chinese newspapers.

The idea for the paper goes back to 1978. Toward the latter part of that year, the first big influx of foreign tourists came to visit China. They proposed an English-language newspaper where they could learn about new developments in this country and up-to-date news from other parts of the world. In answer to their needs, and with government approval, *China Daily* was launched.

It took more than two years of preparation, including a year of trial issues, to determine the format and content of the new paper. Feng Xiliang, today's editor of *China Daily,* was appointed to a special four-member commission to investigate the possibility of an English-language newspaper. He and other pioneers spent one year experimenting with newswriting and layout. They spent a little more than a month in Mel-bourne studying production techniques. At the end of 1980 they began printing periodic trial editions. On 1 May 1981 they put out three trial issues a week for sale in Beijing, Shanghai, and Guangzhou to test readership response and gain staff experience.

China Daily began its official publication on 1 June of that year when it started regular publication of an eight-page broadsheet. It published Monday through Saturday during the first week, but announced plans in its first edition to publish thereafter Tuesday through Saturday. (The paper now publishes Monday through Saturday.) The paper began with 12 English-speaking journalists. These journalists trained Chinese college students who had studied English but who also had journalism training. *China Daily*'s present staff includes Chinese editors who were trained in Western journalism, such as Feng Xiliang, who graduated from the School of Journalism of the University of Missouri; Bill Kuan (Guan Zaihuan), who worked with Agence France Presse (AFP) in China in the 1940s; and Yu You, who was with the United States Information Service in Shanghai and Chongqing.

The paper got substantial help from the Melbourne Age publishing group in Australia and the Thomson Group in England. John Lawrence, group training supervisor of David Syme and Company of Melbourne Age, and Ron Kidd, a Thomson consultant, were among the original foreign experts. *China Daily* also got considerable help from the *People's Daily* in its initial days. But *China Daily* is responsible for itself both financially and editorially. The governing body at *China Daily* during its founding in June 1981 was an executive board whose members included Chairman Jiang Muyue; Editor in Chief Liu Zunqi; Managing Editor Feng Xiliang; deputy editors Zhang Xesun, Li Boti, Luo Qing, Zheng Defang, and Yu You; and Director of the General Office Ai Ling.

Readership and Circulation

Today, eight years after its official launching, *China Daily*'s target readership is still foreigners in China. They include residents, such as diplomatic personnel, business representatives, correspondents, technical advisors, and students, and transient readers, including visiting VIPs, officials, scholars, businessmen, and large numbers of tourists. *China Daily*'s readership also includes overseas subscribers. These are mainly corporate executives, government officials, professionals, and libraries. Results of a survey carried out by the *China Daily* Distribution Corporation in New York show that readers in the business and banking circles account for 60 percent of *China Daily*'s North American subscribers.

The number of *China Daily*'s Chinese readers within the country is growing continuously. Tourist organizations, hotels, government offices, foreign-trade departments and companies, nongovernmental organizations, professionals, and large numbers of students who want to improve their English are the main subscribers.

China Daily was originally meant to be circulated only on the mainland. But there was so much interest in Hong Kong that a Hong Kong edition, printed and distributed by Wen Wei Po, was published simultaneously on 1 June 1981. On its second anniversary, 1 June 1983, a North American edition was launched. It was printed in New York and distributed in the United States and Canada. The U.S. and Canadian cities where the paper is now available are New York, Boston, Washington, Chicago, San Francisco, Los Angeles, Houston, Vancouver, and Toronto. To cope with the growing readership at home, *China Daily* began printing in Shanghai on 1 July 1983, and in Guangzhou on 1 October 1984. At present, all editions have the same content as the Beijing edition.

Overall circulation has grown from 10,000 copies at launching in 1981 to 100,000 by December 1985 with roughly 90,000 copies inside China and 10,000 copies overseas. The price of the paper is 10 fen inside China and $.25 at newsstands in the United States or Canada. An annual subscription fee is $118.

China Daily has a separate department that handles advertising sales. It also has representatives in Hong Kong and the United States. The advertising rate was originally $6.50 per column inch in 1980 and $2,625 for a full page in 1983. But in 1987 the advertising rates had been raised to $8.50 per column inch and $3,000 for a full-page ad. The increase is due to the rising international advertising rates and higher costs. The initial goal to have advertising space constitute one-fourth of the paper has been met; in fact, the situation is so good that the demand for advertising space is greater than the space available. As a solution, *China Daily* has put out special supplements in specific regions. Fifteen such supplements were issued in 1984. Zheng Defang, former deputy editor, has commented that "we get more money from our advertisements than from our circulation."[1]

Editorial Policies

The paper now comes out six days a week, with no Sunday edition. The broadsheet newspaper has eight pages, carrying major news on the front page, financial and economic news on page 2, national and local news on page 3, editorials and opinion on page 4, culture, science, and travel features on page 5, a Life/People column and entertainment on page 6, sports news on page 7, and world news on the back page.

China Daily has a clearly defined readership and tailors its content accordingly. All its reporters and editors write in the English language. All copy is written and edited in English. This is a salient feature that sets *China Daily* apart from other Chinese publications in English. It is the policy of the editorial board to make *China Daily* a newspaper that caters to the needs and complies with the reading habits of foreigners. It is written in modern English and enlivened by the kind of layout to which Western eyes are accustomed. The editorial board pays special attention to selecting and effectively presenting good news photos.

The objectives of *China Daily* as determined by its editorial board may be summarized as follows: to report the latest news at home and abroad, with stress on political, economic, cultural, and social developments in China and relevant Chinese policies, thereby promoting understanding, friendship, and cooperation between the Chinese people and the people of other lands in the service of China's modernization drive and world peace.

The editorial department of *China Daily* is subdivided according to its pages, with the editorial board as the leading body. The subunits of the editorial department are the day desk, the night desk, the reporters' department, the financial page, the national page, the opinion page, the culture page, the Life/People column and entertainment page, and the sports page. The board also oversees the production, advertising, circulation, business, and personnel departments. Today's editorial board members are Editor Feng Xiliang, deputy editors Chen Li, Chen Hui, and Tang Wensheng, former Deputy Editor Zhang Xesun, and Secretary General Lu Ning. Jiang Muyue and Liu Zunqi currently serve as advisers.

At *China Daily* the day begins with the morning news conference at the day desk, which handles inside pages: financial news, national news, stories on the opinion page, the culture page, and the entertainment page. The respective pages' staffs submit to the day desk the stories they have prepared for the paper of the next day from whatever sources they have. These stories have to be approved by the desk before they can appear in the paper. The desk does a layout for each page, edits stories that have been approved, and creates headlines for all stories. Foreign specialists at the desk refine the editing done by Chinese copy editors. Arguments sometimes do spring up in the desk room; the Chinese editors and foreign specialists naturally see things from different perspectives. The night desk handles the front page, the back page, and the sports page, although the sports staff members usually do most of the work on sports news themselves. The night desk simply submits the finished page for approval and waits for the latest sports stories from the wire services.

The front page, needless to say, carries the most important foreign and domestic stories. More often than not, its content is evenly divided between the two. The lead story on the front page is usually domestic, but this is more a matter of news judgment than policy. Domestic stories on the front page are often about news of development in the country, government policies, and specific problems in national development. Sometimes stories are about policy speeches made by state officials on the domestic economy or foreign affairs.

One noticeable characteristic that distinguishes *China Daily* from other Chinese newspapers is that it does not preach. Former Deputy Editor Zheng Defang said in 1981: "We have a different readership, very different from that of *People's Daily*. If we tried to preach, you know what the reaction would be." But she added: "This paper is run in China, and China is a country where the Party leads, so any paper printed in China would be, broadly speaking, under the leadership of the Party."[2]

Foreign news to a large extent depends on AP, UPI, AFP, and Xinhua wire services. The paper often has a human-interest story or a story about the latest development in science as a bottom strip, which is not often found in other Chinese newspapers. This, too, is an attempt to cater to the taste of foreign readers. To meet the needs of foreign tourists and businessmen who travel extensively, *China Daily* often carries a little weather piece in a box on its front page. But occasionally the weather forecast is not accurate. An index, also not found in other Chinese papers, appears on the first page, too, as well as an eye-catching photo designed to attract the attention of the Western reader. Chinese newspapers do not have a tradition of using large pictures, but this front-page photo is also a special consideration for foreign readers, who are used to bright and attractive newspaper layout and graphics.

Almost from the very beginning, *China Daily* attempted a Western format, using short stories and large photos, separating news from comment, and using stories from Western news services and Xinhua. *China Daily* Editor Feng Xiliang said: "At first the newspaper looked rather stuffy because it followed the not terribly lively model of the *People's Daily*. In general, Chinese newspapers have longer articles and lots of background, and opinion is blended with the news. American papers tend to have shorter, sometimes more superficial, stories. Also they have more graphics, which shows the impact of television."[3]

The second page of *China Daily,* the financial and economic page, is an important page because it provides economic and business information for foreign businessmen who would not find such information on a timely daily basis, and in English, if there were no *China Daily*. Stories on this page are about construction of new projects, opportunities for investment, enterprises that earn big profits, and businesses that don't, with analyses of their problems. There are also numerous stories about joint business ventures between the Chinese and foreigners. The development of these joint investments, their successes and their problems, get tremendous coverage that is designed to encourage even more successful joint ventures. Joint ventures are presently an important part of China's economic policies. Such enterprises can attract foreign capital, which is badly needed, without totally forgoing the decision-making powers of the Chinese managers.

The financial and economic page also contains important announcements, such as bids for large-scale offshore oil exploration, and devotes coverage to important, signed business contracts. There are stories about imported new technologies, their advantages, and their problems. Some articles on this page also discuss what kind of new technologies China needs. The government's latest economic and monetary policies and regulations, which are also of great concern to foreign businessmen, are included on the financial page.

The page is not exclusively a domestic economic news page. It has stories about world markets of grain, tin, oil, and so on. It also carries stories about economic problems of other countries. The page is very sensitive to the changes in the exchange rates of currency, which are of course vital news to businessmen, and carries daily exchange rates of major currencies. The page also has a regular, brief column about economic issues and a column called "The Market," which reports the status of stock markets in New York, London, Tokyo, and Hong Kong.

The third page is the national and local news page, which reports all kinds of activities in the country with emphasis on new topics and new directions. It also pays special attention to the problems of the country, including corruption, mismanagement, and natural disasters, as well as questionable trends and practices, such as the recent tendency toward extravagant wedding ceremonies that are beyond the financial resources of both the bridegroom's and the bride's families.

Often, more than half of the news stories on page 3 originate in Beijing, the center of government offices and activities. The page also carries a brief column of human-interest stories and a column entitled "Around. . . . " This column alternates among the four topics of "Around Northeast China," "Around Shanghai," "Around Guangdong," and "Around Beijing." These are well-developed areas in China, pacesetters inside the country. The Northeast and Shanghai areas are also major industrial bases in China. What happens in these places will have great impact on the rest of the country.

Page 4 is the opinion or editorial page, which some Chinese readers consider dull, but some foreign readers like very much. Many of these readers say that one should read the opinion page to understand what is really going on in China, what the Chinese are arguing about and what their worries, anxieties, problems, and hopes are. They are right.

The page is a rare garden where all kinds of ideas blossom. It carries such orthodox pieces as commentaries or long theoretical articles from the Party magazine *Hongqi* (*The Red Flag*) or Xinhua news commentary on some particular world event. *China Daily* has its own commentary, too, signed by a *China Daily* commentator. When this commentary is about foreign affairs, it generally reflects government foreign policy.

Side by side with these orthodox pieces, the paper often carries heated arguments about controversial literary works. There are also articles written in a very personal style, expressing rather unorthodox views. Generally speaking, in Chinese newspapers readers seldom see articles with personal touches, although news stories do take bylines. Opinions instead seem to be expressed anonymously. On *China Daily* opinion pages, however, the "I" often gets into the story.

During the short-lived anti–spiritual pollution campaign, *China Daily* published a translation of *Hongqi*'s article that explained why such a campaign was necessary and how "spiritual pollution" was evident in society. Some reporters at *China Daily,* however, found some of the campaign regulations ridiculous. The Beijing Municipal Government, for instance, demands that women wearing unbound hair longer than their shoulders, whether on a business or a private visit, should not be admitted through the gate of its office building, for such hairstyles are supposed to show the decadent influence of the bourgeois West. One day a female reporter who was wearing such a hairstyle went to the municipal government to get a story. She was politely stopped at the gate and shown the regulation board. She said she wanted to meet a certain official inside the building for her story, so she had to enter. The doorkeeper then handed her a rubber band for her hair; she secured her hair, went in, and conducted her interview. When she finished and went back to the door, she returned the rubber band to the doorkeeper, thanking him, in case other such women should come along.

Back at the *China Daily* her colleagues thought such an anecdote too humorous to be ignored. In the "It Seems to Me" column a few days later, a writer introduced this story to the readers and commented sarcastically that the female reporter had her spirit cleaned for a couple of hours while her hair was in the band. The story was printed at a time when the campaign was still going on. This is one example of the openness and boldness of the *China Daily* style.

"We're the most open paper in China," said Guan Zaihuan (Bill Kuan), the late *China Daily* editorial board member. But in order to make such a boast, the paper must eschew certain important topics. "We don't interfere in Chinese politics," he added. John Lawrence of David Syme and Company, one of the paper's foreign experts, said in 1981 that the news judgments of Chinese journalists on the paper were coming closer to the tastes and needs of a Western audience. "It is essential that Chinese journalists develop a critical approach to news," he said.

On the opinion page of *China Daily* there is nothing in as personal a style as the styles of professional columnists who are popular among the opinion pages of U.S. newspapers. The People's Republic Chinese papers simply have not had the tradition, and *China Daily* is too young yet to give it consideration. But the page does have some columns, such as the previously mentioned "It Seems to Me," which is, comparatively speaking, rather personal and in which the writer can say whatever he or she thinks about whatever societal events or tendencies seem to call for comment. "In the Chinese Press" is a column in which mostly short versions of pithy opinions or comments in the Chinese press appear. "In the Foreign Press" carries summaries of opinions printed in foreign presses. These opinions are either about world affairs important to the Chinese or about social problems in the West that have a bearing on Chinese society. "To the Point" carries very brief comments, written by either editors or contributors, that are often ironic and to the point. "What They Are Saying" is a column that carries the expert opinions of professionals or officials, often selected on the basis of originality.

"Letters to the Editor" is a favorite column of many readers, both Chinese and foreigners. So far, the feedback on this feature has been strong. Besides providing a forum for response to articles in the paper, the column also provides a channel for many foreign tourists either to share the fun and joy of their travels or to vent frustrations and complaints about their journeys. Another distinguishing feature of the page is the picture column entitled "Our Candid Camera," which captures interesting moments in the everyday lives of ordinary people. These sizable pictures often have humorous and witty captions that add to their appeal. The page also carries cartoons or a cartoon series. Single-panel cartoons in most cases have some political import, while cartoon series often carry moral messages.

The fifth page, the cultural page, is the most successful page of the paper. Foreign readers, especially wives of businessmen, tourists, and foreign professors in China, rate it very highly. The page introduces ancient Chinese culture to today's China. Regular articles appear on the subjects of culture, archeology, medicine, science, theater, and travel.

Under "Culture," the page carries articles on a variety of topics including music, dance, movie reviews, introduction of well-known or rising movie stars, book reviews, poetry, latest discoveries of ancient tombs, history, art in carving and painting, and exchanges of cultural activities between the Chinese and people of other countries. These articles trace the ancient culture of China and display the grandeur and magnificence of this civilization at the dawn of human history with splendid language and dazzling pictures. This page also includes a regular piece on cultural trends in today's China.

From the articles on "Medicine" and "Science," readers learn the latest developments in the medical and scientific fields. Underdeveloped as its economy may be, China is very advanced in its medical research and in its pure, theoretical scientific research. Many foreigners are interested in China's acupuncture treatment and in traditional Chinese medicine. In articles introducing the latest results of scientific research, the full significance of the research is explained so that the readers may better appreciate and understand it.

All kinds of plays, including the world-famous Peking Opera, are discussed under the heading of "Theater." These plays usually depict life and problems in society, and the themes are often topical issues. Such plays often predict new trends. Articles introducing new plays or play reviews are written with professional judgment and insight. Here *China Daily* has the advantage in that a majority of its young staff have graduated as foreign literature majors and so have had adequate training in writing quality pieces of literary criticism. Writers who are responsible for poetry have written poetry themselves in English. People who write about art also have had special training in that field.

More foreigners like Peking Opera than young people in China who grew up during the Cultural Revolution and know nothing about art. The opera has developed very sophisticated and fascinating rituals of its own, and the genre is too accomplished for these young people to appreciate. But foreigners are overwhelmed by its unique artistic expression, sophistication, and fascination.

China Daily also has a senior staff whose members are well versed in operatic art. For example, the different makeup designs on the face show what kind of person the character is and what role he is to play in the opera, a very sophisticated distinction. The cultural page publishes articles with illustrations of different facial designs, explaining in detail their inner logic.

Travel is another popular topic among tourists. Under "Travel," the cultural page introduces to its readers all the natural wonders, scenic spots, and ancient civilization sites, such as the Great Wall, the Ming Tombs, the Palace Museum, the Forbidden City in Beijing, and the large-scale terra cotta figures of soldiers and horses in Xi'an. Due to the rapid increase in both foreign and domestic travelers, the page gives special attention to the recently discovered places of interest and new luxurious trains or cruises. China is such a large country with such diversified tourist resorts that a collection of these travel-page articles would make an ideal tour guide.

The culture page also introduces local delicacies and offers suggestions on where to buy special produce. From time to time, the page has a column of Chinese recipes, introducing certain kinds of native dishes. It also describes foreign tourists' experiences in the real Chinese restaurants, which are unlike what they have in their home countries.

As old as the Chinese civilization is, the culture page of *China Daily* is by no means ethnocentric. The exchange between the Chinese culture and foreign cultures occupies a prominent position on the page. The paper gives generous space to introducing foreign novelists, playwrights, and musicians. It also pays attention to the translation of foreign works. When Alvin Toffler's *The Third Wave* swept through the United States, his "wave" and *Future Shock* had impact across the Pacific in mainland China. The page devoted a large amount of space to his two books and their significance. Reporters for the page interviewed the author and his wife while they were visiting China, and publication of the interview shed further light on his two books. The coverage was a major project.

The sixth page in *China Daily* is the Life/People and entertainment page. Articles on this page generally have a rather light tone, telling stories about the lives of ordinary people, their joys, their worries, their problems, and their hopes. People of extraordinary achievements also find their stories published on this page. It is a place where foreign readers get to know the daily life of the ordinary Chinese, while Chinese readers get to know the life of their neighbors and learn to share their feelings.

Entertainment includes the announcement of weekly TV programs, programs on Radio Beijing, concerts, dances, plays, art exhibitions, and movie schedules in the capital. All of this information is very convenient for businessmen and their wives, individual travelers, or even group tourists who want something different from what is planned for them, who prefer entertainment to their own taste.

The page also carries a bridge game every day, and it is said that bridge fan Deng Xiaoping follows it closely. A crossword puzzle is also a regular feature of the page, although a dilemma exists in that professors often say the puzzle is too easy while some beginners in English get quickly discouraged after failing to solve it. However, foreign readers are usually not so particular about all this, as long as it can help them pass time while they are waiting for a plane or train.

The seventh page is the sports page. No other paper in China has devoted such a large amount of space to sports news. Most of the stories on this page deal with world games, but when the Chinese participate, the story is usually highlighted. When there is a breakthrough victory for the Chinese in world games, the story is carried in a front-page box. The results of important games played in other countries are also consistently reported.

The last page is the world-news page. This is the only page where all the stories come from the wire services of AP, UPI, Reuters, AFP, and Xinhua. *China Daily* distinguishes itself from other Chinese papers in its superb coverage of major world events, which may be due to the fact that *China Daily* has better access to information. *People's Daily,* however, may soon have access to Western news agencies as well. Until then, the competition is not equal. Most of the Chinese newspapers depend on Xinhua for their world news coverage. Xinhua is very selective about the nature of the news that it emphasizes, although in recent years, it has opened its door much wider to comprehensive coverage of world news.

China Daily's world news desk is truly news oriented. Editors at the desk judge news according to its intrinsic value rather than its possible impact on society. News is news wherever it occurs. *China Daily* gives considerable space to the coverage of the relationship between the two superpowers — the United States and the Soviet Union — and to the arms race, the Middle East, terrorist activities, economic and political trends in Western Europe, and the development and problems of Third-World countries, especially those of Africa and Latin America. *China Daily* pays special attention to the economic problems common to many developing countries, such as the huge international debt problem. Every attempt to tackle the problem is monitored by *China Daily* and reported. The activities of the delicate oil cartel OPEC are also given special attention. Natural disasters of Third-World countries are closely followed in order to call world attention to the problems.

Covering the struggle for independence and freedom in various countries is another distinguishing feature of *China Daily*. It devotes a large amount of space to the fighting in countries such as Cambodia, Afghanistan, Namibia, and the Middle East where the Palestinian people have yet to fight for their lost homeland, as well as to the mass demonstrations in South Africa against apartheid rule. Disputes between labor and management in any country also receive attention. In covering Central America, unlike its American counterparts, *China Daily* provides much coverage of the Contadora group, hoping for a peaceful resolution to the problems in that region. *China Daily* believes that the wishes of the people in Central America should to be respected.

As a newspaper in an Asian country, *China Daily* opens its eyes wide to the situations or problems in other Asian countries, such as religious and ethnic disputes in India and Sri Lanka, the situation on the Korean Peninsula, and the domestic movement for democracy in South Korea. *China Daily* has also closely followed the situation in the Philippines.

For the rest of its world coverage, *China Daily* includes stories about the trade protectionist wars between the United States and Japan, New Zealand's boycott of the U.S. nuclear ships, the unrest in Northern Ireland, and so on. Alongside stories depicting a gloomy reality, *China Daily* has lighter human-interest stories to lend balance to its coverage. Breakthroughs in science and technology are always highlighted.

Perhaps the one part of the world that *China Daily* does not cover adequately is the Soviet Union and Eastern Europe. The five news agencies available to *China Daily* do not provide comprehensive coverage on this part of the world, and the paper at present does not have access to TASS, the Soviet news agency.

Gathering the News: Accesses and Sources

How does *China Daily* get its news stories? It has, in fact, several channels for doing so. The first of these are channels for gathering domestic news. *China Daily* has a highly competent reporters' department filled with reporters who are mostly young and energetic and have received journalistic training in Britain, Australia, and the United States. Usually they will get their domestic news stories from various branches of the government, including ministries, commissions, committees, and offices; the beat system is not clear-cut. *China Daily*'s staff is rather limited, and it is hard pressed to produce stories every day. In addition to the reporters' department, however, each page has its own staff, some of whom interview people and write stories, but usually for that page only.

Apart from staff-generated news stories, a large number of *China Daily* stories are translations or reedited stories from other Chinese newspapers that prove to be good sources of information. Reediting of these pieces is quite important. Chinese papers tend to include long pieces without clear-cut or fresh leads, and with a lot of interpretation and "empty talk." To render these pieces readable to foreign readers, *China Daily* must often perform some heavy editing.

A considerable proportion of *China Daily*'s domestic news, especially from outside Beijing, depends on the Xinhua News Agency, because *China Daily* has only three domestic bureaus inside China, while the Xinhua staff is all over the country. However, Xinhua pieces often need heavy editing also. And sometimes Xinhua stories are not so timely. When a Xinhua story is somewhat different from a version in a local newspaper, *China Daily* has real problems. Often checking the simplest facts can be very difficult; local leaders, at times, seem painfully unaware of the impact the mass media can have.

China Daily's three domestic bureaus are located in Shanghai, Guangzhou, and Hangzhou. Except for the largest office in Shanghai, only a couple of people are stationed in these bureaus. All have been trained at the paper in Beijing for about a year before they are sent to their bureaus. This method of training proves to be very successful; the rate of publication is high for stories submitted from these bureaus.

The three cities with bureaus are modern cities in China, cities opening up to the outside world. Foreign businessmen and overseas Chinese have invested heavily in Shanghai and Guangzhou. The economic situation in these two cities is of at least some interest to most foreign businessmen in China.

So far, *China Daily* has no foreign bureaus to cover news events outside China. But *China Daily* will send reporters to cover such special events as the 1984 Olympic Games in Los Angeles, major sports games in Canada, or the fighting in Cambodia. When a high-ranking official such as the president of the state or the premier pays an official visit to another country, *China Daily* usually sends a reporter with the official's entourage so that the paper can offer its own version of what has happened. More stories with staff bylines will, of course, enhance the paper's image.

For world-news coverage, *China Daily* depends almost entirely on Xinhua and the wire services of the Big Four Western news agencies. The limitations of the Western news agencies are inherited by *China Daily,* which does not have the capabilities to redress them yet. However, the newspaper expects to gain access to more world news agencies in the near future. Besides its staff and the wire services, *China Daily* also gets stories from contributors, who offer their expert opinions on specific topics.

Access to information has been increasing in the last couple of years in China. Now the Foreign Ministry offers weekly news briefings to foreign and Chinese reporters, during which it answers reporters' questions. Although occasionally the answer is "no comment," even this is progress. Within the context of a long history of feudalism, it is progress when the government deems itself accountable to the press, the representative of the general public. Other ministries, furthermore, have followed suit. Ministries, commissions, and committees under the State Council have held press conferences and news briefings for the press when there are major policy changes, when major projects are planned, or when there is much publicity or rumor about what is going on in the ministry.

And this is only the beginning of what is sure to be greater progress in the future. David Dodwell of the *London Financial Times,* who once worked as a foreign specialist on *China Daily,* has commented that most news comes from formal briefings, from government ministries, or from state corporations. Officials in China are not yet accustomed to answering reporters' questions, but will surely grow more comfortable with the system as time goes on.

Photography and Graphics

The Photography Department of *China Daily* is the pride of the paper. From the paper's early days, Feng Xiliang, the current editor, has paid special attention to the quality of news photos. His Western journalism education must have heavily influenced him, for most Chinese newspapers do not usually pay as much attention to pictures as do their Western counterparts. Feng, in one of his interviews with the Western press, talked about the impact of television on newspapers in the West. His attention to pictures in the paper can be traced to his awareness of the importance of graphics to Western papers, and in turn to *China Daily,* which targets Westerners as its readers.

China Daily has pioneered the use of large photos. On special occasions, such as the opening ceremonies of the National People's Congress and the birthday of late Party Chairman Mao Zedong, *China Daily* has carried extra-large pictures of the ceremony across all six columns on the front page. Such pictures often have tremendous impact on the readers and are not easy to forget. These kinds of pioneering experiments have shaken press circles. *People's Daily,* for instance, timidly followed suit and eventually began to use larger and livelier photos.

China Daily's daring and successful experiments with pictures were possible because of its first-class photographers. Members of its photo staff have tried hard to be innovative. The meeting scene inside the Great Hall of the People has been photographed by Xinhua photographers so many times, and the pictures have been so dull and so monotonous, that a picture taken by a *China Daily* photographer from a new angle awakened readers to the grandeur of the meeting hall and the significance of the meeting in session. The photographers of *China Daily* have since become well known in the circle of Chinese photography.

The Subtle Problems

China Daily has benefited from its unique position in the Chinese press, but it also has a number of problems and dilemmas that editors from other Chinese papers do not have to face. Everything has its compensation. The biggest dilemma is that *China Daily* tries to make itself a paper of Western taste to cater to its readers—but, after all, it is a paper published in a socialist country. Staff members have wracked their brains to reconcile these two realities.

The *Wall Street Journal* once commented on the situation: The *China Daily* treads a careful path between its editors' desires to emulate a Western-style newspaper and its need to keep a low profile on political matters.[4] Guan Zaihuan has been quoted in the *New York Times* as saying, "We are not a party organ, and we do try to be as objective as we can. In other words, we don't deviate from the party line, but we do have our own editorial policy."[5] Government control of information is indeed a favorite topic of Western journalism scholars. The foreign specialist at *China Daily,* David Dodwell, has written, "As a foreign friend, one was rarely aware of the hand of the party in editorial decision-making. In fact, I was pleasantly surprised at the extent of editorial freedom allowed to the staff. Only occasionally did one come face to face with the authoritarian aspect of Chinese society."[6]

Another problem arises from using Western wire services. Because *China Daily* depends almost totally on the Western news agencies for its world-news coverage, the tone of these agencies sometimes sets the tone of the world-news page. Some foreign readers consider *China Daily* pro-West, or worse still, pro-American. The paper, for instance, covers much more news of the United States than of the Soviet Union. The U.S. version of any world event is offered first, for the simple reason that its version comes out first. Although Western journalists claim to be objective and to stick to the separation of facts and opinion, they often belie their intentions by their selection of material and choice of words.

Editing is not easy for the night news desk, which handles wire copies. It is relatively simple to deal with blatant bias, but difficult to redress bias built into the interpretation of a story, particularly if editors do not have firsthand material. In extreme cases, the staff turns to Xinhua for help. Unfortunately, Xinhua pieces often do not have the necessary background material to present the full meaning of an event. And *China Daily* is too young to have a good morgue.

China Daily has done its best to give the Third World its fair share of coverage. The paper has a special column on the world-news page called "Third-World Notes," which includes such stories about the Third World as the cooperation of developing countries in education programs, the construction of major power plants, agreements between countries for joint development, and so on. Most of these pieces come from Xinhua. Western news agencies do send some stories about the Third World, and the staff at the paper tries hard to extract something positive enough to publish. But too often even pieces introducing progress in developing countries are filled with disdain and ethnocentrism.

Foreign specialists offer valuable second opinions in the newsroom, as the editor of the paper, Feng Xiliang, has noted. But opinions there occasionally clash. Newsroom debates can be very illuminating. Some foreign specialists take a purely Western approach, especially young ones who refuse to understand the limits and realities of another country. Well-experienced foreign journalists are more understanding and know better how to put forth a suggestion. But on the whole, the paper benefits greatly from all these specialists.

Still another problem *China Daily* has is that its readers sometimes endow it with an official status that it does not have. Chinese are polite people and so are their papers. Chinese papers carry a lot of stories about official visits of heads of state from other countries. Sometimes the embassy staff of a country will compare the space that *China Daily* reserves for such stories, as if such editorial decisions have something to do with the status of their own country. Some diplomats complain because a certain story is too short compared with a story about their neighbors. Sometimes the misspelling of the name of a sensitive country can actually result in a formal protest to the Chinese Foreign Ministry. Such things do happen and *China Daily* cannot afford to ignore them.

Human-interest stories can be risky, too. Once the paper ran a piece from AFP reporting survey results that indicated the French use the least amount of soap among Western Europeans. The headline, which may have been too flip, was "A Stain on French Character." The story hurt French journalists in Beijing, and they called in to protest. *China Daily* explained to them that the story was intended as a human interest story and that it was from AFP. They refused to believe it was from AFP. *China Daily* learned a lesson: Do not offend your readers by hurting their national pride.

Developments

China Daily is developing along with its country. In light of increasing interest in China's economic news among American readers, a "Business Weekly" section was added in June 1985 to the North American edition as a special Wednesday supplement. The paper is now working on preparations for the publication of a "Student Weekly" section, designed to attract readers of high-school age, whose enormous numbers will likely boost circulation.

From time to time, *China Daily* issues special supplements about a particular region, introducing its industry, development, natural resources, and investment opportunities. Advertisements in these supplements come exclusively from that region. Local officials are quite enthusiastic about such supplements.

The Staff

China Daily now has a staff of more than 200 people, with about 80 editors and reporters and 5 photographers. There were 4 foreign specialists during the early days, and now there are 5 to 6 all year around. In 1981 Editor Feng Xiliang said, "Originally, I would have told you this paper would eventually be run exclusively by Chinese, but now I believe we'll always need one or two experienced foreign journalists."[7] He said it was important to have a "second opinion—otherwise I think we would tend to get too subjective." He described involvement of foreign journalists as necessary to act "as a representative of the voice of the readers." He also knows that news recruits at the paper need training by foreign specialists.

A few of the senior Chinese staff at the paper have prior experience in journalism. Most of them are, however, English teachers or people who were recruited because of their English skills. The new recruits at the paper are mostly English or English-literature majors, who know next to nothing about journalism. Only a small number now come from the graduate school of the Institute of Journalism under the Academy of Social Sciences of China. Therefore, the majority need professional journalistic training.

China Daily has sent quite a number of its staff abroad to study journalism. It currently has people at the University of Hawaii, Stanford University, East-West Center in Hawaii, University of Minnesota, Columbia University, and the University of Missouri. It has also sent young journalists for training at Thomson Editorial Study Center, the *Financial*

Times, Newcastle Evening Chronicle, Edinburgh Evening News in Britain, *Canberra Times, Newcastle Herald* in Australia, and *Seattle Post-Intelligencer* in the United States.

A Trailblazer in China

China Daily seeks to be a trailblazer. It is the first newspaper in China to introduce a computerized photo typesetting process in newspaper production; it is also the first newspaper in China to adopt a satellite telepress transmission system to transmit its pages to overseas printers. On 12 August 1985 *China Daily* began telepress transmission via satellite to Hong Kong. In October 1985 the paper began satellite transmission of its pages to New York and, a few months later, also to San Francisco, where the North American editions are printed and distributed. So far *China Daily* is the only newspaper in China that devotes, on the average, 25 percent of its total space to advertising.

Although the newspaper is barely eight years old, *China Daily* has established itself as an important and reliable source of information from China. It is widely quoted by the world media. Many friends, including the late British writer Felix Greene, have rated *China Daily* one of the best English-language newspapers produced in non-English-speaking countries. In the past five years, *China Daily* has won awards from both Chinese and foreign institutions. In March 1982 the Population Action Council presented the Award for Media Excellence to *China Daily* for the best developing world coverage.

In April 1984 the University of Missouri's School of Journalism awarded *China Daily*'s editor Feng Xiliang the Missouri Honor Medal for distinguished service in journalism and for his contribution to publishing *China Daily,* the first English-language national newspaper in the People's Republic. In 1983 and 1984 *China Daily*'s Photography Department and Features Department each won the honored title of National Advanced Unit awarded by the All-China Journalist Association. In 1984 Editor Feng Xiliang was awarded the Perceptive Eye Prize by the National News Photography Society for the newspaper's selection and handling of exciting news photos.

5 ☒ *World Economic Herald*
(*Shijie Jingji Daobao*)

Introduction

China has marched into a new historic era under the leadership of
Deng Xiaoping since the end of the Cultural Revolution. In the past ten
years, tremendous changes have taken place all over the country. The
new leadership has advocated that all the Chinese people strive to modernize China. Along with the modernization drive a nationwide economic reform movement was launched in all walks of life with the support and cooperation of the Chinese people.

The Chinese mass media, propaganda and agitation tools of the
leadership, are used to promote the economic reforms and to motivate
the Chinese people to help carry out that task.[1] The press has devoted
considerable attention and enormous space to economic news and issues
with the advance of economic reforms in the country. Amid the winds of
change in China's journalism since the late 1970s, a conspicuous phenomenon is the rise of economic news, especially the plethora of economic newspapers that had disappeared from the Chinese press during
the Cultural Revolution and that have now regained prominent attention
at the national, provincial, and local levels.

Economic newspapers are playing an increasingly significant role in
the nation's economic development, and they are closely integrated with
the nation's recent economic reforms.[2] The flourishing of economic
newspapers in China's press has broadened the news scope and depth to
an unprecedented degree, providing the Chinese people with economic
information that used to be unavailable.

The *World Economic Herald* is one of China's many economic
newspapers that appeared in the nation's modernization drive. It mainly
covers world economic news and important economic issues in China,
comments on current economic situations, popularizes economic knowl-

edge, introduces new economic developments and economic management both at home and abroad, and exchanges research results concerning both the national economy and world economic situations and relations.[3] It is distributed not only in China but also to many other countries and regions.

The *World Economic Herald* has been regarded as an authority on both world and national economic issues. Because of its influence, the Chinese government uses the newspaper to test the practicability of new policies. By leaking information concerning new policies through the *Herald* to the general public, the government often tries to gauge public response before the official implementation of those new policies. The *World Economic Herald* has become a window through which the authorities watch for a suitable time for making either political or economic changes.

Background of Economic Newspapers in China

As China has opened its doors to the outside world, new things from around the world have flooded into China's vast territory. As a result those in all walks of life have been affected in one way or another. This has inevitably influenced the country's newspaper industry as people are no longer content with the Party papers at all levels. Demanding novelty and variation, they feel the need for specialized newspapers. This increasing public demand has resulted in the appearance of many newspapers with totally new formats and content catering to different needs of the public in virtually every corner of the country.

Caimao Zhanxian (Finance and Trade Front) was first published in 1978, though it later changed its name to *China Finance and Trade,* and then again to *Economic Daily.* It was soon followed by *Market, Economic Reference, World Economic Herald,* and many more economic newspapers in the Chinese press.[4] In the past few years, economic newspapers have thrived in China. According to incomplete statistics submitted by the Ministry of Posts and Telecommunications, 130 economic newspapers existed in the country by April 1985, excluding hundreds of smaller economic newspapers run by grass-roots units and distributed in small cities, towns, or counties. This figure is based on the publications registered through the post service in Beijing and other major cities.[5]

In general, economic newspapers in China can be divided into the following five categories.

1. *Comprehensive Economic Newspapers.* These kinds of economic

newspapers cover economic activities and affairs in all fields both at home and abroad and also serve to propagate and explain the policies of the Party and the government. They normally answer to, or are operated by, the direct leadership of Party or government organizations at various levels. They also cover current political, cultural, and sports events and news.

The *Economic Daily* is one representative paper of this type. This paper, under the direct control of the Finance and Economy Subcommittee of the Party and the Party Central Committee Propaganda Department, is responsible for reports of the nation's economic activities, reflecting the views of the Party and the government on economic affairs and guiding the practice of the nation. Its content includes both domestic and foreign economic news and reports, and important political, cultural, and sports news. Its Sunday editions carry a great deal of entertainment information centering on arts and literature. Since the paper is under the direct leadership of the Party, the *Economic Daily*'s news and commentaries reflect the intentions of the leadership and carry a tone of authority. The paper also plays the role of explaining policies and guiding economic practice. Even though this paper offers comprehensive news coverage, it falls easily into the stereotype of the "Party paper." That is why it does not have a large audience, except for some Party and government departments and large enterprises that must subscribe to it.

2. *Purely Economic Information Papers.* Newspapers of this kind carry only comprehensive economic news paying no attention to other news such as politics, culture, or sports. They emphasize the practical and educational aspects of the economy. These papers are usually run by news agencies or economic departments. A large number of economic newspapers in the country belong to this category. Most economic papers operated at provincial, municipal, or county levels fall into this category. *Economic Reference* published by the Xinhua News Agency and *Shanghai Economic Information* operated by *Jiefang Ribao* are typical of this kind of economic newspaper.

3. *Specialized Economic Newspapers.* This type of economic newspaper specializes in information about certain businesses or economic fields. Such papers carry information concerning only economic activities, scientific and technological development, and theories. Their readers usually cluster in specific businesses. *Zhongguo Shangye Bao* (*China Business Journal*), *Guoji Shangbao* (*International Business Journal*), *Jishu Shichang* (*Technology Market*), and *Dianzi Shichang* (*Electronic Market*) are of this type.

4. *Newspapers for Consumers.* These papers are purely for consumers' use. They provide information on conveniences and service in the interest of consumers, and they meet the needs of the general public.

Market information, introductions to new products, and advertisements are the main content of these papers, which are informative, practical, and entertaining. One successful paper of this type is *Jingji Shenghuo* (*Economic Life*). There is a saying among the people: If you watch television, better read *TV Weekly,* and if you want to do shopping, don't forget to read *Economic Life.*

5. *Newspapers Published by Economic Research Institutes.* These papers are normally published by economic research institutions and have a strong academic orientation. They not only cover economic news and issues but also carry in-depth discussions and analyses of both domestic and international economic issues. They focus their attention on economic problems that need to be resolved quickly and try to provide information to their readers. Readers usually regard the views of these papers as authoritative since many of their stories are written by economic specialists. They help readers better understand current economic problems and topics, and they guide them in their day-to-day affairs. The *World Economic Herald* in Shanghai and the *Jingji Xuebao* (*Economic Journal*) are considered to be representative of this type of economic newspaper. Even though economic newspapers have historically been very active and have had an influential position in Chinese society, only two economic newspapers existed until the 1970s. In recent years, however, economic newspapers have flourished all over the country. It is necessary and meaningful to examine the three developing phases of economic newspapers in Chinese society; prosperity, depression, and revival.

The key to understanding the unusual phenomenon of the growth of economic newspapers in China is to comprehend the relationship between the features of economic newspapers and the socioeconomic system. China had no economic newspapers in feudal societies. Though *Di Bao* had a history of over one thousand years, it covered mainly activities of the emperor and his family and other court affairs. It was intended to disseminate information from the top to officials at all levels so that they could act accordingly.[6] Ordinary citizens were satisfied with their own lives without knowing the political or economic situations outside their daily affairs.

The entry of Western powers to China in the 19th century brought about an advance in industry and trade. Along with the country's economic development, economic newspapers developed rapidly in China. The contemporary commodity economy led to economic newspapers in China, and, in turn, economic newspapers aided the growth of the nation's economy.

During the period from the early 19th century to the middle of the

20th century, the socioeconomic system in China was that of a commodity economy, though China's economy was developing at a slow pace and on a small scale and was highly dependent on the West. Various economic information was in high demand among privately owned businesses, and economic newspapers that provided the necessary information had a tremendous audience.

Since 1949, when the Communist Party came to power and gained control of the country, China has taken a new road to development. The Party strove to rebuild and reform the existing socioeconomic system and to consolidate its regime. Marxism-Leninism became the official ideology governing the country. Strenuous efforts were made to nationalize the economy. The political and power structure also became even more centralized, with the result that the Party and government began to control every aspect of society.

During the first three years after the founding of the People's Republic, China was successful in rebuilding the economy left by the Nationalist regime and restoring social stability and the people's confidence. Beginning in 1953, the new government began to carry out its first five-year economic plan and the "socialist reforms" of the country's economic structure and ownership. Privately owned industries were eventually transformed into completely state-owned operations through a "buying off" policy.[7] The most important program enacted by the government from 1950 to 1953 was land reform. In the 1953–54 period, one step in this countryside reform was to set up agriculture production cooperatives. Later the final step of the socialist collectivism was the founding of the people's commune system, which had long been the basic form of production in China's countryside.[8]

Beginning in the middle of the 1950s the Party and the government embarked on a rapid industrialization program. This period was a key factor in forming China's social and economic system. It constituted a distinct phase in the history of the new China. For ideological reasons and because of China's isolation in the international community as well as the hostility between China and the United States, a Soviet development strategy of long-term centralized planning was adopted to promote industrialization. Central to the Soviet model was the rapid buildup in heavy industry by means of centralized allocation of investment into capital goods industries. This required that the central government determine targets and quotas for various economic sectors to meet.[9]

Since the nation's economy was developing under the control of the government and all economic activities were planned by the central government, local units had no freedom in their production and management but carried out the tasks set forth by the government. They did not necessarily need any economic information because all economic factors had been considered by the central planners, and because the tasks for every economic sector had been decided by those in charge at high administrative levels who obtained economic information from reports sent by grass-roots units. The central government set targets and quotas for those at the lowest levels to fulfill.

All economic sectors were therefore run and controlled by the central government, all economic activities were well planned in advance, and there was no competition among different enterprises. Therefore, economic newspapers, whose role is to provide economic information to help people benefit from economic activities, especially in the competitive market of the economy, were not regarded as essential to the nation's economy. The two economic newspapers existing during that period simply reported how the plans were being worked out and more often than not reflected only the positive aspects of the nation's economy.

With the start of the Cultural Revolution, China's economy immediately turned into chaos. All economic sectors were greatly affected, and the only two economic newspapers soon disappeared from the Chinese press. After the death of Chairman Mao Zedong and the arrest of the four chief radical leaders, the Cultural Revolution finally came to an end. The ten-year-long "revolution," which turned out to be a national catastrophe for China, exposed fundamental weaknesses in the system—a fact that the Party itself admitted. The revolution was regarded as a serious mistake, "the most severe setback" with "the heaviest losses suffered by the Party."[10]

Deng's rehabilitation after the Cultural Revolution was a key to the occurrence of later reforms in China. With the development of economic reforms launched after the ten-year turmoil, the new leadership together with some theorists and specialists analyzed the economic and political situation in China and summed up the experience, both positive and negative, in socialist construction, and particularly that of reform of the economic structure in the urban and rural areas over the past few years. They systematically probed into problems existing in socialist construction. What they were concerned with most was the issue of a commodity economy.

Concerning the establishment of a new socialist economic system, the "Decision on Reform of the Economic Structure," passed at the Third Plenary Session of the Twelfth Central Committee of the Chinese Communist Party, stated:

> In the reform of the planning system, it is necessary, first of all, to discard the traditional idea of pitting the planned economy against the commodity

economy. We should clearly understand that the socialist planned economy is a planned commodity economy based on public ownership, in which the law of value must be consciously followed and applied. The full development of a commodity economy is an indispensable stage in the economic growth of society and a prerequisite for our economic modernization. It is the only way to invigorate our economy and prompt enterprises to raise their efficiency, carry out flexible operations and promptly adapt themselves to complex and changing social demands. This cannot be achieved by relying only on administrative means and mandatory plans.[11]

The decision adopted at that meeting went on to say:

We must also realize that the extensive growth of a socialist commodity economy may also lead to certain disorder in production, and there has to be guidance, regulation and administrative control through planning. Therefore, a planned economy by no means excludes the application of the law of value and the growth of a commodity economy; they in fact form a unity.[12]

Proceeding from these principles, the decision goes on to summarize the nature of China's planned economic system:

First, ours is on the whole a planned economy, that is, a planned commodity economy, not a market economy that is entirely subject to market regulation. Second, production and exchange completely subject to market regulation are confined mainly to certain farm and sideline products. Small articles of daily use and labor services are in the service and repair trades, all of which play a supplementary but indispensable role in the national economy. Third, our planned economy does not necessarily mean the predominance of mandatory planning, both mandatory and guidance planning being its specific forms. Fourth, guidance plans are fulfilled mainly by use of economic levers; mandatory plans have to be implemented, but even then the law of value must be observed.[13]

Social existence determines social consciousness, and social needs bring about new things. Economic newspapers were a by-product of the development of a commodity economy; they were the inevitable outcome of the commodity economy and also aided in the development of the economic system.

Meanwhile, other general purpose newspapers paid more attention to economic news as well as to social needs. For example, the four-page *Renmin Ribao* (*People's Daily*), which was expanded to eight pages in January 1980, allotted more coverage to economic news. In January

1980 out of the 29 news stories given the greatest prominence on the first page, 21 were economic reports. In the corresponding month of 1979 only 3 economic stories out of a total of 27 occupied the same place on page one. Also, out of the total 312 stories appearing on the first page in January 1980, 173 were economic reports. In the corresponding month of 1979 only 49 economic stories out of the total 151 news reports were carried on page one.[14]

Apart from page one of the *Renmin Ribao,* nine other pages were devoted to economic reporting every week including agriculture, industry, and commerce. Reports in other fields such as politics, science, education, literature, and art focused on economic aspects. The coverage of a stable political situation, economic laws, economic sanctions, development among national minorities, the training of scientific research personnel, and newly published works of literature and art all served the interests of economic reporting.

Not only were the economic reforms fully covered, but so were the changes they brought about. In rural areas the system of contracted responsibility for production with remuneration linked to output promoted agricultural production. As a result, the living standard of peasants was improved, bringing about changes in their attitudes — demands that their cultural life should be improved.

Economic activities have become the overwhelming center of attention in Chinese society. An increasing number of people are involved in this type of activity and they are demanding more economic-related information. Economic newspapers have been developing rapidly to meet the social needs.

In China, the mass media are under the control of the Party and the government. The role of the media is to agitate and motivate the people to support and follow the line and policies of the Party.[15] On 8 February 1985 Hu Yaobang, former general secretary of the Chinese Communist Party Central Committee, said at a meeting of the Party Secretariat: "The journalist should serve as the organ of the Party by its very nature. This is justified and must not be abandoned. The journalist work of the Party must speak for the Party and government, and provide opinion and guidance in accordance with the line and policy of the Party."[16] The situation is no different concerning today's economic reforms. If change has taken place during the past few years regarding the Party's control of the press, it is simply a matter of *degree* of control.

The characteristics of the sociopolitical system in China have been reflected in China's economic newspapers. In the West, economic newspapers, a kind of commodity themselves, do not represent the government or interfere directly in the operation of enterprises or businesses.

They merely sell economic and business information to those who need it in their day-to-day affairs. Unlike their Western counterparts, Chinese economic newspapers are owned and administered by the Party and the government or concerned economic departments. They do not simply provide information, but they also propagate and explain economic policies and directives of the Party and the government while helping to guide the development of the nation's economy. In this context, the term *propaganda* cannot be defined or explained according to Western standards. In China this term means presenting the country in a good light to its people—in other words, favorably introducing China's economic, political, and social developments on domestic and international issues.

Economic newspapers in China also function as a channel through which the demands, opinions, problems, and questions of manufacturers and consumers can be delivered to the concerned departments. Economic newspapers in China are regarded as both information sources and tools of adjustment and control.

World Economic Herald as a Leading Economic Newspaper in China

Among all the economic newspapers that came into being in the Chinese press along with the last decade's economic reforms and development is an economic newspaper that has received great attention from the government and people in all walks of life with its distinctive characteristics and style—the *World Economic Herald*. This newspaper has been regarded as a "forerunner" and a "pioneer" among economic newspapers in China and has been praised by Chinese journalists as a model for journalism.[17]

In commemoration of the fifth anniversary of the founding of the *World Economic Herald,* the Party organ *Renmin Ribao* (*People's Daily*) spoke highly of the *Herald* in a congratulatory message:

> You have made great achievements in the past five years. Being prompted by the mission of the time, you have tried every means possible and have done your utmost in exploring the road which would lead China to economic prosperity. You have demonstrated your global perspective, high strategy, and incisive views with a lively style and distinctive characteristic in your coverage and content. You've developed a school of your own in Chinese journalism. You spare no efforts in advocating reforms, and you have offered good ideas and opinions for the modernization of our nation. . . . You are a good teacher for your counterparts and a helpful friend of readers. You are worthy of the name of the *Herald.*[18]

Origin of the *World Economic Herald*

Like other economic newspapers in China, the *World Economic Herald* emerged in the Chinese press in association with the nation's economic development and increasing social demands. Behind a closed door for several decades, the Chinese people had a very limited understanding of the outside world obtained only through some restricted international contacts. When China opened itself to the outside world under the leadership of Deng Xiaoping after the Cultural Revolution, the government and the people felt a great need to learn from the developed West and to incorporate the advanced experience of other countries into China's modernization program.

As China greatly increased its economic exchanges with foreign countries, it not only had to study the historical development of other nations' economies, but also had to catch up with the current global economic development. Therefore, fragmentary and nonsystematic coverage of global economic news could not meet the needs of China's socioeconomic life. There existed a great need for an economic newspaper of global orientation to offer comprehensive and systematic coverage of current economic developments around the world, to introduce new experiences and lessons learned by other nations in their economic development, and to conduct penetrating analyses of current economic conditions and issues.

As the reforms proceeded, there was a need for an overall adjustment of China's economic development and for systematic guidance in its macroeconomic development. Therefore, economic newspapers could not limit themselves to covering only economic activities of individual departments, sectors, or units. China's nationwide economic reform is a massive experiment, and a wide range of problems could appear needing resolution. Reform, and constant review of that reform, must progress carefully as the government calls on economists to explain different economic policies in the modernization movement. There is a pressing need for a specialized newspaper to carry the views, opinions, and situational analyses of these economic specialists so that people engaged in economic activities can be better informed on economic matters. There is also demand for information about foreign economic theories.

General-purpose economic newspapers have proved unable to provide the Chinese people the necessary information, principally because of their specific orientation and their limited space. Thus social needs have determined the essential prerequisite for the birth of the *World Economic Herald,* an unprecedented economic newspaper in the Chinese press. In a sense, the *World Economic Herald* was an inevitable outcome of China's historical development. "A Message to Readers" in the trial edition of the *World Economic Herald* stated:

> As China is opening itself to the outside world, China needs to understand the outside world. Construction of China's socialist modernization is closely linked with the world's economy. To meet the needs of changing circumstances, the *World Economic Herald* has been founded. . . . We hope that this economic newspaper will become a window through which our readers can see and understand the outside world and make some contributions to the construction of the socialist modernization of our nation.[19]

The *World Economic Herald* is based in Shanghai, a city that has developed rapidly and has gradually become the largest industrial and commercial center in China. By the 1930s and 1940s, Shanghai's economic importance had already been recognized abroad. Since the founding of the People's Republic, the great production capacity in the Shanghai area has played a significant role in China's economy and occupies a special place in China's economic development. Shanghai's fiscal income accounts for about 8 to 10 percent of the nation's annual revenue. According to 1984 statistics, the average per capita income in Shanghai was $1,400, far above the national average per capita income of $300.[20]

As China's biggest industrial and business center Shanghai has a strong newspaper industry with a long history. *Shen Bao* (*Shanghai Gazette*), one of China's earliest and most influential modern newspapers, and *Xinwen Bao* (*News Gazette*), China's first business newspaper, were both started in Shanghai.

Before the creation of the People's Republic, Shanghai was the center of China's newspaper industry around which assembled a large group of professional journalists. Even though the city lost its role as the center of China's newspaper industry after the new China was founded, Shanghai still has the potential for supporting a large number of newspapers. Whenever conditions are ripe, new newspapers may appear at anytime.

With China opening its door to the West, Shanghai immediately became an open port city. This industrial and commercial city had a great demand for more specific business information for its development as an increasing number of foreign business people entered the city. Especially in the past few years, with the rapid development of the national economy and the urgent modernization drive, Shanghai sensed the need to add more economic newspapers to meet the demand for new information. In 1980 one year after the Chinese Communist Party Central Committee approved the decision on China's economic structural reforms, the *World Economic Herald* was born in Shanghai.

The *World Economic Herald* was first published on 21 June 1980. At that time, it was only a biweekly newspaper, but beginning in 1981 it became on eight-page weekly. By the beginning of 1982, the paper added four more pages and became a specialized economic journal. The *World Economic Herald*'s content is comprehensive, focusing mainly on world economic news; important economic issues in China; comments on current economic affairs; economic principles; new economic developments and economic management both at home and abroad; and research results on both the national economy and international economies.

The *Herald* is run jointly by the China Association of World Economics and the World Economic Research Institute of the Shanghai Social Science Academy. Its circulation in recent years reached six hundred thousand and it was distributed not only in China but also to 57 different countries and regions of the world. Its foreign distribution lags behind only that of the *People's Daily,* the largest and most authoritative newspaper in China.[21]

The *World Economic Herald*'s Support for Government Economic Reforms

The *World Economic Herald,* a product of the economic reforms promoted by the Party and the government, ardently propagates principles and policies of the reforms and actively defends and explains government policies on a theoretical basis. It uses a lot of evidence to prove the correctness of the Party's policies determined by the Third Plenary Session of the Eleventh Party Central Committee and the Third Plenary Session of the Twelfth Party Central Committee. The *Herald* has been regarded as the by-product of the Third Plenum of the Eleventh Party Central Committee.[22] The *World Economic Herald* has thoroughly reported economic activities under the guidance of the Party, has paid great attention to Party policies, and has provided large amounts of space to news about economic reforms.

From early 1980 to the middle of 1981, guided by the Party's policy of economic reform, the *World Economic Herald* used more than 20 percent of its space to advocate the construction of Chinese-style socialism and the modernization of the country through reforms, to popularize government policies on changes in the national economy, and to emphasize the shift of the central task of the nation from "class struggle" to economic development.[23] It also used economic theories and sufficient evidence to criticize the previous leadership's economic policies. In 1982 when the Party and the government advocated an increase in economic, scientific, and technological cooperation and exchanges with foreign countries, the *Herald* gave wide publicity to their efforts, tried to explain the necessity and importance of foreign contacts, and helped resolve the puzzles and questions concerning China's "open-door" policy.

Moreover the *World Economic Herald* held a series of symposia in such major cities as Shanghai, Fuzhou, Guangzhou, Beijing, Tianjin, Shenyang, Dalian, and Wuhan discussing the practicability of improving economic relations with foreign countries through cooperation and exchange programs on the basis of each city's unique conditions and circumstances. In 1982 the *Herald* used one-fourth of its space to report and discuss issues concerning economic relations with foreign countries, such as foreign capital, imports of advanced technology, joint ventures, compensation trade, labor exchanges, joint oil discoveries in the seas, and construction of special economic zones.[24]

In 1983, in accord with the policy of the Party and the government, the *World Economic Herald* stressed the reforms of the country's economic structure through its news coverage. In line with the Party's policy of systematic and overall reforms of the national economic structure, the *Herald* carried eye-catching headlines such as "China's Future Belongs to Reformers," and "Destroy the Old and Establish the New." From 1984 to 1986 the *World Economic Herald* paid full attention to the progress of economic structural reforms in the nation and provided comprehensive coverage of those reforms.

Characteristics of the *World Economic Herald*

Although the *World Economic Herald* tries to popularize Party and government economic policies, it opposes simply printing the actual texts of Party and government decisions. The *Herald* maintains that the paper should be practical and realistic and that it should voice its own views and opinions. The *Herald*'s editors often say they would close the newspaper if they could not make it vivid and appealing to its readers. They also say that running a newspaper is not just a profession but a cause.[25]

Shi Ximing, former deputy director of the Propaganda Department of the Chinese Communist Party Central Committee, and a high-level official responsible for the press, said that newspapers should have their own voices and definite views and that their positions on issues should be clear. He praised the *Herald* by saying, "You've done a very good job in this respect. You're very appealing to readers and there is a strong voice in your pages."[26]

The style of the *World Economic Herald* has become a model highly esteemed by its counterparts in the Chinese press. Qian Junrei, editor in chief of the *Herald* and a famous economist, summarized, "The *Herald* has created its own distinctive style which should have existed a long time ago in Chinese journalism, and the *Herald* has set a good example for other newspapers to follow."[27]

As a newspaper jointly run by an academic institution and a research unit, the *Herald* has some disadvantages. First, it lacks a well-established network of correspondents. The *Herald* has no correspondents in other parts of the country or abroad except in Beijing. Second, the paper is a weekly and cannot provide some of the timely information a daily newspaper can. Third, many of its staff members are not economic specialists. However, the *Herald* has done its best to overcome these disadvantages.

The *World Economic Herald* has taken advantage of some its relations with other organizations and its own position as a "nongovernmental" newspaper. It maintains a close relationship with the economic sectors and economic departments of the government that supply the *Herald* with a substantial amount of economic information. In order to overcome the shortage of correspondents, the *Herald* has reached an agreement with the Xinhua News Agency by which all Xinhua foreign correspondents serve as special correspondents of the *World Economic Herald*. They not only cover economic news, but also write features or special reports concerning international economic issues. Meanwhile the *Herald* has also tapped world economic specialists as special reporters.

In 1981 while most periodicals avoided mentioning the study of contemporary Western economic theories, the *Herald* published an article arguing that it is very helpful to study modern Western economic theories in promoting the modernization of China's economic development.[28] While a theory spread in the country that the faster the economy develops, the better it is for the nation, the *Herald* argued that blindly seeking speedy development will lead to problems in resources, transportation, raw materials, and capital and will harm the nation's economic development.

Unlike most other Chinese newspapers, the *World Economic Herald* does not neglect economic activities and affairs in the Soviet Union, some East European countries, and Taiwan, with which China has a delicate relationship. Instead of biased coverage, the *Herald* has tried to accurately depict their economic situations. Before the 1980s most newspapers in mainland China either played down the realities of economics in Taiwan or paid little attention to its economic situation. Since the *Herald* was founded, it has realistically and accurately reported Taiwan's situation.

The *Herald* tries to provide solid information filled with facts and substance rather than vague and general views or opinions. Its underlying philosophy is to "let the facts speak for themselves." Within the first year and a half of its establishment, the *Herald* published more than 120 lengthy articles providing information on China's economic conditions and statistics and economic affairs in more than 100 countries or regions. The paper intends not only to help general readers gain knowledge of the world but also to provide useful reference materials to economic departments or economic research institutions. Editors of the *Herald* make full use of news and stories supplied by foreign news agencies, newspapers, magazines, and reports presented by authoritative economic organizations or research institutions.

The *Herald* searches for exclusive news. It does not carry any news or articles published by other major Chinese newspapers, and tries to avoid using economic news released by the official Xinhua News Agency, upon which the majority of Chinese newspapers depend heavily. The *Herald* reaches its sources through the channels it has established so as to guarantee the exclusiveness of its content. It often invites well-known economists to present their views on current economic affairs and also interviews visiting economic specialists, scholars, entrepreneurs, bankers, and business people from other countries.

A large part of the *Herald* is devoted to coverage of world economic news. It watches the changes in the world economy and frequently reviews and analyzes situations and also makes predictions. In the past few years the *Herald* has focused its coverage on the following issues: effects of the world political situation on economic development; state interference in other countries' economies; the world crisis of overproduction; economic structures and the imbalance of economic development in different nations; the change of economic policies in other countries; and the influence of modern technology on today's world. It has also offered a large number of analytical discussions on major issues such as the relationship among the United States, Japan, and Europe; the monetary and energy crisis; and the new world economic order. In comparison to other economic newspapers in China, the *Herald*'s coverage of world economic news and issues is more complete and penetrating.

Meanwhile the *Herald* has made efforts to relate China's economic situation with economic situations outside the country in the hope that China's economy can develop faster by learning from other countries' experiences. It has introduced advanced administrative and management techniques from the West and reported experiences of other Third-World countries that share similarities with China as far as economic systems are concerned. The *Herald*'s coverage has emphasized how other countries have solved problems of overall economic balance, made use of foreign capital, established special economic zones, and adjusted economic structures.

Compared to other major newspapers in China, the *World Economic Herald* usually addresses major economic issues quickly, providing more timely information. Not only is the *Herald* a step ahead of its counterparts in news coverage and discussion of issues, but it also provides more in-depth information. A deputy editor in chief of the *Herald*, Lu Ping, once said, "Our report must be deep and profound and give the reader all dimensions of the issues."[29] The *Herald* always attempts to approach an issue from all respects, presenting both positive and negative views, background information, explanations, and comparative materials. It tends to supply sufficient statistics, normally in the form of charts, to make it easy for the reader to understand. Readers have referred to its news and reports as "holographic coverage."[30]

While covering a meeting held in March 1981 concerning economic effectiveness, the *Herald* published the following articles on the subject in its 13 April issue of 1981:

First page: Economist Sun Yifang on economic effectiveness (occupying one-fourth of the page)
Letters to Editors, "Invisible Waste Is More Dangerous Than Visible Waste" (one-fourth of the page)
Second page: "Draw a Lesson from History—Summary of the First National Symposium on Economic Effectiveness" (one-fourth of the page)
Sixth page: "Japanese Benefited from Foreign Capital," (one-third of the page)
"Lessons Learned from Blindly Using Foreign Capital in Poland," (one-third of the page)

These articles clearly indicate that the *Herald* provided diverse coverage ranging from news reports to readers' opinions, a summary of the issue, a theoretical article, an analysis, background information, and other countries' experiences. The *World Economic Herald* believes that the general public needs not only news about economic activities but also information that can help enhance its understanding of certain issues. Accordingly, the *Herald* has made great effort to conform to this belief.

Because of its outstanding and distinctive characteristics, the *World*

Economic Herald has become successful in China's newspaper industry. Its informative and novel content and its unconventional style have attracted millions of readers and helped this economic newspaper establish a strong position in Chinese society, especially in the development of the nation's economy.

The *World Economic Herald*'s Participation in Social Activities

The *World Economic Herald* maintains that it should not simply involve itself in news reporting but should actively participate in social activities and serve the society in a broader sense. Because the newspaper has good relations with economic departments and institutions that serve as its news sources, the *Herald* never neglects to use its connections with these organizations.

Regional economic development has been considered an important part of the nation's modernization program. In helping to accelerate the nation's modernization, the *Herald* has tried to make some contribution to the economic growth of certain regions. Consequently the *Herald* has jointly sponsored symposia with local economic research institutes on the subject of socioeconomic development in Wuhan, Hangzhou, Dalian, and Shenyang. Economic specialists and other influential people in economic sectors were invited to attend discussions on cooperation and exchanges with foreign countries, economic structural reforms, and long-range economic development in those regions. The symposia offered valuable suggestions for policymakers in the regions. In May 1985 the *Herald* invited many economists and high government officials from a dozen major cities to Shanghai to attend a national conference on regional economic improvement. The *Herald* believed that it could provide further service to society by sponsoring such conferences and symposia.

A long-existing problem in China's economic structure has been the predominance of administrative affairs over economic matters, which has obstructed regional economic development. In January 1983 the Party and the central government decided to break up the former East China administration division and form a new Shanghai and special economic zone which included the city of Shanghai and the provinces Shandong, Zhejiang, Jiangsu, Anhui, Fujian, and Jiangxi. As a result, there was no more jurisdictional relationship among these provinces and the city, which now made up an economic-cooperation network. The change was an adventurous attempt by the Chinese government.

Immediately the *Herald* started a discussion about the change, exploring strategies of dealing with the new situation and strengthening economic cooperation in that area. Meanwhile, the *Herald* also helped establish the Shanghai Economic Zone Research Association, which tried to justify on a theoretical basis the significance of the special economic zone.

It has also been part of the *Herald*'s policy to boast local economic development and to train economic personnel for different regions. After opening ports to foreign countries, the fourteen coastal cities faced an urgent need for business people who specialized in foreign trade. Witnessing the urgency of this social need, the *Herald* immediately set up a center for training foreign-trade personnel with the support of concerned government economic departments. A special training class on using foreign capital and importing technology and equipment was held three times, and more than eight hundred business people in foreign trade were trained in the class. The training center's textbooks have been distributed around the country.[31]

Today, many readers yearning for knowledge about basic economic theories and principles refer to the *World Economic Herald*. In response to readers' demands, the *Herald* has established a special educational column and offered a substantial amount of information in its special editions. In the second half of 1981, the *Herald* published 14 articles in its special columns concerning principal economic theories, 14 lectures on business administration and management, 13 columns for a "Self-study University" (which also offered lectures), 5 discussions on special economic issues, 6 lectures on the local economy, 11 on finance and banking, and 7 on foreign trade. The content ranged from the basics of economics to special academic issues.

In the seven years since its birth, the *World Economic Herald* has shown great vitality and has received considerable praise from authorities in political, economic, and academic circles. As a consequence, it has developed into one of the leading journals in the country. During this time, other economic newspapers have experienced cyclical ups and downs in terms of readership and circulation due to severe competition. Such large national economic newspapers as the *Economic Daily, Market,* and *Economic Reference* were no exceptions. The *World Economic Herald,* on the other hand, was the only economic newspaper that enjoyed a steady increase in readership and circulation. Its circulation has increased from over one hundred thousand copies when it was established to six hundred thousand.[32]

With its increasing influence and enhanced social position, the *Herald* has become a leading force in the nation's development and modernization and has often touched on sensitive areas or issues in society. When economic reforms became part of the modernization drive, some specialists argued that the country's political system was not compatible with the economic structural reforms, that it would hinder the nation's economic growth, and that reforming the economic structure alone was not enough. In late 1986 the *Herald* began printing discussions on increased freedom and democracy in the nation's political life. It published the following articles written by specialists on the issue:

30 May 1986:	"Academic Prosperity Cannot Be Achieved without Freedom and Democracy" by Fen Lanrei (a well-known economist)
2 June 1986:	"Develop Socialist Democracy in Economic Reforms" by Li Hongliu
	"Give Reformers a Relaxed Social Atmosphere" by Wen Yuankai (Chairman of China Reformers' Association)
	"Some Thought about Cultural Liberation" by He Zhu (influential reportage writer)
30 June 1986:	"On Elimination of Party Committees in Enterprises"; "Su Zhizhi on Marxism" (president of the Marxism-Leninism Research Institute)
7 July 1986:	"Solving Urgent Problem Is the Essence of Political Reforms"
	"Reader on Relaxed Social Political Environment"
22 Sept. 1986:	"The Cause of the Cultural Revolution"
29 Sept. 1986:	"Review of the Cultural Revolution and Political Reforms" by Wang Huning (professor at Fudan University in Shanghai)
6 Oct. 1986:	"Economic Source and Results of the Cultural Revolution"

Such a large number of open discussions on political reforms by professors, economists, historians, and sociologists had heretofore been a rare occurrence in Chinese newspapers. Their influence and effect on society as a whole is difficult to measure.

China, however, is still a socialist country even though the nation is experiencing widespread economic and political reform and some elements of the Western world have been imported into the country. China's planned commodity economy is still different from the Western free economy; the features and roles of newspapers in China remain different from those in Western countries. The most obvious difference between the West and China remains government involvement in the media. Chinese newspapers are all under the control or surveillance of the Party and the central government. Their main task is issuing propaganda;

explaining Party and government policies, laws, and directives; and guiding social development. They are not merely information sources but also tools of control and adjustment. Although the *Herald* is jointly operated by the China Academy of World Economics and World Economic Institute of the Shanghai Social Service Academy, the newspaper is actually under the direct supervision of the Propaganda Department of the Shanghai Municipal Party Committee. Relatively speaking, the *World Economic Herald* enjoys a great degree of freedom provided it does not stray too far from the Party's principles.

The *Herald*'s readers include people who will, to a large extent, have a great deal of influence on China's future—Party and government leaders, economic department officials, economic specialists, university professors, and students. Because the success and failure of the economic reforms will be in the hands of such readers, the *World Economic Herald* will have enormous impact on the future of China.

Conclusion

China's current political and economic reforms, which began in 1979 and are still under way, are part of a great revolutionary movement. Having experienced a decade of political instability and a highly centralized economic planning system during Mao's period, China is still faced with poverty, and it lags far behind advanced nations. In order to maintain its leadership and to enlist the support of the masses the post-Mao leadership found it essential to change the 30 years of unsuccessful practices and to seek other options. Reforming the economic system became part of an inevitable trend and reflected the people's will.

In order to seek legitimacy for the reform policies and ensure success for the reforms themselves, the leadership reevaluated and corrected orthodox ideology and practice left over from the Mao period. Measures drawn from capitalism were introduced to reshape the centralized economic structure and to improve the economic management system. The door to the outside was opened to welcome advanced technology and funds necessary for modernizing the nation's economy. A great deal of freedom was granted to peasants to spur their initiative and desire to work hard and produce more. Strenuous efforts were made to ease the considerable political controls, establish relatively democratic politics, and maintain political and social stability.

The change in China's political and economic systems would inevitably affect the mass media, which are integrated with the nation's socioeconomic system. The nationwide pervasive reforms have brought about changes in the mass media in China, which have shifted their focus from that of "class struggle" to economics. Economic newspapers in the Chinese press have proliferated as a by-product of the current reform movement.

In the winds of these far-reaching reforms, the *World Economic Herald* appears to be an active and strong supporter of the economic reforms. Indeed, the *Herald* has attempted to play an important role in the nation's economic development. In order to create a new newspaper style and establish a model that differs from most Chinese newspapers concerning news sources, the *World Economic Herald* boldly created its own style instead of following the traditions of the Chinese press. The *Herald* insists on a policy of self-reliance in news sources rather than a policy of copying news releases of the Xinhua News Agency and the *People's Daily*. The *Herald* has also avoided publishing a large number of government documents and speeches of government officials in order to avoid the label of a "government organ economic newspaper."

As a whole the *World Economic Herald* has supported the policies of the Party and the government through its news coverage and the treatment of its news content. It has actively advocated the economic structural and management reforms and reflected the progress of reforms which has benefited the national economy. Meanwhile, the *Herald* has presented itself as a showcase in which the general public, especially those involved in economic activities directly related to foreign trade, could see the changing economic situations outside China. The paper has also functioned as a window through which the outside world can observe China's economic development. As China continues to implement the policies of pervasive political and economic reforms, as well as the policy of opening itself to the outside world, the *World Economic Herald* can play an increasingly important role in propagating the economic policies of the Party and the government, reporting on foreign trade, and conveying economic information to both the Chinese people and people outside China.

6 ▩ China Public Broadcasting System

▨▨▨▨▨▨▨▨▨▨▨▨▨▨▨▨▨▨▨▨▨▨▨▨▨▨

Historical Background

From the first radio station run by the Chinese Communist Party before the founding of the People's Republic, to the present well-developed nationwide radio broadcasting system in China, the Communist Party has understood the significance of this kind of modern communication, using it to help carry out the task of the Party by propagandizing Party policies and decisions, educating the general public, and instructing them to abide by the Party's intentions. Radio broadcasting has developed into the number-one mass medium in the country and currently functions under the direct leadership of the Chinese Communist Party.

The Early Days of Radio Broadcasting

The first radio station was established by the Chinese Communist Party in 1940 to coordinate mass support on a broad scale. In the flames of the anti-Japanese war the Chinese people's broadcast emerged under the direct leadership of the Central Committee of the Chinese Communist Party. Even before the outbreak of the War of Resistance against Japan, Mao Zedong, chairman of the Chinese Communist Party Central Committee, proposed that a radio station be set up in Yan'an, the revolutionary headquarters during the anti-Japanese war. By means unknown, the Party purchased a radio transmitter in Hong Kong. Unfortunately, on its way back to Yan'an, the transmitter was detained by the Kuomintang Nationalists, a development which defeated the effort of the Chinese Communists to establish their own station.

In March 1940 Zhou Enlai, former premier of the People's Republic, brought back a radio transmitting set when he returned to Yan'an from Moscow. The Party Central Committee once again issued a directive to establish a radio station. In the meantime, a broadcasting commission was formed, and Zhou Enlai was appointed to head the commission. The appropriate departments under the Third Bureau of the Military Commission of the Party Central Committee immediately selected more than 30 people, divided them into nine groups, and gave them the task of constructing the station.

On the evening of 30 December 1940 a voice announced from a cave house in a small village northwest of Yan'an: "This is Yan'an Xinhua Broadcasting Station. We are now on the air. . . ."

The announcement solemnly proclaimed the birth of the radio service under the leadership of the Chinese Communist Party. The day marked the inauguration of the Chinese people's broadcasting undertaking, the founding of the Yan'an Xinhua Broadcasting Station—the predecessor of the Central People's Broadcasting Station(CPBS).

In the 1920s and 1930s, dozens of broadcasting stations were built in some major cities in China by foreign capital, China's private capital, warlords, the Kuomintang government, and the Japanese aggressors. The newly established Yan'an Xinhua Broadcasting Station, characterized by its revolutionary content and national style, began to disseminate news among the people, who were suffering in an abyss of misery, and to give them hope and confidence. This signified the beginning of a new era in the history of broadcasting in China.

The station, with the call letters XNCR, was housed in several cave dwellings halfway up a mountain. Its electricity was generated by the motor of a used car fueled by gas that was made from burning charcoal. At the beginning the station had a transmission power of only three hundred watts. It broadcast twice a day, one hour each time. The content of the programs consisted basically of statements and announcements by the Party, important domestic and foreign news, and some entertainment. The broadcasts were interrupted in the spring of 1943 because a tube in the transmitter was out of order and could not be replaced until 1945.

With the triumph of the anti-Japanese war, the Yan'an Xinhua Broadcasting Station resumed its service in the middle of August 1945 in a temple about 19 miles from Yan'an. The station broadcast news, bulletins on the war, official announcements, and art and literary programs. The latter at first consisted only of revolutionary songs and mouth-organ music played by announcers. Because the broadcasting room was quite small and there were no recording devices, musical programs could be aired only by assembling choruses and orchestras outside the station and transmitting from there. It was not until later that the station began to play a small number of records on a hand-operated gramophone.

Soon after the war against the Japanese, the civil war broke out between the Kuomintang Nationalists led by Chiang Kai-shek and the Communists headed by Mao Zedong. The radio network owned by the Communists immediately became part of an all-out offensive strategy against the Nationalist government.[1] The programs, intended for audiences in Kuomintang territories, disseminated news and commentary about Communist-controlled areas and Party policies. Radio played an important role in encouraging the people during those war days. It served as the voice of the people, "a guiding light in the darkness" and "a comfort in agony" for the listeners in those areas ruled by the Nationalists.[2]

In March 1947 the Eighth Route Army evacuated Yan'an as the Nationalist troops attempted to annihilate the revolutionary headquarters. The XNCR moved out of Yan'an after it finished its noontime program on 14 March 1947. But the station never stopped its service even though it was forced to move around. On 21 March XNCR changed its name to the Northern Shaanxi Xinhua Broadcasting Station. In September of that year, the station's daily broadcast was extended to three hours.

With the development of a favorable situation and an increase of its military forces, the Communists became aware that they should make themselves known not only to Nationalist-occupied areas but also to people outside China. On its seventh anniversary, the XNCR added an English-language service, and on 11 September 1947, the voice of Red China reached the outside world in English for the first time. The broadcast was made in a village in Shexian County, Hebei Province, marking the beginning of the external broadcasting of Communist China. Working under difficult conditions, the station moved four times before it entered Beijing in 1949—the year the People's Republic was born.

Ever since the inauguration of radio broadcasting led by the Chinese Communist Party, the people working for it maintained a revolutionary spirit of self-reliance despite the hard struggle.[3] In those days they had only extremely simple and crude equipment at their disposal. Their output was small, and they had a shortage of personnel trained in broadcasting. Yet their staff members displayed a spirit of perseverance and tenacity and overcame numerous difficulties to preserve and develop their broadcasting service. Unswervingly loyal to the Party spirit of proletarian journalism, those journalists propagated Marxism-Leninism and Mao Zedong thought, the guiding principles and policies of the Chinese Communist Party, and news of major developments both in China and abroad, thus encouraging and educating the soldiers and people in the Communist-controlled areas. Underground Party organizations and progressives in the Kuomintang and Japanese-occupied areas also were influenced by the voice from Yan'an. They secretly listened to and took notes on the broadcasts, and distributed and displayed posters carrying radio messages from Yan'an. The people regarded the Yan'an Broadcasting Station of XNCR as "a beacon in a vast sea."[4]

With the triumphant progress of the anti-Japanese war and then the civil war (or, it was called, the Liberation War), other Xinhua radio stations were built in the Northeast China Communist-controlled areas and in Zhangjiakou and Handan. By the end of 1948, 16 stations had been established in Manchuria, Xinjiang, and eastern and northern China. The Communists claimed that broadcasting from these stations had a tremendous impact on the morale of Nationalist officers, many of whom joined the People's Liberation Army as a result. The Yan'an Xinhua Broadcasting Station and all the other Xinhua radio stations made concerted efforts to expand their influence and made remarkable contributions to the victory of the Communists in the anti-Japanese war and later the Liberation War.

Radio Broadcasting after the Founding of the People's Republic

When the Communists took over the mainland in October 1949 and founded the People's Republic, 49 government-operated stations with a total of 89 transmitters existed. Of those, 17 were newly established, while the others were confiscated Kuomintang stations.[5]

Privately owned stations permitted to operate during the earliest stage of the New China included 33 outlets with a total power capacity of 13,000 watts in 1950. Located in Shanghai, Guangzhou, Chongqing, Ningbo, Beijing, Tianjin, and Qingdao, these stations were ultimately taken over by the Bureau of Broadcasting Affairs. Their facilities were handed over to Communist people's broadcasting stations throughout the country.

In 1950 the number of radio sets was estimated at over one million, half of which were Japanese-made mediumwave receivers.[6] Metropolitan residents and those in industrial areas of northeastern and eastern China were the typical owners, as broadcasting was almost nonexistent in rural areas before 1950. To facilitate broadcasting in rural areas, cadres in the countryside began using loudspeakers for collective listening.

The founding of the People's Republic opened up a new era for the development of broadcasting. After moving to Beiping (now Beijing), the Yan'an Xinhua Broadcasting Station (now renamed the Northern

Shaanxi Xinhua Broadcasting Station after it withdrew from Yan'an) began to operate in the capital on 25 March 1949 and use the call name Beiping Xinhua Broadcasting Station. When it was officially renamed the Central People's Broadcasting Station (CPBS) on 5 December 1949 it broadcast 15½ hours daily; 50 percent of that time was devoted to news, 25 percent to public education, and another 25 percent to culture and entertainment. As part of its educational content, in late 1949 the station began a natural-science series featuring lectures by scientist and professors. In January 1950 a social-science series, with emphasis on Marxism and Leninism, was added. Entertainment programming included revolutionary and folk songs, drama, and foreign music, mostly Russian. Choruses and opera troupes from schools, factories, and People's Liberation Army units were invited to present shows. The Central Station's news program included the editorials of leading national newspapers and news stories provided by the Xinhua News Agency and as well as by its own reporters.[7]

In 1950 the Central Station began to broadcast to minority nationalities in their own languages. At first it broadcast in Mongolian and Tibetan one hour a day. Later on it added Uygur, Zhuang, and Korean. In 1954 the Central Station launched a broadcast aimed at listeners in Taiwan. It carried a four-hour daily program in Putonghua (standard spoken Chinese) and Amoy.

By 1956 the station operated on five channels for 38 hours a day, and the broadcasting schedule increased to about 60 hours daily in 1965. As a result of the hard work and concerted effort made by the staff members, and concern and attention from the Party, the Central People's Broadcasting Station greatly expanded its service and became the nerve center of the nationwide broadcasting network.

CPBS now operates on six channels for 96 hours daily (102 hours on holidays and festivals). The first and second channels present comprehensive programs for the mainland, including the four categories of news, education, entertainment, and service. The third channel offers FM stereo programming for the capital and adjacent areas. The fourth channel broadcasts in languages of minority nationalities — Mongolian, Tibetan, Uygur, Hazak, and Korean. The fifth and sixth channels are beamed to Taiwan in Putonghua, Amoy, and Hakka.[8]

At provincial, municipal, and local levels, stations are required to transmit news, commentary, and other important political programs relayed from the Central Station, as well as to produce shows to meet the needs of the people, government, and Party units at various levels. In the 1950s one of the most significant programs at many local stations was "Russian Forum," designed to teach the Russian language. Fourteen stations at the local level presented this program, with an estimated audience of 40,000.[9]

Despite a shortage of equipment and professional personnel, the development of provincial, municipal, and local stations made steady headway in the 1950s. The number of stations increased from 54 in 1951 to 73 in 1953 and 97 in 1958.[10] By June 1959 the deputy director of the Central Bureau of Broadcasting Affairs reported 107 stations in operation, with a combined radiating power nearly 33 times that of 1949. By the end of 1959, 122 radio stations existed under the supervision of the bureau. Most of this growth occurred during campaigns of agricultural collectivization, the 1955–56 campaign of "agricultural producers' cooperatives," and the 1958–59 "People's communes."[11] The broadcasting industry in the People's Republic continued to grow in the 1960s; by 1967 there were 151 stations.[12]

The Eleventh National Radio and Television Work Conference in 1983 laid down the principles of four-level administration of radio service and four-level mixed coverage, consolidating and developing the national radio network, which integrated the central with the local stations, and combining the wireless with the wired stations. Up to the end of 1984, the various provinces, autonomous regions, municipalities directly under the central government, cities directly under the provincial government, counties, and towns had a total of 167 radio stations, more than 2,570 rediffusion stations, and more than 50,467 amplification stations.[13]

In 1965 there were reportedly more than 11.5 million radio receivers, or 16 per one thousand inhabitants.[14] During the next two decades, the popularity of radio receivers increased greatly. By the end of 1984, there were an estimated 220 million radio sets and cassette radios, and more than 86 million loudspeakers across the country.[15] The scope of coverage and the multitude of listeners in China are unparalleled in the world.

Monitoring and Wired Broadcasting

A person in China may hear radio programs either on an ordinary radio receiving set or over wired speakers located in his home, office, dormitory, school, recreation center, or street corner. Radio is extremely popular in China and has been used as a major propaganda tool by the Party and the government since the early days of broadcasting in the country. Radio ensured that the Communist Party expanded rapidly, both at the national level and in services to grass-roots units. After the founding of the People's Republic, the Communist Party was aware of the serious problem of insufficient radio facilities and the limited number of radio receivers. Nevertheless, these technical handicaps did not prevent the Chinese from making radio a major propaganda instrument. Their solution to the problem was to develop *radio-receiving networks*.

The document "Decisions Regarding the Establishment of Radio-Receiving Networks of the Information Administration under the State Council," issued in April 1950, recognized the importance of radio as an instrument of mass education and propaganda that could obviate the problems of illiteracy, newspaper shortage, and vast, expansive territories. The directive ordered government agencies at county and municipal levels, People's Liberation Army units, and all organizations, factories, and schools to appoint broadcasting monitors.[16] The duties of monitors were to listen and record news, political instructions, and other important contents broadcast by central and provincial stations; to announce the programs broadcast by stations in advance; and to organize people within a unit to listen to the programs collectively. The monitor might interrupt the programs to make statements, in the form of announcements or cultural and educational materials designed especially for the audience.

Two similar directives were issued by the central administration. As a result, radio monitoring teams were organized at various units of the lowest level of political, military, economic, and educational structures in the country. The monitors worked under the dual leadership of the local government and the provincial and municipal information administration. In fact, they were supervised by local party cells or by mass organizations such as trade-union locals in factories. On 29 April 1950 the Central People's Broadcasting Station, in its statement "Regulations on the Work of Monitors," commanded monitors to place emphasis on speeches of Chinese Communist leaders, lectures by outstanding social-science scholars, and news and government decrees, in order to raise the political consciousness of the audience. They were also instructed to report to their local broadcasting stations the contents that had been selected and distributed and the public's reaction to them. Thus monitors provided audience feedback and enabled stations to adjust programs.

As part of this monitoring system, the Chinese Communists in the fall of 1950 developed *wired broadcasting networks*. These networks have two distinctive features. The first, called *line broadcasting,* is technical. The networks are not, strictly speaking, broadcasting systems, but systems of point-to-point radio communication using wired loudspeakers. This is known as the "radio diffusion exchange system" in the Soviet Union, or "community listening" in some other countries.

The operation is very simple. The system uses primarily a transformer, a switchboard housed in a studio. Station broadcasts are picked up by a powerful off-the-air receiver, amplified, and sent through the switchboard to loudspeakers connected to the wired broadcasting distribution point. These wired broadcasting loudspeakers have penetrated almost every corner of the country. They were installed everywhere—in village squares, school playgrounds, marketplaces, rice paddies, factories, mines, communal mess halls, dormitories, households, and even on treetops and telephone poles. Of course, under such a system people don't have much choice but to receive the messages selected by the operators.

Although wired broadcasting networks started as early as 1950, and the press frequently reported various kinds of accomplishments, between 1951 and 1955 the government concentrated on the development of the monitoring system or relay stations and collective-listening groups in factories, mines, enterprises, and the army. According to an incomplete report, the number of monitoring stations increased from 20,519 to 51,200 between 1952 and 1955, while the number of monitors jumped from 14,260 in 1951 to 42,722 in 1952.[17]

In December 1955 the Third National Conference on Broadcasting Work held in Beijing emphasized the development of wired broadcasting networks. The conference mapped plans for building more than nine hundred wired broadcasting distribution centers in the country in 1956, with a total of 450,000–500,000 wired loudspeakers, 80 percent of which were to be installed in rural areas. A report on the conference explained:

> By the end of 1957, there will be more than 1,800 [wired] broadcasting stations [i.e., receiver-distribution units] in rural areas throughout the country, with 1,360,000 loudspeakers. In some provinces . . . broadcasts will reach every *cun* [village] and every cooperative. By 1962, there will be more than 5,400 [wired] broadcasting stations in the rural areas of the whole country, with 6,700,000 loudspeakers.[18]

The policy on constructing the rural network, as set out by the Third National Conference on Broadcasting Work, called for "reliance on the masses; use of existing equipment; development by stages and gradual regularization of the network; access to the villages and the cooperatives first, and later the homes of the peasants."[19] Those unfamiliar with the Chinese language or with Communist expressions may need some explanation. "Reliance on the masses" actually means that the peasants were supposed to contribute actively to the project: "Reliance on the masses not only refers to the question of the construction cost, but after the broadcasting network has been built, the masses must further be relied upon for inspection, repairs, maintenance, and management."[20]

"Utilization of existing equipment," according to the Party, "is in keeping with the practice of thrift and practicality, the promotion of the spirit of economy."[21] In practice, that means using existing telephone posts, cables, and buildings. "Development by stages," the Communists continuously pointed out, "does not mean spreading over several quarters or years the work that can be accomplished within a single quarter or a single year."[22]

Acting as an instrument of Party propaganda and agitation at the local level, the wired broadcasting system has been used for "the political and cultural education of the peasants, the dissemination of advanced experiences in agricultural production, and the advancement of cultural life in rural areas."[23] In February 1959 the Sixth National Conference on Broadcasting Work further declared that the major functions of wired units in rural areas were "to guide production and to relay programs of the central and provincial stations." The conference recommended wired broadcasting units "not hurry in making their own programs."[24]

Peasants in communes were encouraged by the Party to bear the major burden of the construction cost, maintenance, and management of wired broadcasting units. The Xinhua News Agency once described the "spirit of self-reliance" in developing wired broadcasting units as follows:

> The setting up of a broadcasting station [i.e., units] by a commune, the installation of rediffusion lines by a production brigade or team depends mainly on collectively accumulated funds. Many areas use local materials to produce the facilities themselves. The poor and lower-middle peasant of the Kuomintang production brigade of Mihsien County, Hunan Province, used indigenous methods to produce well over three hundred loudspeakers, and rediffusion reaches every household.[25]

The agricultural collectivization period of 1955–59 marked a rapid growth of wired broadcasting in China. The number of wired broadcasting units increased from 835 in 1955 to 11,124 in 1959; the number of loudspeakers from 90,500 to 4,570,000.[26] Between 1958 and 1959, the number of wired broadcasting units almost doubled. By 1959 in the province of Shandong, the wired broadcasting system reached every county and 66 percent of the communes in the province, with a total of 193,000 loudspeakers.[27]

With the frustration of the Great Leap Forward movement in 1959, the development of wired broadcasting systems came to a standstill. In

1960 Liu Shaoqi, then president of the People's Republic, issued a decree called "expert-operated broadcasting" policy, which further hampered development of wired units in rural areas.[28] "As early as 1958, the year of the Great Leap Forward," the Xinhua News Agency reported, "all 12 production brigades under the Wangwa People's Commune in Kuyuan County (Ningxia Province), were linked by radio rediffusion." The official news agency continued: "In 1963, the rediffusion system stopped operation, on orders from the 'capitalist roaders in power,' " meaning Liu and his followers. They were accused of opposing "the masses' studying and applying Mao Zedong thought in a living way" and of doing "their utmost to prevent the masses from hearing Chairman Mao's voice" by disrupting the operation of rural radio networks.[29] As a result, by 1964 the number of wired broadcasting units in the nation declined to 1,975.

Despite the enormous efforts of pro-Mao revolutionary committees to bring wired broadcasting networks under their control, the system suffered some damage during the Cultural Revolution from 1966 to 1968. Wires were cut and equipment destroyed by the rampage of the rival Red Guards. Wired units in Inner Mongolia stopped operating for more than two years; many units in rural areas of Anhui, Hebei, Hunan, Zhejiang, Sichuan, Guizhou, Yunan, Shandong, Henan, Jiangxi, Fujian, Shanxi, and Heilongjiang also ceased to operate during this period.[30]

In 1968 the Ninth National Congress of the Chinese Communist Party decided to "strive to do broadcasting work well" in order to send the latest instructions from the central leadership to the grass-roots units. Since then a mass movement to restore and expand rural wired broadcasting networks has been promoted. According to a Xinhua News Agency news release of 21 September 1971 radio rediffusion networks covered over 98 percent of the production brigades and over 87 percent of the production team throughout the nation. Along with the movement, radio manufacturers in China have distributed large quantities of loudspeakers, transistor radio sets, and three-purpose transistorized sets (radio-phonograph-amplifier) to meet the increasing demand of rural wired units.

As for programming, it was decided in 1956 that, "while it is necessary to relay certain programs of the Central People's Broadcasting Station at specific hours, a more important task should be to strive to improve locally originated programs. Furthermore, local programs were to be designed to publicize and promote agricultural producers' cooperatives, to constantly stimulate the enthusiasm for labor among the peasants, to agitate for high agricultural production, and to satisfy the peasants' demand for cultural life."[31]

After several decades, the rural communes today have fully developed to become production organizers and grass-roots political units. The broadcasting systems in rural China now connect every peasant home by a web of wires to the central government, the commune leadership, or the county station. The system allows leaders to deliver messages directly into each home loudspeaker and to relay radio programming across the wires to the peasants, many of whom do not own radios.[32] There are now about 95 million loudspeakers scattered across the country.[33]

Nantong County provides an example of wired broadcasting communication in the rural areas of the country as it has developed to its present stage. Besides the programs relayed from the Central People's Broadcasting Station and provincial station, the local stories broadcast by the Nantong County–funded broadcasting center indicate close links with the local people in that cotton-growing area on the lower reaches of the Yangtze River. The center has some three thousand part-time reporters from different trades among the county's 1.5 million people, most of whom are peasants. They write stories, supply tips, relay audience reaction to particular programs, and comment on the general effects of the broadcasts.

On an ordinary day, the center receives some one hundred articles and a dozen or so letters from listeners. These are its main sources for the 40-minute local news and special feature programs broadcast three times a day. Listeners also provide material for a three-hour art and literature program. Listeners' contributions often become brief news items or commentaries on topics such as how a village selected its wheat seeds, how another called an on-the-spot meeting to popularize duck-weed planting, the successful trial operation of a new machine in a farm-tool plant, and so on. Four editors with diverse backgrounds are responsible for the wired broadcasting center.

The center's "Listeners' Box" program answers a letter every day about the problems of policy, production, or life-style. The station also carries regular five-minute news summaries gathered from the national news media and local sources. This news coverage is so efficient that listeners once learned the results of a county-head election only 10 minutes after the votes were counted. Another time, when the price of pork was to be lowered for seasonal reasons, the station announced the news a day in advance and reassured the peasants that the state's purchasing price for pigs would not change. Once when the weather station forecast an unusually strong wind, the home loudspeakers not only carried the news, but suggested preventive measures.

The success of such wired broadcasts can, in large measure, be attributed to the contributions of the peasant and worker reporters scattered in every corner of the county. The more the editors come into contact with the people, the better and more insightful stories they seem to broadcast. Despite the increasing prevalence of transmitter radios these days, the peasants are reluctant to part with the tiny loudspeakers in the corners of their homes.[34] Although many of their programs are politically oriented, the wired stations scattered in the rural areas certainly have widened the horizons and cultural lives of rural inhabitants. The wires stretch far and wide, connecting remote villages with the outside world.

The Central People's Broadcasting Station

The Central People's Broadcasting Station (CPBS) is the state radio station of China. It is the nerve center of China's widespread national broadcasting networks. It is the largest and probably the dominant organization within the central sector. Its preeminence stems from its origin, from the tacit acceptance of radio as the most important broadcast medium, and from its size.

CPBS is considered the mouthpiece of the Chinese Communist Party and the government. It has been used, to the greatest possible extent, by the Party and the government to popularize their policies and decisions and to help motivate the general public to act in line with Party directions and objectives. In a sense, it acts in a management function to help define the objectives and philosophy of the Communist Party and the central government.

In order to promote its objectives, the Chinese Communist Party has redefined the tasks of CPBS at different times for different purposes. During the war years before the founding of the People's Republic, the party made it clear that the tasks of the Northern Shaanxi Xinhua Broadcasting Station, predecessor of the CPBS, were to propagate and explain the policies and positions of the Communist Party, to tell the outside world about the conditions and development in the liberal areas, to disintegrate the enemy forces, to educate and agitate the people toward unity, and to overthrow the policies of imperialism, feudalism, and bureaucratic capitalism so as to establish a new China. After the establishment of the People's Republic, the Central Information Bureau in 1950 set three tasks for the CPBS: to broadcast Party and government policies and decisions, and domestic and international news; to educate the general public; and to provide entertainment. Its task in the new era is, as stated by the Chinese Communist Party in 1981, to educate and agitate the Party, the army, and all nationalities in the country to mold socialist material and a spiritual civilization.[35]

So CPBS policies and programs are very much part of the daily routine of the Communist Party. They are embedded in the Party's consciousness and they are among the purest expressions of Party policy and politics. CPBS policies and programs are therefore matters Party leadership would naturally keep under its control.

Ideological Context

The functions of broadcasting in China are determined by the Chinese Communist Party's philosophy of mass media, which flows directly from Marxist-Leninist doctrine. It emphasizes the effective manipulation of coercive and persuasive mass media as an instrument of power and control. Marxism-Leninism hold that the media are tools of class struggle and, as such, must assume such roles as collective propagandist, collective agitator, and collective organizer.

According to Mao Zedong, the functions of the mass media are to publicize Party decisions, educate the masses, and form a link between the Party and the masses. Through the mass media, the Party strives to develop in the masses the socialist characteristics that will make them loyal and useful citizens of the country. To achieve those missions the mass media must become the Party's "loyal eyes, ears and tongue," an important bridge for daily contact between the Party and the people, and a powerful instrument for the Party to guide socialist revolution and construction.[36] It is considered "an art of Marxist-Leninist leadership" to be good at translating the Party's policies into the actions of the masses.[37] In the view of Mao, this is not merely journalistic work, but Party work. Accordingly, the press, radio, television, and other mass media must be run by the Party. Mao believes it necessary to subordinate mass media to the leadership of the Party.[38] The mass media have always been used to define the objectives of the Chinese Communist Party and the government. Radio broadcasting is no exception.

The Communist Party took effective measures to consolidate its position by establishing a stable government after the success of the revolution in 1949. These measures included much wider use of the broadcasting system to promote its objectives. Thus China's broadcasting system became an integral component in the Party's national management system.

Until recently most journalists in China seemed to be so devoted to the promotion of the Party and state objectives that the Party seemed to take it for granted and never considered writing out specific guidelines. However, recent criticism in China's journalist circles charged that journalism in China has been negatively influenced by the dogmatic tendency of the Soviet stereotype.[39] Some critics raised questions about the "party tool" concept.[40] Others advocated that the ideas of young Marx and Engels, who were then in favor of the free press and against Russian military censorship, should be used as guidelines for the Chinese-style socialist journalism.[41]

Facing new challenges, the Secretariat of the Party Central Committee began to pass resolutions, restating the status of Chinese journalistic institutions. One such resolution reads: "Radio and television are the most powerful modern tools for the purpose of educating and inspiring the Party, the army, and people of all nationalities to build socialist material and a spirited civilization. This is the fundamental nature and task of radio and television."[42]

So the broadcasting system is still regarded as an important tool of political influence. "It must function to propagate the Party line, its principles and policies, and serve the main Party objectives of the time. It should voluntarily keep in line with the Central Party Committee politically and avoid deviating from it."[43]

Also related to the resolution is the degree of attention the Party has given the broadcasting system, which was further discussed by Yang Zhaolin, director of the Central People's Broadcasting Station:

> According to the resolution, the tool [broadcasting] is not only powerful but the most powerful. Our responsibility is great and lofty. Our task is glorious and also arduous. With the strengthening of leadership over radio by the Party Central Committee and the State Council, the political and professional standard of our unit will be raised. The material and technical conditions will be greatly improved. Any skepticism as to the significance of radio work is groundless.[44]

The ongoing discussion serves to (1) remind radio journalists of the historical responsibility imparted to them by the Party; (2) ensure that radio will not lose out to newspapers and television in the competition to win support of the Party and the government, both of which administer financial as well as personnel resources; (3) convince the public and the broadcasters that strengthening of leadership by the Party and the state is essential to the development of the radio system in China. The Central People's Broadcasting Station, the center of China's broadcasting system, operates within the confines of the resolution. Under the direct leadership of the Party and state, CPBS takes upon itself the responsibility of propagating the Party's policies and decisions and carrying important information or messages into the homes of the Chinese people through the well-developed wired and wireless broadcasting networks.

Administrative Structure

The administrative structure of China's broadcasting system, like all Chinese institutions, reflects the nation's ideological context, the core of which is the centralized leadership of the Party and the government. It is also a reflection of China's socioeconomic structures, Chinese ideas, and Chinese traditions that stress the authority of the Party and the state over individuals. The horizontal structure follows the administrative territorial geographic patterns. Vertically, the system is organized to perform various specialized functions. Centralized administration is vested in the Department of Propaganda of the Chinese Communist Party Central Committee, which is under the supervision of the Secretariat and the Political Bureau of the Central Committee. The department determines policies and issues operational directives: policy control is carried out through the Party chain of command from the Central Department of Propaganda to the various provincial, municipal, and local party propaganda departments; administrative, or operational, control is carried out through the central government's agencies, from such central agencies as the Ministry of Radio and Television to their provincial, municipal, and local subdivisions (Fig. 6.1.).

The Central People's Broadcasting Station reports directly to the State Council; but it is, in practice, regulated by the Communist Party at the highest level. The formal regulatory body is the Central Propaganda

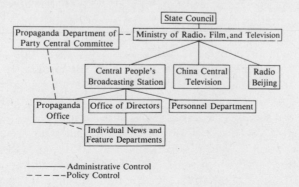

Fig. 6.1. Administrative structure of China Public Broadcasting System.

Department, which reports directly to the Communist Party Central Committee.[45] The organization of the CPBS is rather complicated, both because of its size and because of the sensitivity of its task. The CPBS's administrative structure is a miniature of the structural patterns of the national broadcasting system. The centralized administration is vested in the director of the CPBS, who is responsible to the Minister of Radio and Television.

The horizontal structure can be divided into three sections: the administrative section, the editorial and news distribution and gathering section, and the logistics section. The administrative section consists of the Propaganda Office, the Office of Directors, and the Personnel Department.[46] The Propaganda Office and the Office of Directors set policies and tones of the broadcasting according to the directives of the Central Propaganda Department and the Ministry of Radio and Television. But this section has little direct impact on the program production process of the CPBS. However, the Personnel Department of the section has the power to appoint, promote, dismiss, and assign duties to professional people such as editors and reporters. The criteria for appointment are concerned not only with professional skills, but also with political background, though that aspect is becoming less important.

The editorial and news gathering and distribution section is composed of the General Editorial Office, and 16 individual news and program departments. The highest body of the section is the General Editorial Office, which is also part of the Central Broadcasting Service. This office is responsible for the 16 news and program departments: the news department; the department for industry and business; the department for peasants; the department for culture and education; the department for ideological theories; the international department, which handles foreign news; the department for military affairs; the department for youth and children; the department for literature and the arts; the department for nationalities (in China, that means the national minorities); the department for broadcasts to Taiwan; the presentation department (continuity and announcers); the department for local correspondents; the department for current events; the commentary department; and the program department.[47] Some of these administrative departments contain their own sections for production, engineering, and so on.

The logistics section includes all the departments the are not directly involved in the news and production and distribution processes. They are the Editorial Office for making broadcasting programs, the department for correspondence work, information and data reference department, and the Broadcasting Service Company. The Editorial Office for

Broadcasting Programs is responsible for the publication of the weekly radio program guide that prints weekly programs as well as stories about certain programs and events sponsored or initiated by the CPBS. The correspondence department deals daily with listeners and letters. From time to time it reports the criticism, commendations, suggestions, and advice from listeners to the administrative section and the editorial and news gathering and distribution sections, to help them improve their work. Each year the correspondence department receives two to three hundred thousand letters from listeners both at home and abroad. The Broadcasting Service Company is responsible for the station's advertising and other service businesses.[48]

In addition, the CPBS has stations at the provincial and municipal levels to work as "collective correspondents" to provide news and features for the CPBS. Though it doesn't have any foreign correspondents stationed abroad at present, the CPBS does send its own reporters to other parts of the world to cover important events. In all, the CPBS has more than eight hundred employees, over seven hundred of which are news people. The rest are administrative people and technicians.

Rules and Operational Directives

There are many rules for Chinese journalists to follow in their daily practice. Most of them are in accordance with the concept of Party journalism. For instance, a journalist is required to study the fundamental principles of Marxism and Leninism and have a regular understanding and knowledge of Party lines, policies, and decisions. "An editor in charge of culture and education should know about Marxist teaching on culture and education and be familiar with the Party policies on the subject."[49]

A reporter is also required to follow the principles of "positive propaganda." The textbook of the Beijing Broadcasting Institute defines positive propaganda in this way:

> "Positive propaganda" means news that deals with models and excellent situations that can mobilize and inspire the people. . . . News that is typical in this respect should be used. Disaster news can be reported. However, emphasis should be placed on the activities and brave endeavors that serve to recover from the disaster. . . . But positive propaganda does not mean exclusion of criticism. Stories of criticism should be: (1) truthful; (2) typical; and (3) constructive, to give people confidence, inspiration, and strength rather than make them depressed and pessimistic. Stories solely for the purpose of exposure should be dumped.[50]

Another rule for reporters is to protect Party and state secrets. The quantity and quality of information the average person can have access to is regulated and classified. The same textbook explains what material is to be openly published, what material is to have limited circulation, what stories should be temporarily restrained, and to what extent certain subjects can be reported. All are to be in line with the policies of the Party Central Committee. Statistics, defense industry matters, results of scientific and technical research, and national resources information are state secrets and are generally prohibited from being openly published. Instructions should be obtained from the next higher authorities about when and how news with sensitive content can be published.[51]

When unforeseen situations arise that general rules do not anticipate, the authorities issue specific directives to cover changes in policy, new policies, or new interpretations of old policies and to correct errors and inadequacies or fill in gaps in the propaganda mainstream. Current and timely directives or guidelines help editors and reporters adapt to change. Three different kinds of directives can be issued.

GENERAL DIRECTIVES ON CENTRAL ISSUES FROM THE PARTY CENTRAL COMMITTEE. Instructions from the CPC are not specifically associated with the functions of the media, but are used as directives for the general news selection process. A description of such a directive appeared in the 19 February 1985 issue of the *Broadcasting Editors' Daily,* a publication limited within the Ministry of Radio and Television:

> The leading comrades of the Party Central Committee pointed out recently that no more campaign months are to be organized. Campaign months such as "Quality Month" and "Civilization Month" did not have the desired effect. Building socialist spiritual civilization is long-term work; a few campaigns cannot build it up. Frequent campaigns can only foster formalism, which in turn may lead to new unhealthy tendencies.[52]

Another instruction given by an anonymous leader of the Party Central Committee dealt with foundations. The instruction read as follows:

> Too many such organizations are harmful to the development of our work. No more foundations should be established from now on, because they are also a financial burden on our people.[53]

After the release of these instructions, no news about campaign months or new organizations was heard on radio or seen in newspapers.

SPECIFIC DIRECTIVES FROM THE CENTRAL PROPAGANDA DEPARTMENT OR OTHER CENTRAL AGENCIES. Some directives deal specifically with the function of the media. One such directive appeared in the 19 February 1985 issue of *Broadcasting Editors' Daily:*

> The General Offices of the Party Central Committee and the State Council issue this notice, requesting that the unhealthy tendency of extravagance, waste, and ostentation be stopped during the Spring Festival of this year. The Party Central Committee may hold a New Year's Greeting Party with a cup of tea for each participant, but no other party, government, or army agency or unit or organization may hold a party of any kind. News media must not report any activity against this regulation. Instead, the media should report any of these activities to the Central Committee.[54]

Another directive issued by the Central Propaganda Department reads as follows:

> Some media organizations recently reported on activities such as "beauty contests." At present these kinds of activities should not be reported too much.[55]

The Ministry of Radio and Television issued at the end of 1984 a document summarizing the year's work and setting directives for its propaganda task in 1985. The document states:

> Radio and television are pieces of the Party and the government. They must serve to define the Party's general task and objectives for the new historical era. . . . They should be careful in handling the news of the economic reforms in 1985, especially news about reforms of the price and wage systems. They should consult the State Council and receive permission before releasing any news about the specific reform measures of the government.[56]

DIRECTIVES FROM THE HEAD OF THE ADMINISTRATION. Directives can also be issued by the head of the administration. These directives are concerned with the performance of media organizations, operational departments, and groups. For instance, when the Secretariat of the Chinese Communist Party Central Committee established new guidelines for the work of radio and television in 1981 — to educate and agitate the Party, the army, and people of all nationalities in building up a socialist spiritual and material civilization — the director of the CPBS immediately defined the work of radio broadcasting in response to this call:

Broadcasting propaganda should center on the central task set by the Party. . . . We should give wide publicity to the great achievements and deeds of those advanced units and individuals in building up the two civilizations; we should point out directions for the people, give them confidence, courage, and strength, and inspire them to constantly open up new prospects. . . . Concerning coverage of mistakes, shortcomings, and evil persons or deeds, we should also make sure that this would be beneficial to the construction of the civilization.[57]

Within such rules and directives the Central People's Broadcasting Station produces its daily programs. In addition, regular examination and criticism are required of the final broadcast products. Grass-roots editors may receive criticism not only from their own officials, but also from every level above them. Postproduction review serves as a final check for editorial faults and deviations, both in content and performance. This criticism may furnish the basis for a new regulation or for calling a conference of professionals to help improve the product.

Programming and Content

The Central People's Broadcasting Station currently broadcasts in six channels for 85 hours a day (more hours are added on holidays and festivals). The first two channels in Putonghua (standard Chinese) are broadcast throughout the mainland for a total of 40½ hours a day. A third is aimed at national minorities and uses Mongolian, Tibetan, Uygur, Kazak, and Korean languages; it broadcasts 13 hours a day. Each broadcast in a particular language lasts one hour, and normally is broadcast two or three times a day. The fourth and fifth channels in Putonghua, Amoy, and Hakka are transmitted to Taiwan for about 25 hours of broadcasting a day. The fifth channel is beamed to the overseas Chinese. An FM channel offers stereo programming for the capital and adjacent areas for 5½ hours a day.[58]

The content of programs on the first two channels can be broken down into news (15 percent), features (20 percent), entertainment (more than 60 percent), and service or advertising (less than 5 percent). The bulk of the news, especially international news, is supplied directly by the Xinhua News Agency, which provides the CPBS with more than 50,000 words a day of national and international news and news summaries. The CPBS organizes this news into 28 bulletins a day, many of which run for 30 minutes. A typical long bulletin would have 15 minutes of "soft" news, 5 minutes of news in brief, and 10 minutes of background information. The most influential news programs are "Nationwide Hook-up," broadcast in the morning, "News and Newspaper Clippings," transmitted in the morning, and "News and Summaries," beamed at noon.[59]

The features are broadly educational. Programs even have intended audiences, such as "Broadcasts to the Countryside," "Friends of Youth," "Xingxing Huoju" (which literally means "a single spark can start a torch fire") for children, and "Little Trumpet" for preschoolers. Popular special feature programs are "Learning," "Life of the People's Liberation Army," "Science and Knowledge," "On Hygiene," "Sports," "Across the Motherland," "Around the World," "Current International Events," "Reading and Appreciation," and "Listeners' Letter Box." Other educational programs are "Central Agricultural Radio School," "Learning English," and "English on Sunday".[60]

The largest component of entertainment programming is music, both Chinese and foreign music. It constitutes 30 percent of entertainment time and 10 percent of total air time. Other popular entertainment programs are drama, opera, literature, folk art, radio plays, and information about literature and the arts.

The service programs are basically commercials as well as announcements, radio broadcasting exercises and advance program notices. Advertising was first put on the air by the CPBS on 1 January 1980 and is currently broadcast one hour a day. Each advertising segment is 5 to 10 minutes in length. Commercials can never interrupt programs, but are aired between programs.[61] Even though advertising is becoming popular in the Chinese media and drawing wide attention, it is still being used cautiously. A mixture of news, administration, and advertising is not tolerated, and commercialization of radio and TV programs is totally forbidden.[62]

Programs broadcast to minorities in their own languages consist basically of news commentary, special features, and a small amount of entertainment. The minorities can enjoy their own kind of cultural entertainment on local stations. Programs beamed to Taiwan consist of news, developments on the mainland, letters to relatives and friends in the Taiwan area, and explanations of policies concerning the Taiwan issue. They also include entertainment programs aimed at army officers, soldiers, and government officials. The FM channel programs are composed of Chinese and foreign music, operas, and sometimes folk art.

The programs of the CPBS are subject to change whenever the Party and government policy changes and the Party needs to propagate new decisions or issues. Meetings and conferences of the Party Central Committee and the National People's Congress may get extensive coverage, which often breaks up regular programs. Following the Second

Session of the Fifth National People's Congress in 1979, the CPBS planned to readjust the proportions of program output in accordance with the needs of the modernization drive. In practice, that meant more educational programs. A major plank in the new policy was for a Radio University to match the highly successful Television University. The Radio University began its courses in late 1980.

Content Analysis of CPBS Programming

The study in this section involves a content analysis of the programs of the CPBS in December of 1985. The objective of this analysis was to determine the nature of the station's coverage of foreign and international news, with specific emphasis on how CPBS's attitude toward different nations compared with China's foreign policy, a policy shaped, to a certain extent, by Mao Zedong's concept of the "Three Worlds." The study also compares news attitudes of different sources, or news agencies, toward different nations and examines the program arrangement of CPBS's news.

Two of CPBS's important news programs were selected for the study. They were the 30-minute "Nationwide Hook-up," which is broadcast at 8:00 PM and rebroadcast on the same channel at 10:00 PM, and the 10-minute "International News" transmitted at 11:00 PM. The two news programs were taped from 1 December to 31 December 1985, and the international and internationally related news of the programs was analyzed. December 1985 was the most recent month available for analysis at the time at the selection.

A large number of Chinese turn on their radios for news during the evening. A survey conducted in northwest China in 1981 showed that 60 percent of the population in that area listened to newscasts in the morning and 50 percent at noon, but 80 percent of the people turned to the radio for information at night.[63] This is one of the reasons that two evening news programs were selected for the study. "Nationwide Hook-up," furthermore, is the most wide-reaching news program of the day. This program has the largest audience of all CPBS programs. It was launched on 13 June 1949, and has been beamed to local stations all over the country. All radio stations at various levels, including more than two thousand wired broadcasting services at the country level, now relay the program, which covers the most significant news of the day. It is the only CPBS news program that is rebroadcast two hours later on the same channel. "International News," at 11:00 PM is one of three 10-minute foreign news programs on CPBS. It deals exclusively with events taking place outside China and transmits the key world events that CPBS gate-keepers think necessary to tell the Chinese audience.

In this content analysis, one of the first problems was to determine the coding units. The common coding units for content analysis are words, sentences, paragraphs, or entire articles. The decision about the coding unit depends primarily on the purpose of the study, whether the project goal and the category system employed are of a general nature, and whether using the entire article as the coding unit is acceptable. The entire news story was deemed appropriate for the basic unit of the study in order to determine what subjects were dealt with in the news broadcasts and whether news treatment was favorable or unfavorable toward particular subjects.

An acceptable precedent for choosing categories is that the categories yield information pertinent to the research questions. The three major requirements in establishing categories are that they be functional, manageable, and pertinent to the objectives of the research. Categories must also be comprehensive and mutually exclusive. An initial scheme for dividing categories was developed based upon review of (1) statements made by the Chinese Party and the state leaders and high officials on China's foreign policy; (2) findings and studies about China by Western scholars; (3) foreign news stories broadcast in CPBS's programs; (4) discussion with several Chinese students and visiting scholars. About four hundred stories in CPBS's two chosen programs fell into four categories during the one month-long period. Those categories included the following:

1. *The First World* (the United States and the Soviet Union): All events concerning Sino-United States and Sino-Soviet relations and United States and Soviet activities in other parts of the world fell into this category. Even though the relationship between China and the United States has improved since the normalization of diplomatic relations, and China and the Soviet Union are trying to normalize their bilateral relations regardless of existing problems, China still considers the two countries global superpowers "menacing world peace at any moment."[64] So the United States and the Soviet Union fit naturally into this category.

2. *The Second World* (the developed countries): According to Mao's Three-Worlds Theory and China's political foreign policy, Western Europe, Japan, Australia, and Canada are within the Second World. Although Eastern Europe never seems to fit into this world very well, an

obviously authoritative elaboration of the Three-World Theory in 1977 did include Eastern Europe. So everything concerning those countries was included in this category.

3. *The Third World* (all developing countries): Developing countries scattered throughout a vast area in Asia, Africa, Latin America, and Oceania belong to the Third World. News stories about those countries were included in this category.

4. *Others:* All news items that did not fit into the preceding three categories were included in this category.

In order to measure the attitudes reflected in each story in terms of category, or theme, a three-point scale was designed: favorable, neutral, and unfavorable. Each story was coded on a sheet according to its theme. The intensity of attitude also was recorded on a scale of attitude measurement. The source or origin of the story was indicated on the coding form, and finally, the program in which the story was broadcast was marked.

The two researchers who conducted the analysis coded all articles independently of each other, and yet produced virtually identical results. This high level of agreement indicates not only the suitability of the four-category system for the research, but the degree of clarity of the working definition of each category. Even the researchers' measurement of story attitude was almost perfectly matched.

Findings

During the designated month, 427 pieces of international and internationally related news were broadcast on those two important news programs by the CPBS. Data from this study showed that the CPBS did present a wide spectrum of news about the world. But the number of stories devoted to different countries or regions varied tremendously, depending on the importance of the country or region in the eyes of the Chinese government (Table 6.1).

TABLE 6.1. Content of Foreign-News Programs Produced by the Central People's Broadcasting Station

Theme	Number of Stories	Percentage
First World	81	18.97
Second World	148	34.66
Third World	178	41.69
Others	20	4.68
Total	427	100.00

THE THIRD WORLD. The data show that news about the Third World or the relationship between China and the developing countries received most coverage in comparison with coverage of developed countries. Of the 427 news stories, 178 (more than 41 percent) were devoted to the Third World, or to developing countries scattered throughout Asia, Africa, Latin America, and Oceania. Furthermore, the stories about Third-World countries appeared to be very favorable (Table 6.2). Over three-quarters of the news (79.78%) about the Third World was favorable; only 36 stories, or just over 20 percent, were neutral in attitude.

TABLE 6.2. Attitude toward Subject Matter in CPBS Foreign-News Programming

	Favorable	Neutral	Unfavorable	Total
First World	19	26	36	81
	23.46%	32.10%	44.44%	100%
Second World	101	45	2	148
	68.24%	30.41%	1.35%	100%
Third World	142	36	0	178
	79.78%	20.22%	0	100%
Total	262	107	38	407

A high proportion of the favorable stories about Third-World countries was about the good relations between China and those countries. Visits to those countries by Chinese leaders and leaders from other developing countries always received extensive coverage. Favorable stories also included news about Third-World countries' safeguarding their national independence and state sovereignty while developing their national economies. News about the efforts of Third-World nations to prevent war and maintain world peace appeared to be very favorable as well. Favorable stories were also devoted to showing how the Third-World countries overcome difficulties, problems, and backwardness in their national development and modernization. They related how those countries were helping one another develop and improve mutual relations, regardless of existing problems or differences.

Stories about unrest, dissent, war crimes, coups, assassination, and disasters in Third-World countries were treated with a neutral attitude. The CPBS presented simple facts or objective descriptions about the events. No comments, criticism, or unfavorable statements were made. Neutral stories about Third-World countries amounted to only 36 out of 178, or a little over 20 percent. No news in the Third-World category was regarded by the researchers as unfavorable.

This favorable coverage of Third-World countries is quite understandable if one considers China's foreign policy toward those countries. The Three-World Theory of Mao Zedong that shaped China's foreign policy is a source of pride in the Third World. The Third-World countries, according to this theory, are a great force pushing forward the wheel of history. The geopolitical role and the global significance of the Third World have been underscored by Qian Qichen, vice foreign minister of China:

> The Third-World countries possess three-fourths of the world's population. The emergence and growth of these countries is a major event in contemporary world history, and their influence on the whole international situation is growing. The Third-World nations are the main force for the prevention of war and maintenance of peace. They are also an indispensable factor in the struggle for the development and common prosperity of the world.[65]

It is China's basic foreign policy to strengthen its unity and cooperation with the other Third-World nations. Qian Qichen has further stated that the Chinese people

> share a common destiny with the other Third-World countries, and show good faith in our dealings with them. We support their joint struggle and their legitimate rights and interests in international affairs. We respect their domestic and foreign policies and back their efforts to strengthen solidarity and cooperation among Third-World nations.[66]

Ironically, China's Third-World policy in practice has often shown a Janus face in response to changing domestic conditions and external constraints. China has come to rely less and less upon the Third World as a main factor in its putative anti-Soviet international united front.[67] In its modernization drive, the main focus of its attention has been directed toward the United States and Western European countries and developed countries in the Asia-Pacific region.

In spite of this foreign-policy practice, state leaders continue to claim a common identity with the Third World. And it is predicted that whatever the extent of change in the new historical era in China and in certain aspects of its foreign relations, there can be little doubt that the geopolitical thinking underlying the strategic dimensions of foreign policy are still very much within the framework established by Mao.[68]

Accordingly, the CPBS has kept itself in line with what the Chinese leaders have constantly claimed is their policy toward the Third World, regardless of actual political practice. What emerges from the news coverage of the developing countries is a favorable overall picture.

THE SECOND WORLD. In the foreign-news coverage of the CPBS, Second-World countries also received great attention, with only slightly fewer stories than the Third World. About one-third (34.66 percent) of the total number of stories broadcast during the period of time studied were about the developed countries and China's friendly relations with those countries. The news turned out to be quite favorable toward those countries. Nearly 70 percent of the news (101 stories) was favorable; 45 news items, or 30 percent, remained neutral in their attitude; and only 2 stories appeared to be unfavorable.

Most of the stories about the relationship between China and the developed countries were favorable. Stories of this type also included the efforts of those countries to strive for world peace, to protest the arms race, to strengthen themselves in the face of momentous world problems, to help developing countries, and so forth.

The Communist bloc appeared to be more favorable to Western Europe and Eastern Europe, not so much in amount of coverage as in news attitude. Romania and Yugoslavia received a lot of attention, and news about the two countries was quite favorable. Achievement and development in other Eastern European countries did receive a great deal of coverage, though exchanges between China and those countries were rare or nonexistent. News about problems among the Second-World countries and any crisis the Second World was facing tended to be neutral. Unfavorable stories concerned the involvement of some Western European countries in the developing countries' internal affairs.

THE UNITED STATES AND THE SOVIET UNION. In comparison with the Third and Second worlds, coverage of the United States, and especially the Soviet Union, was minimal. Eighty-one stories, or nearly 19 percent of the total 427, were about the First World. Attitudes varied from favorable to unfavorable in news stories about the United States and the Soviet Union. A high proportion of such news (32 percent) remained neutral, but the number of unfavorable stories about the two superpowers was the highest among all the news items (36 stories out of 81, about 45 percent).

Since the normalization of diplomatic relations between China and the United States in the early 1970s, the relationship between the two countries has improved considerably, especially in the areas of trade, cultural exchange, and so forth, despite the fact that some dark clouds still hang over the Sino-American relationship. The Chinese leadership has realized that its interests may best be served by emphasizing only those aspects of the United States connection that promise to be of clear benefit to its modernization program.[69] This development of the Sino-American relationship has been reflected in the CPBS's news. The favorable stories show that a beneficial exchange between the two countries in trade and culture has developed. But the progress of the official relationship seems ambiguous, because some obstacles—mainly the Taiwan issue—have complicated and impeded the development of Sino-American relations. China also is unequivocally opposed to the arms race between the United States and the Soviet Union.[70] Any effort made by the United States to halt the arms race was praised in the news stories.

The United States and the Soviet Union are seen by the Chinese as two superpowers that threaten world peace with their arms race, or with contests in some of the "hot spots" of the world, where troops invade other countries, wage prolonged war there, and suppress the resistance of weak nations.[71] China is strongly against any nation that interferes in another nation's affairs, under whatever pretext or to whatever extent. Any such activities conducted by the United States were treated very unfavorably in the CPBS's news.

Scientific and technological achievements in the United States also received a lot of attention. News of this type made up a large proportion of news about the United States and was handled with a neutral attitude.

Although the Soviet Union did not get as much coverage as the United States, the attitudes towards that country were not necessarily any worse. Most of the stories about the Soviet Union were devoted to discoveries, creations, or innovations in the fields of science and technology. Neutral attitudes were prevalent in this type of story.

Before the 1980s the relationship between the Soviet Union and the People's Republic of China was marked by a degree of conflict so severe, so persistent, and so pervasive that there appeared to be little or no cooperation between them. Yet in recent years Sino-Soviet relations have improved somewhat, especially in the areas of economy, trade, and technology. Personnel exchanges are also increasing. The talks between Beijing and Moscow to settle the outstanding issues between the two countries and improve bilateral relations have resumed. The three favorable stories broadcast by the CPBS during that period of time enabled us to catch a glimpse of the trend in Sino-Soviet relations, though the small number of stories could hardly provide an overall picture of the improving relationship between China and the Soviet Union.

Despite the recent improvement of Sino-Soviet relations, the Chinese leadership is still unhappy about the fact that Sino-Soviet political relations have not been normalized due to the existence of three obstacles: massive concentrations of Soviet troops along the Sino-Soviet border and in Mongolia; Soviet backing of Vietnam in its aggression against Kampuchea; and Soviet armed occupation of Afghanistan. China blames the Soviet Union for the slowdown of the normalization of political relations. What is incomprehensible to China is that the Soviet Union, while expressing a desire to improve relations with China, has tried under various pretexts to dodge discussions about how to remove the three existing obstacles. That country agrees to talk about easing international tensions and eliminating regional conflicts, but at the same time shows an unwillingness to talk about the Afghanistan and Kampuchea issues. The CPBS's unfavorable stories provided a faint impression of the unfavorable attitude of China's government toward some of the words and deeds of the Soviet Union in dealing with international affairs.

SUMMARY OF DATA ON THE THREE WORLDS. Clearly, then, the CPBS's treatment of the First World compared to the Second and Third worlds appears to be unbalanced. Comparison of news attitudes among the articles shows that the difference in news about the three worlds is statistically very significant (see Table 6.1). Much more time was devoted to the Second and Third worlds, about 35 percent to the Second World and over 40 percent to the developing countries, yet less than 20 percent of the stories were devoted to the United States and the Soviet Union. The Second World and the Third World were also treated much more favorably than the two superpowers (see Table 6.2). The majority of the news items about the developed world and the developing countries were handled favorably (the Second World nearly 70 percent, and the Third World almost 80 percent). However, only about 20 percent of the stories about the First World were treated in a favorable manner. Although about 30 percent of the unfavorable stories were about the three worlds, there were no unfavorable stories about the Third World and the majority of the unfavorable news items were about the First World. But about 45 percent of the stories about the United States and the Soviet Union were treated unfavorably. And that, to a great extent, reflects China's foreign policy toward the three worlds.

Although news concerning the developed world was treated quite favorably, the comparison between the news attitude toward the Second World and that toward the Third World showed a statistically significant difference. More attention was devoted to Third-World countries than to the Second World. There were 178 stories (over 40 percent) about the developing countries, and 148 stories (less than 35 percent) about the developed world. Furthermore, the Third-World countries were treated more favorably. Among all the stories concerning the Third World, almost 80 percent were favorable and the rest remained neutral. There were no unfavorable stories about those countries. Of all the stories about the developed countries, less than 70 percent were favorable, more than 30 percent of the stories remained neutral, and two stories were treated unfavorably.

It is no surprise that the Third World was treated more favorably in the CPBS's news coverage. China considers itself a member of the Third World. Nevertheless, the Second World holds a significant place in China's global politics. The Chinese theory is that by cooperating with the Third World, the Second World could become a force to counter the alleged hegemonism of the two superpowers that constitute the First World. And the Second-World nations can help to change the unfair international economic order and promote the common development of the world economy.

At the purely political level, China now enjoys formal diplomatic relations with all Western European governments, Japan, Australia, and Canada. China's links with those countries were regularly buttressed in the 1970s and 1980s by visits of senior Chinese leaders. On the economic level, the Second-World countries, especially Western Europe and Japan, are excellent partners for China and have been important sources for access to advanced technology. Notwithstanding China's decision to purchase advanced foreign weaponry, Western Europe is still the best place for China to buy weapons should the need arise.

Chinese diplomacy toward the Eastern European countries has shown the most development and change in the post-Mao era. Chinese foreign policy toward the Eastern European countries after Mao reflected a unique combination of both strategic and domestic interests.

China's foreign policy toward the Second World has been clearly reflected in the CPBS's foreign news coverage. The disadvantages of China's dealings with the Second World seem very few indeed. In theory, there is but one problem: the charge that European nations engage in neocolonial ventures damaging to the Third World. This problem was evident in the two unfavorable stories about some Second-World countries.

All news in the final category of "others" comprised only 20 items, or 4.68 percent of the total number of news items. This type of news dealt basically with activities of international organizations such as the United Nations instead of with particular countries. Attitudes in those news stories varied from favorable to neutral.

NEWS SOURCES OF THE CPBS. In designing a coding form, the author established two categories for classifying news sources or origins. These categories are: CPBS's editors and correspondents, and the Xinhua News Agency. Of the total number of the 427 stories used in the study period, only 80 items, or 18.74 percent of the total, originated from the CPBS's own staff reporters. The self-gathered news basically dealt with internationally related events that happened almost exclusively inside China.

Most of the CPBS's foreign news came from the Xinhua News Agency. Xinhua news was the source for 347 items, or 81.26 percent of the total. It is not difficult to understand the CPBS's heavy dependence on Xinhua for foreign news, because the Central People's Broadcasting Station has no foreign correspondents or foreign bureaus. The Xinhua News Agency is also the official news agency, and what it reports reflects Chinese foreign policy accurately. There is no risk if the state-owned station relies on Xinhua as the primary source for its foreign news, for Xinhua is responsible to the Party and the government for its news dissemination.

COMPARISON OF CPBS AND XINHUA. As a whole, CPBS treated these stories with a more favorable attitude than Xinhua regardless of the great difference between the number of stories gathered by the two sources (Table 6.3). Nearly 80 percent of the CPBS's self-gathered news turned out to be favorable, while only 60 percent of Xinhua's stories appeared favorable. But Xinhua handled the news with more of a neutral attitude (about 30 percent of its total stories) than did CPBS (about 17 percent). Xinhua also carried more unfavorable news (about 10 percent) than CPBS (about 6 percent).

There was not much difference between CPBS's attitude toward the First World and that of Xinhua's. Unfavorable stories from both sources came to more than 45 percent of their respective totals. CPBS's favorable and neutral stories were equally divided; but Xinhua's stories were 20 percent favorable, and the rest (about 33 percent) remained neutral.

Concerning CPBS's and Xinhua's attitudes toward the Second

TABLE 6.3. Comparison of Attitude toward Subject Matter in CPBS- and Xinhua-Generated Foreign News

		Favorable	Neutral	Unfavorable	Total
First World	CPBS	3	3	5	11
		27.27%	27.27%	45.46%	100%
	Xinhua	15	23	32	70
		21.43%	32.86%	45.71%	100%
Second World	CPBS	29	5	0	34
		85.29%	14.71%	0	100%
	Xinhua	65	47	2	114
		57.02%	41.23%	1.75%	100%
Third World	CPBS	25	5	0	30
		83.33%	16.67%	0	100%
	Xinhua	117	31	0	148
		79.05%	20.95%	0	100%
Others	CPBS	4	1	0	5
		80%.	20%	0	100%
	Xinhua	8	7	0	15
		53.33%	46.67%	0	100%
Total	CPBS	61	14	5	80
		76.25%	17.5%	6.25%	100%
	Xinhua	205	108	34	347
		59.08%	31.12%	9.79%	100%

World, CPBS's news appeared to be more favorable, as about 85 percent of its news items were favorable toward those countries. Only 57 percent of Xinhua's stories were favorable out of a total of 114 stories about the Second World. The only two unfavorable stories about the Second World were from Xinhua; CPBS had no unfavorable stories about the Second-World countries.

However, both CPBS and Xinhua handled stories about the developing countries pretty much the same way. CPBS had about 83 percent favorable news stories concerning the Third-World countries, and Xinhua nearly 80 percent. The rest remained neutral for both news sources, with no unfavorable stories about the Third World.

PROGRAM CONTENT. Coverage of international or internationally related news on CPBS was not the same for the two news programs during the study. The "Nationwide Hook-up" carried 164 stories or over one-third (38.4 percent) of the total, while the evening "International News" broadcast 263 items or 61.59 percent of the total.

The "Nationwide Hook-up" normally had 5 to 8 international or internationally related news stories, aside from the domestic news it carried in each newscast. And the "International News" had 8 to 12 items in each newscast. But the news on the "Nationwide Hook-up" carried more important information about Chinese foreign policy than that used in the evening "International News." Sometimes there were repetitions of news items in the two programs.

Conclusion

The mass media in China function, in general, within the bounds set by the Chinese Communist Party and the government, and they are under the tight control of the Party and the government. It is not surprising that the Chinese mass media function in this manner, as they are all run or owned by the state.

Radio broadcasting is no exception, because the Chinese Communist Party has long understood its importance in propaganda. Ever since the birth of the first radio station run by the Communist Party, the Party has used this modern communication tool extensively to help carry out the tasks of the Party by propagandizing the Party's policies and principles, educating the masses, and instructing the people to follow the leadership of the Party and the government. The Party and the government have paid great attention to radio broadcasting in the country, and have always emphasized its significance in the Chinese revolution. As a result, radio broadcasting has grown to be the first ranked of the country's mass media.

The Central People's Broadcasting Station is the mouthpiece of the Chinese Communist Party and the government. It is the center of China's radio broadcasting networks and always sets the tone of propaganda for radio stations scattered across the country. Although a medium that offers the people a variety of services, it always functions as an effective propaganda instrument to popularize Party policies and decisions and to help motivate the masses to act in accordance with Party directions and objectives.

Data obtained from a content analysis of two selected CPBS news programs indicates that coverage of international news on the Central People's Broadcasting Station reflects the attitude of the Chinese government and is faithful to Chinese foreign policy. The Third World, which is regarded as a force propelling the wheel of history forward, received the most coverage on these two programs and was treated most favorably. China always claims to support Third-World countries shaking off the yoke of colonialism, as they simultaneously safeguard their national independence and state sovereignty and develop their national economies. No news unfavorable to those nations could be tolerated by the Chinese government, and indeed, no unfavorable news about the Third World was found during the selected study period.

Although the Second World did not receive as much coverage as the Third World, and was handled less favorably, the Second World did gain much more attention than the United States and the Soviet Union, and was dealt with more favorably than these two countries. The Second World is a force China can count on in its global politics, a force that could help build a peaceful, stable world. It is also an important source for China's national development.

The First World was treated much less favorably than the others. In theory, China regards the United States and the Soviet Union as superpowers that threaten world peace and stability. But in reality, the issue is far more complex and delicate. China does not necessarily want to make these two countries its enemies; rather, it wants to enhance its relations with them. But China would never hesitate to criticize or condemn the deeds of the two superpowers when China disagrees with their policies. The data show that the unfavorable news items and the favorable ones were relatively balanced. Even though about 45 percent of the news stories about the First World were unfavorable, almost 25 percent of the total still appeared to be favorable. For both countries, a large quantity of news remained neutral (nearly 35 percent).

Clearly, then, the foreign-news broadcasts of CPBS reflect Chinese foreign policy quite accurately, and function as an avenue by which Party and government policies and decisions can be carried to the general public.

7 ░ Radio Beijing

Radio Beijing and the Chinese Revolution

The Chinese Communist Party established its first radio station on 30 December 1940 and started transmitting in a temple about 19 miles from Yan'an, the revolutionary base of the Communists in northwest China. The station was part of an all-out offensive strategy against the Nationalist government in the country. The station was called the Yan'an Xinhua (New China) Broadcasting Station, which soon became better known as the Northern Shaanxi Xinhua Broadcasting Station, and it was equipped with a three hundred–watt transmitter. The programs were intended for audiences in Kuomintang-occupied territories, and they disseminated news and commentaries about the liberated areas and policies of the Chinese Communist Party.

The men and women who put down their guns more than a quarter of a century ago to operate at the level of power in the world's largest and oldest civilization retain fond memories of this first effort. There are tales about its first years and the difficult circumstances endured by those who struggled to keep it on the air. One such tale was about how the director of Radio Beijing, Ding Yilan, radio announcer at that time, withdrew from the cave where she was doing a newscast seconds before the cave was demolished by Japanese bombers. Another legendary account, printed in the *Beijing Review* in 1982, conveys much of the pride of those who express it most often when they discuss this first radio station. It also conveys some sense of identity with the old guard:

> The station broadcast news, bulletins on the war, and official announcements as well as art and literacy programs. The latter at first was comprised of only revolutionary songs and mouth-organ music played by

---

This chapter was written with the assistance of Yu Xuejian and Liu Hui of Radio Beijing.

announcers. Because the broadcasting room was quite small and there were no recording devices, music programs could be aired only by assembling choruses on the slopes outside the station and transmitting from there. It was not until a year after the station was established that it began to play a small number of records on a hand-operated gramophone.

However, the station played an important role in encouraging people during those war days. It served as a voice of the people, a "guiding light" in those areas ruled by the reactionaries. . . . The broadcasting room had neither doors nor window glass, only a homespun woolen blanket covered the doorway. The victory of the People's army was broadcast time and again from a room like this.[1]

The victory of the People's army was part of the reason Radio Beijing was launched. Wu Lengxi, minister of radio and television, explained in a recent speech:

When the People's Liberation Army led by the Party was switching from strategic defensive to strategic offensive, and its successive victories stunned the international communities, the Xinhua Radio launched its English-language broadcast. This was the beginning of China's international radio broadcasting under the leadership of the Party. The overseas service is the product of the victorious development of the Chinese revolution. And it grows with this revolutionary cause.[2]

The emphasis here is on the leadership of the Party over Radio Beijing and Radio Beijing's kinship with the legacy of the Chinese revolution.

One of the tales associated with the legacy and the early days of Radio Beijing is told this way: A Nationalist military plane was forced to land in the liberated area; a navigational transmitter on the plane, with a capacity of only one thousand watts, was captured; the comrades of Xinhua Radio worked 24 hours a day for a week to remodel the transmitter into a shortwave radio transmitter; it was with this transmitter that the first English-language program was launched in 1947.

Another story is that Deng Xiaoping, then the commander of an army group of the People's Liberation Army, paid a visit to the Xinhua Radio in 1947. During the visit, Deng instructed:

As the army is advancing about a hundred li (40 kilometers), we are further and further away from the Central Party Committee. How can we commanders get an idea about the general war situation? How can we get access to the principles and policies of the Central Party Committee? The most effective tool we can rely on for these kinds of information is your radio.[3]

With the development of a favorable situation and an increase of military forces, the Communists became aware that they should make themselves known not only to Nationalist-occupied areas, but also to the people in other countries. Seven years later, the Northern Shaanxi Xinhua Broadcasting Station added its English-language service. On 11 September 1947 the voice of Red China reached the outside world in English for the first time. The broadcast was made in a village in Shexian County, Hebei Province. That marked the beginning of external broadcasting from Communist China.

At that time the civil war imposed on the Communist Party by the Kuomintang had entered its second year and a news blockade was enforced in the liberated areas by the Kuomintang. An English-language program was inaugurated to break that blockade and to inform the outside world of the truth of the Chinese people's revolution. The program began under very harsh conditions. The studio was in a doorless cave with no proper equipment to speak of, and when broadcasting time came, a coarse felt blanket was hung up as a "door" to keep out the noise. The transmitter was one converted from a U.S.-made, one thousand–watt navigational transmitter captured from the Kuomintang air forces, and the transmitting power was generated from the motor of a truck. The air time was 20 minutes a day, 2 hours and 20 minutes a week. The studio was some 40 miles away from the editorial department.

Every day the news scripts had to be delivered to the studio on horseback. The Huto River was right between the two places. When the river flooded, the deliverer had to wrap the scripts with oilcloth and swim across the river with the parcel on his head. On urgent occasions, news was sent by telephone, and the people in the studio transcribed it and handed it over to the announcers. The broadcast was aimed at popularizing the policies and principles of the Chinese Communist Party, and at transmitting news about the Communist-controlled areas and the civil war between the Communists and the Nationalists.

The following is the announcement made when Radio Beijing began its English service in 1947.

> Good evening, everybody. This is XNCR, New China Broadcasting Station, North Shaanxi. Today, September eleventh, marks the premier broadcast in a new series of regular daily English-language newscasts, presented by New China News Agency and designed to inform our English-speaking friends on Chinese affairs. It is our aim to present over this station every evening at eight forty o'clock, or twenty-four hours, Shanghai time, a concise factual picture of Chinese events, in the belief that such material is not readily available elsewhere to the English-speak-

ing world. We plan to bring to our radio audience the March of China—one-fifth of humanity—over all obstacles towards a new domestic life, which profoundly affects the future course of world events. Our aim is to serve YOU—we heartily invite your suggestions and criticisms. Station XNCR broadcasts daily on a wavelength of forty meters, at a frequency of seven five zero kilocycles. This newscast is simultaneously retransmitted by Shanxi-Chahar-Hophe Station XCNR, on thirty-five meters at a frequency of eight six six zero kilocycles, and Hatan Station XCHT, at forty-nine point two meters, on a frequency of six zero nine six kilocycles. Now, here are the headlines in today's news: People's Army recovers ten North Shaanxi cities. Thirty-sixth Division gone, Hu Tsung-nan is on the spot in North Shaanxi. From feudal peasant to free farmer in Manchuria. Guerrillas expand role in support of People's Army.[4]

Although the broadcasts could not reach beyond the borders of China, they were heard in Peking (now Beijing), Shanghai, and other Chinese cities where there were large English-speaking communities. Through the people in these communities, information about the Chinese revolution spread to other parts of the world. In this way the broadcasts helped win international support and sympathy for China's revolution.

The founding of the People's Republic of China on 1 October 1949 paved the way for the rapid growth of the country's external broadcasting services. The service changed its name to Radio Peking after nationwide liberation and was later renamed Radio Beijing, when the spelling of Chinese names and places was standardized according to the Chinese phonetic system.

The few foreign-language transmissions initiated shortly before and after the birth of New China were in the languages of China's immediate neighbors—Japan, Korea, Indonesia, Vietnam, Thailand, and Burma. The broadcasts in local Chinese dialects were also inaugurated during that same period. By 1950 Radio Beijing had already initiated broadcasts in seven foreign languages and four local dialects, including Guangzhou, Hakka, Xiamen, and Chaozhou, for 17½ hours a week for overseas Chinese.

The English broadcasts to Southeast Asia, North America, and the South Pacific began in the early 1950s. A blockade was being imposed on the Chinese mainland at the time by forces hostile to the new socialist republic. Hardly any publication from New China could reach its readers overseas. Once again radio played an important part in breaking the blockade by transmitting information on China to people abroad.

After the Korean War, the Chinese government showed direct interest in the cause of revolution outside China. And China began to actively participate in international conferences of nonaligned countries. The trend was reflected in the sizable expansion of the external broadcasting service. In 1956 broadcasting time to overseas Chinese was increased to over 45 hours a week. Programs to Cambodia and Laos, English broadcasts to the Near and Middle East, and English and Spanish broadcasts to Europe were beamed over the air. Transmissions in Arabic, Persian, and Turkish, as well as French broadcasting to Africa were initiated in 1957 and 1958. By June 1958 Radio Peking was airing programs in 15 foreign languages for 22 hours a day.

Ten years later, Radio Peking's programs were transmitted in 31 foreign languages, ranging from Tagalog (the native tongue of the Phillippines) to Swahili. Programs reached North America, Northeast Asia, South and Southeast Asia, Europe, Africa (sub-Sahara), the Arab world and North Africa, and Latin America. Apparently the single country receiving the most attention from Radio Peking at that time was the Soviet Union. With the deterioration of relations between the two Communist parties and governments, Radio Peking's Russian-language programs increased dramatically from 1966 to 1968.

Like external broadcasting services in other countries, any sudden increase in broadcasting time to a particular area usually reflects China's specific foreign-policy moves. For instance, China's active diplomatic offensive in Europe in 1970 corresponded to an increase in broadcasting time to Italy and Turkey. China eventually established diplomatic relations with Italy in November 1970 and with Turkey in August 1971. An international crisis can result in a significant shift in Radio Peking's schedule. During the French student riots in May and June of 1968, for example, Radio Peking increased its French broadcasting to Europe from 14 to 56 hours a week to voice its strong support of the antigovernment activities. Following the Soviet invasion of Czechoslovakia in August 1968, Radio Peking started a program in Czech, lasting 3 hours a day, to denounce the "revisionist imperialism," meaning the Soviet Union's foreign policy.

At present, Radio Beijing broadcasts to the five continents of the world in 38 foreign languages plus Putonghua (standard Chinese) and 4 local dialects (Guangzhou, Hakka, Amoy, and Chaozhou). The 38 foreign languages are: English, French, Japanese, Russian, Spanish, Arabic, Korean, Mongolian, Filipino, Indonesian, Malay, Vietnamese, Laotian, Kampuchean (Cambodian), Thai, Burmese, Bengali, Nepali, Hindi, Urdu, Sinhalese, Tamil, Pushto, Persian, Turkish, Swahili, Hausa, Romanian, Serbo-Croatian, Polish, Czech, Hungarian, Bulgarian, Albanian, German, Italian, Portuguese, and Esperanto. The total broadcasting time is 140 hours a day, or 980 hours a week. The service now ranks third among worldwide networks in terms of language and air time.

At peak hours, Radio Beijing puts into operation more than 40 different transmitters with power outputs of up to 240,000 watts. Those transmitters are scattered throughout the country. At the beginning, the station had no more than 10 news people, apart from several technicians. Since then, it has developed rapidly and expanded enormously. There are now more than one thousand people working in the editorial, language, and administrative departments of Radio Beijing.

Ever since the start of China's external broadcasting service, listeners abroad have been responding warmly to its programs. Now Radio Beijing has enthusiastic listeners all over the world. Some of them have written to the station to give their comments or suggestions on the content and quality of the programs, and to express their friendly feelings for the Chinese people. The letters pouring into Radio Beijing have increased greatly during the past few decades. In 1951 Radio Beijing received 650 letters from 18 countries and regions. In 1955, 7,365 letters from 43 countries and regions arrived at the station. And during the calendar year of 1965, 28,600 letters arrived from 135 countries and regions. In 1983, however, the station received more than 80,000 letters from 140 countries and regions throughout the world. Those letters keep Radio Beijing in contact with its audience abroad and are a constant source of inspiration for improving its programs.

In the past few years, especially since China opened its door to the outside world, a lot of foreigners have been invited to work in China to help its modernization drive. A large number of foreign business people have gone to China engaging in foreign trade. And tourists from other countries have flocked to the country, group after group, to see the historic sites and scenic beauties. In order to help those people know more about China, Radio Beijing added in 1984 a special English-language program directed at foreigners in China's capital. Later that year, English programs were also transmitted to Shanghai and Guangzhou (Canton) through microwaves. Mediumwaves instead of shortwaves have been used to broadcast to foreign listeners inside China.

Radio Beijing currently has foreign correspondents stationed in Tokyo, Islamabad, Belgrade, Paris, Mexico, and Washington. At present Radio Beijing has established friendly ties with broadcasting stations and organizations in more than 10 countries and regions, supplying them with radio programs and exchanging personnel with them.

Ideology, Structure, and Functions

The structure and functions of broadcasting in China are determined by the Chinese Communist Pary's philosophy of mass media, which flows directly from Marxist-Leninist doctrines. It emphasizes the effective manipulation of coercive and persuasive mass media as an instrument of power and control. Marxism-Leninism holds that the media are tools of class struggle and, as such, must assume such militant roles as "collective propagandist," "collective agitator," and "collective organizer."

Communications have been considered extremely important ever since war times. All armies depend on communications, and guerrilla armies especially so. In its initial years during China's first civil war (1920s) and the war with Japan (1937–45), and during the second civil war (1946–49), the Chinese Communist Party required communications to survive and knew that good communications would assist greatly toward victory. After the founding of the People's Republic in 1949, the Chinese Communist Party was faced not only with establishing its government in one of the world's largest and most fragmented countries, almost ruined by years of fighting, but also with gaining the support of its people, many of whom were either indifferent or hostile. Knotty problems, ranging from the economy, which was on the brink of bankruptcy, to intense oppositions from both inside and outside, were waiting for solutions. To consolidate its position in New China with a stable political and economic situation and a united and effective government, the Party took all necessary measures, including a broad expansion of its mass media, to define its objectives. From the very beginning the media system became an integral component of the Party's overall system.

According to Mao Zedong, late chairman of the Chinese Communist Party, the functions of the mass media are to publicize Party decisions, educate the masses, and form a link between the Party and the masses. Through the mass media the Party strives to develop in the people the socialist characteristics that will make them loyal and useful citizens of the country. The mass media must therefore become the Party's "loyal eyes, ears, and tongue" and an important bridge for daily contact between the Party and the people, as well as a powerful instrument for the Party to guide socialist revolution and construction. It is "an art of Marxist-Leninist leadership" to be good at translating the Party's policies into the actions of the masses. In the view of Mao Zedong, this is not merely journalistic work, but Party work. Accordingly, the press, radio, television, and other mass media must be run by the Party.

The ideological context of the mass media in China was very much shaped by Soviet Communist ideology. Lenin wrote in 1901 that

> the role of the newspaper . . . is not limited solely to the dissemination of ideas, to political education, and to the enlistment of political allies. A newspaper is not only a collective propagandist and a collective agitator, it is also a collective organizer. In this respect it may be likened to the scaffolding around a building under construction, which marks the contours of the structure and facilitates communication between the builders, enabling them to distribute the work and to view the common results achieved by their organized labor.[5]

Later Stalin enlarged on this statement:

> The press is a most powerful weapon by means of which the Party daily speaks in its own language, the language it needs to use, to the working class. There are no other means of stretching spiritual threads between the Party and the class, there is no other apparatus of equal responsibility.[6]

Mao Zedong combined the Marxist-Leninist theories with the realities of China and developed theories suitable for China.

But changes have taken place under new leadership. In the wake of the reforms going on in all walks of life in the country, some people began to challenge the old structure of the mass media. Some objected that journalism in China was influenced strongly by the dogmatic tendency of the Russian stereotype. Other critics raised questions about the "Party tool" concept. Some advocated a free press without any censorship as a guideline for Chinese-style journalism. They even held discussions to change the name of "the Propaganda Department" of the Chinese Communist Party Central Committee.

In order to deal with the changing situation, the Party has restated its position on the functions of the mass media. Broadcasting is still considered the most important and effective medium in China, and the role of radio and television in China has been strongly emphasized by the Party. The essential role of the electronic medium became, in the words of a November 1981 resolution issued by the Secretariat of the Chinese Communist Party Central Committee, the most powerful modern tool of educating and inspiring all the Party, the army, and the people in the country to build socialist material civilization and spiritual civilization. And radio and television are also two of the most effective tools to link the Party and the government with the people. This thinking establishes the fundamental nature and task of the electronic medium in China. It also defines the political direction, audience, and the basic content of programs.

1. *Political Direction:* Broadcasting is regarded as an important tool of political influence, so it should adhere to the direction of socialism. It must function to propagate the line, principles, and policies of the Party and the government, and to serve the main objectives of the time. It should voluntarily keep in line politically with the Party Central Committee and avoid deviating from it.

2. *Audience:* The broadcasting service, whether news, educational, cultural, or other programming, whether it is nationally oriented or locally oriented, should be in the fundamental interest of the people and the government. It is set up for the Party, the army, and the people. As a result, it should do its utmost to serve them all.

3. *Content of Programs:* The medium should provide abundant informative and educational programs that are vivid and vigorous and appealing to the audience. It should become a source from which people are able to gain ideas and knowledge. It should be an inseparable companion to its audience.

As part of China's broadcast system, Radio Beijing generally operates within the context of this theoretical and ideological guidance. However, as Radio Beijing is the overseas service with an audience quite different from that of the domestic service, its task and guidelines, which remain within this context, are somewhat different. These guidelines, as outlined in 1983 by Wu Lengxi, former radio and television minister, are as follows:

> Work hard to serve the people of the world by presenting truthfully and vividly the image of socialist China. For this end, it is necessary to give the listeners of various countries a factual picture of China and publicize China's policies and stands, so as to promote their understanding of China and develop friendship between the Chinese and other peoples. It is also necessary to support the just struggles of the people of various countries, the Third World in particular, oppose hegemonism, and safeguard world peace.[7]

The guidelines suggest the dual mission of Radio Beijing: providing listeners with accurate information on China and its viewpoints, and giving timely coverage to international events. But the emphasis is on the first, and there is good reason for that. Letters from listeners still tell of inadequate or biased information about Chinese affairs in some countries and many people overseas continue to have little knowledge of China. Since China adopted its policy of opening to the outside world in 1979, however, many people have become interested in this ancient country with a new social system. They have been trying to find out, by various means, what is really going on in China, and Radio Beijing is one of those means. By emphasizing information about China, Radio Beijing is meeting a primary need of its listeners.

It is natural, therefore, that reports and features on Chinese affairs dominate Radio Beijing's programming. Major events in the country, such as the trial of the Gang of Four, the different sessions of the Communist Party Congress and the National People's Congress, the adoption of the revised constitution and the restructuring of the economic system, have all been given full and timely coverage. The two-hour parade held at Tiananmen Square to celebrate the 35th anniversary of the founding of the People's Republic was broadcast live in English. Problems that have cropped up in the course of the country's modernization have also been given timely coverage. In addition to news, regular features with topics ranging from Chinese history, geography, education, and economic construction to music, sports, and tourism, give insight into all aspects of life in China. Some language services broadcast as many as 18 regular features a week. Many listeners describe Radio Beijing as a "window" through which they can get a clearer view of China.

In line with its guidelines, Radio Beijing highlights statements by the Chinese government and Chinese leaders expounding China's policies and views on specific world issues. China has always been against hegemonism and for peace. Being a Third-World country, it gives particular support to other developing nations in their fight for complete political and economic independence. Radio Beijing clearly reflects these Chinese positions.

In its coverage of world events, Radio Beijing emphasizes the views and affairs of Third-World countries. For instance, it has broadcast many stories on the south-south dialogue and the proposed establishment of a new international economic order. It has sent its reporters deep into Kampuchea and Afghanistan to gather firsthand information on how the people in these countries are fighting against the invaders. And it sent three teams of reporters in 1983 and 1984 to a dozen Asian, African, and Latin American countries to report on their efforts to safeguard national independence, develop their economies, and promote regional cooperation.

Radio Beijing's regular features on the Third World have received favorable response from audiences in the developed and developing nations alike. Listeners in industrialized countries such as Sweden describe these programs as good channels for them to learn more about Third-World countries, as the few reports on these countries carried by their own media are often very limited in scope. Listeners in the developing countries, such as the Philippines, often comment that Radio Beijing's programs show that at least one big country – China – "cares about the developments in Third-World countries."

In its commentaries on international affairs, Radio Beijing interprets China's views and attitudes. The aim is to help its audiences understand China's position better. Radio Beijing, however, has had its setbacks and has not always been able to keep to a realistic approach in presenting China and interpreting its views. During the 10 chaotic years of the Cultural Revolution, the ultraleftist forces dominated all mass media in China, Radio Beijing included. As a result, the broadcasts were often filled with idle talk, exaggeration, and even false statements. The programs consisted mainly of lengthy political lectures. The listeners did not like it, and many showed their dissatisfaction by ceasing to correspond with the radio station. The number of letters dropped sharply. In 1965, the year before the Cultural Revolution took place, the number of letters received exceeded 286,000, but in 1970 it dropped to 21,000. Since the downfall of the Gang of Four in 1976, Radio Beijing has been back on the right track and has restored its credibility.

Administrative Structure

The administrative structure of China's radio system, like all Chinese institutions, reflects its ideological context – the core of which is the centralized leadership of the Party and state (Fig. 7.1). It is also a reflection of Chinese social structures, Chinese ideas, and Chinese traditions that stress the authority of the state over the individual. The horizontal structure follows the administrative territorial geographic patterns. Vertically, the radio system is organized to perform various specialized functions. Centralized administration is considered fundamental and is vested in the Department of Propaganda of the Chinese Communist Party, the Xuan Chuan Bu, which is under the supervision of the Secretariat and the Political Bureau of the Party Central Committee. This department determines policies and issues operational directives by two principle means: The first is the party chain of command from the Central Department of Propaganda to the various provincial, municipal, and local party propaganda departments. The second is the

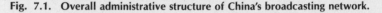

Fig. 7.1. Overall administrative structure of China's broadcasting network.

Central Government's agencies, from such central agencies as the Ministry of Radio and Television, to their provincial, municipal, and local subdivisions.

China's radio system is compared by the officials to "an army group of the revolutionary cause."[8] It is under the governmental supervision of the Ministry of Radio and Television. The booklet issued by the Ministry of Radio and Television for foreign circulation defines the relationship in this way:

> The Ministry of Radio and Television of the People's Republic of China is an organ under the State Council, in charge of the administration of the radio and television broadcasting services throughout China. It gives direct leadership to the Central People's Broadcasting Station (internal service), Radio Beijing (overseas service), and China Central Television (CCTV). Local radio and television stations come under the direct leadership of the radio and television bureaus of provinces, autonomous regions, and municipalities.[9]

The other side of the story is that the radio system also comes under the supervision of the Party Central Committee through its Propaganda Department. Both the Ministry of Radio and Television and the Propaganda Department determine the nature, scope, policy, and operation of the radio network. The following is a good example of this dual leadership: When Radio Beijing was to launch its English-language capital service on middlewave frequency 1 January 1984, it had to get approval not only from the Ministry of Radio and Television but also from the Propaganda Department of the Party Central Committee. When Radio Beijing commemorated its 35th anniversary, leading figures from the Propaganda Department gave most of the guidance speeches.

If China's radio system is considered an "army group of the revolutionary cause," Radio Beijing can be considered a division of this army group. And its administrative structure is a miniature of the structural patterns of the national radio system. Now Radio Beijing broadcasts worldwide in 38 foreign languages as well as in Putonghua (standard Chinese) and four local dialects (Guangzhou, Hakka, Amoy, and Chaozhou). Every language group broadcasts independently to audiences in its target areas. The administrative structure of Radio Beijing is illustrated in Figure 7.2. Its horizontal structure can be divided into three sections: the editorial and news gathering and distribution section, the language broadcasting section, and the administrative section.

The administrative section is considered to have little direct impact on content selection. However, the personnel branch of this section has the power of appointment, promotion, dismissal, and assignment of duty for professional people such as editors and reporters. The criteria for appointment cover not only professional skills but also political and ideological background, though this aspect is becoming less important.

The editorial and news gathering and distribution section consists of the Office of General Editor, the Domestic News Department, and the International News Department. The Domestic News Department is responsible for gathering domestic (nationwide) news and feature stories, and distributing them in Chinese to language departments. The International News Department assumes the responsibility of gathering international news and foreign-feature stories through Radio Beijing's foreign correspondents. Radio Beijing has correspondents stationed in Tokyo, Islamabad, Belgrade, Paris, Mexico, and Washington. The Office of General Editor is often compared to the nerve center of Radio Beijing and functions to supervise the content of the daily Radio Beijing pro-

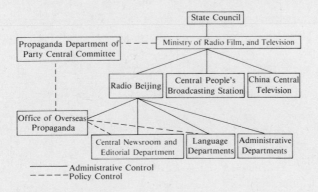

Fig. 7.2 Administrative structure of Radio Beijing.

grams. It publishes a postpublication review known as the Overseas Broadcast Daily, and gives functional principles and directives for program production.

The language broadcasting section includes all the departments that correspond to the geographical locations of the program destination. The pattern is the same as that in the Voice of America and the BBC External Service. The various language departments and groups have their own editors and reporters. However, their dependence on Xinhua news wirecopies and materials from the news-gathering section of Radio Beijing is still great. A considerable number of professional people in each department share the duties of translation, typing, presentation, and maintenance.

Gatekeeping Function of Editors and Reporters

The operational principles and guidance for editors and reporters lie within the general theoretical and ideological context already discussed. The exception is that these principles are more specific; some are even technical. In this section, three different kinds of principles will be discussed: principles for editors, general principles for news selection, and specific guidelines for news selection. All three categories of principles directly influence how an editor goes about selecting content.

Principles for Editors

The responsibility of a journalist in China, as described earlier, may make him or her feel lofty and honorable. But that's not enough to become a good editor:

> An editor should study the fundamental principles of Marxism, Leninism, and Mao Zedong thought, and have a regular knowledge and understanding of Party line and policies. This in turn will help him to keep the gate of theory and policies. For instance, an editor in charge of culture and education must know about Marxist teachings on culture and education, and be familiar with the Party policies towards the social superstructure.[10]

A good editor is also required to have a good handle on words and grammar, in addition to general and professional knowledge. The same article said:

> A working style of precision and rigor should be developed. The edited

story should be clearly written, grammatically, rhetorically, and punctually correct.[11]

Another requirement is to go into the masses and do investigation and study. The same article explained:

> An editor is the ear and mouth of the Party and the people. The pen is the people's pen that must tell the true feelings and demands of the people. Only if an editor goes into society, makes friends with the people, understands and learns from them can he handle stories to reflect the advancing pace of the people, and let every story play its effective role of propaganda and guidance in the four modernization drives.[12]

The implication is that an editor should become the link between the Party and the people. By conducting social investigation, an editor reflects the people's desires and provides evidence to help the Party make correct policies.

General Principles for News Selection

There exist certain criteria that define news. A discussion of these criteria may help to explain the Chinese definition of news and other media content.

The political inclination. The political inclination must be reflected in the coverage of events. The textbook of the Beijing Broadcast Institute explains:

> This inclination is supposed to be in line with the Party policies, guidance, and principles and be beneficial to the modernization drive. . . . If the story has a good theme, even though it's not well written, it should be given priority to be on the air after being polished. Those stories that seem well written but have some obvious defects should be dumped. Political criterion should be put in the first place for an editor to select a news story. The aftereffect and the political influence of a published news story should be taken into consideration.[13]

The significance of the news story. The same textbook gives a definition of *significance:*

> The significance of a news story is defined as an event or an issue that can make significant impact on international and domestic affairs. . . . Also

to be regarded in this category is an event or an issue that reflects common tendencies in the life and work of the broad masses. Some stories that do not reflect certain significant issues, but that are closely linked with reality, have direct bearing on the people's interests and reflect people's demands should also be given priority. . . . An important principle here is that news should be geared to the needs of reality and the people.[14]

Timeliness of the news. According to the same textbook, two principles are recommended in considering timeliness:

The story should be timely and deal with an event that has just happened or is happening. Timeliness should be an important principle for selecting news. The style and the angle of approach to the story should also be new. This is another principle of selecting news.[15]

Educational news. The textbook specifies the following about news that enriches knowledge:

Attention should be paid to selecting educational or instructional stories to cater to the diversities of human interests and people's quests for knowledge. As a kind of attraction, this kind of news also serves to increase the credibility of radio news programs.[16]

In conclusion, the textbook states:

A broadcast editor should be flexible, stick to the principle of "finding truth from facts," and not be blinded by dogma.[17]

Specific Guidelines for News Selection

The textbook of the Beijing Broadcast Institute also provides more specific guidelines to help direct the actual process of selecting news.

Positive propaganda. Most of the news stories in a news program should be devoted to positive propaganda.

Keeping Party and state secrets. The quantity and quality of information to which the average person has access is selected and regulated. The textbook points out:

What's to be openly published, what's to be carried in publications for limited circulation, what issues shouldn't be reported temporarily, and to what extent a certain issue can be reported, are all to be in accordance with the policies of the Central Party Committee. . . . Statistics, defense industry, scientific and technical research results, and national resources are state secrets. They're generally forbidden to be openly published. When and how news with that sort of content is published should be decided by the next higher authorities.[18]

Balanced reporting. The textbook says:

> A broadcast editor should adhere to the principle of seeking a balance among different fields and geographic areas that are reported.[19]

Optimum arrangement of the news program. There are certain rules that should be followed regarding the arrangement of a news program.

1. The key issue should be highlighted. The textbook explains:

> The key issue should be stressed and highlighted on which momentum should be built. In addition to the news, there should be commentary and opinion on the issue. . . . The first three stories of the news program must be associated with the latest political trend and with issues that reflect problems arising from reality and that indicate solutions.[20]

2. A variety of styles should exist. A variety of styles is recommended, such as "on-spot newscast, news feature, reportage, correspondence from reporters, or news in brief."[21]

3. A rank-order should be followed. The textbook states:

> Domestic news is required to be put ahead of international news. For the overseas service, it is desirable to put international news ahead of domestic news. Generally speaking, economic news should be put in front of other news; political and foreign news follows news about education and sciences for the domestic service.[22]

An editor is supposed to have political sensitivity. "He not only knows the sequence of arrangement for a news program in normal situations, but he must also resolutely make flexible arrangements under unexpected circumstances."[23] The textbook goes on to say that

> The goals of the Party change in different historical periods. As a result, the rank-order of the news program changes.[24]

Content Selection

Everyday news from various sources, through different channels, flows into Radio Beijing, whereupon editors carefully select suitable stories and beam them across the air. Before we talk about news sources and how the news flows, we should take a look at the arrangement of Radio Beijing's daily programs.

Every language group at Radio Beijing broadcasts independently to audiences in its target area. Each transmission carries a comprehensive program, which includes news, commentary on international issues, feature programs about China, and cultural programs. Programs in each transmission can generally be divided into two categories: news and commentary, and features and music. News and commentary comprise about 30 to 35 percent of program time, and the rest of the time is devoted to features and music. Each transmission lasts for one hour.

News falls into three categories: international news (usually about 10 minutes), domestic news, and sports news (each about 5 to 7 minutes). Commentary on international issues usually lasts 3 to 5 minutes. Features account for a large portion of each transmission. Programs vary greatly from one language group to another. Some of the regular programs about China are: "China in Construction," "Dispatch from the Countryside," "Current Events," "Topics in the Press," "Pages from Chinese History," "Public Affairs," "Culture in China," "Travel Talk," "Young Friends," "Music from China," and "Sports Fans."

Every language service also produces programs especially for its target audience or at the request of its listeners. Among them are "Listeners' Letter Box" in more than 20 languages (including English, French, Spanish, Arabic); "Learn to Speak Chinese" (English and Japanese); "Chinese Cooking," "The Third World Marches On," "Chinese Ethnic Minorities," "China Anthology," "Profile," "Music Album," and "Chinese Savings and Stories" (English); "News About China" (French); "Friendship Square" and "Topics" (Japanese); "Friendship Page" and "Programs for Sinologists" (Russian); "Chinese Muslim" (Arabic); "Those Years of Friendship" and "Reading from Novels" (Vietnamese); "The Capital—Beijing" and "China in the Eyes of Foreigners" (Korean); "Esperanto in Progress" (Esperanto); "Hometown Today" and "Returned Overseas Chinese in the Motherland" (Overseas Chinese Service).

As for the daily news gathered at Radio Beijing, most international news and a large amount of domestic news are supplied by the Xinhua News Agency. News of various kinds flows constantly into the central newsroom of Radio Beijing through Xinhua's wire service. Some international news is sent back by Radio Beijing's foreign correspondents stationed in six countries. Other domestic news is gathered by its own reporters. Things happening in the capital are mainly covered by Radio Beijing staff reporters. Events occurring in other parts of the country are reported either by its own reporters or stringers, or by Xinhua reporters in the bureaus in different provinces and cities. The final proof of the *People's Daily* also arrives at the central newsroom of Radio Beijing early every morning.

Commentaries on international issues are usually written by staff commentators. But now and then the *People's Daily* and Xinhua commentaries are used if they are important and strongly reflect the views of the Chinese government. Sometimes language groups produce commentaries directed at audiences in their target areas. For instance, if the United States government makes any change in its foreign policies, Radio Beijing's English service might comment specifically on the American government's new policies. However, this commentary may not be used by other language groups unless it is considered extremely imperative. Under the International News Department at Radio Beijing, there are two sections: the central newsroom and commentary sections. The latter provides commentaries on international affairs of common concern. This means they are suitable for virtually all language groups. These commentaries are in Chinese and must be translated by the language groups.

Sources for feature stories vary greatly. Unlike daily news, which is largely supplied by the Xinhua News Agency, features are nearly all produced by Radio Beijing staff members. Because of their specific programs and audiences, language groups produce feature programs appealing to their own listeners. In the meantime, the Domestic News Department also supplies general features or features for the most popular programs, such as "China in Construction," "Culture in China," and "Public Affairs." Sometimes language groups cooperate with the Domestic News Department to help write particular features needed by language groups for their special programs. The bigger the language group, the more independent it is. It usually has its own news and feature sections. Newspeople in small language groups have to deal with both daily news and regular feature programs, and can't be divided into specific sections for there are fewer people available. As a result, they are more dependent on features provided by the Domestic News Department.

Some feature scripts are rewritten from Chinese publications printed in English like *Women in China, China Reconstructs, Sports in China,* or *China Daily.* Occasionally, special features appear from Xinhua already written in English. They are usually substantial, exploring the complexity of current problems and issues clearly and cogently. However, they comprise a small part of the feature programs.

To Americans who live abroad, Voice of America's programming may sound less hectic and diverse than its home counterpart. Voice of America is more cautious and puts more emphasis on the virtues of the American way. Likewise, China's domestic service radio programming offers a richer variety of humor or music and information than does Radio Beijing, which concentrates on the virtues of the Chinese way.

Any international or domestic news broadcast by Radio Beijing has to pass several gatekeepers before it goes on the air. Every day a large amount of news flows into the central newsroom. Copy editors there immediately divide the news items into four categories: international, internationally related, domestic, and sports news. Then, among all the news stories, they choose a certain number according to their importance and timeliness, and newswriters rewrite them into radio news. Before those news stories are distributed to different language groups, they must be sent to the news editor for approval. Each day the central newsroom sends out approximately 100 to 120 news stories. International or internationally related news takes up about 65 percent of total news time, domestic news 25 percent, and the other 10 percent is sports news.

When those selected news stories reach the language groups, the program editors will pick up stories suitable for their target areas. When the stories are decided upon, they are handed over to newswriters who will translate or rewrite them. Then the stories are turned over to the news editor, who reedits all the stories. Finally, all the stories are recorded in the order of international or internationally related news first, then home news, and finally sports news. Everything is prerecorded before broadcasting.

The English Department is the biggest department and quite different from the other language groups. The English Department is considered the most important department at Radio Beijing, because English is widely spoken and because the English service has the largest audience. The authorities pay much attention to it. The English Department is a model for the development of Radio Beijing and is far less dependent on the central newsroom. To a certain extent, it is independent. It transmits news faster than all other departments because not much translation is involved.

Apart from the news stories provided by the central newsroom, the English Department receives Xinhua's English-language wire service. If there is anything important going on in the capital, the English Department will dispatch its own reporter to cover the story. It also has its own foreign correspondent stationed in Washington. Except for urgent news sent by Xinhua in Chinese, most news is in English. Thus the people working the newsroom of the English Department save a lot of time by writing or editing those stories in English instead of translating them from one language into another.

News at the English Service is changed three times a day according to the target areas of each transmission. Thus the working hours of the newspeople are divided into three shifts. On each shift, the program editor will select the news stories for listeners in the areas to where the transmission is beamed. Then newswriters will rewrite those chosen wire-copies. All those rewritten stories are polished by a copy editor from an English-speaking country. All the Xinhua stories can get on the air with the approval of the news editor alone. Stories done by staff reporters are approved by the director or deputy director of the department before they are broadcast. Much more power and freedom have been given to the English Department by Radio Beijing authorities.

What kind of news programs does Radio Beijing's English Service have? Here's a content analysis of English-language news programs from 11 February to 17 February 1985. Thirteen different categories are used to classify the different kinds of news (Table 7.1). The sequence of the categories in the table represents the actual structure of the daily news program. These categories are as follows:

Foreign relations. This category includes what is nicknamed "ban-quet news," stories dealing with important policy, both domestic and foreign. It can include implied remarks made by government and Party leaders when attending banquets for, or receiving, foreign leaders. Also included are foreign ministry news releases and other internationally related activities.

Southeast-Asian conflict. In addition to the war in Cambodia, this category includes China's reaction as well as Thailand's reaction to Viet-namese military offensive in Cambodia.

Korean situation. This category refers to the situation in the Korean Peninsula.

Middle-East conflict. Apart from events taking place in the Middle East, this category includes stories relevant to the conflict, such as "Saudi Arabian King Fahd Asks Reagan to Play an Active Role in the Settlement of the Conflict," "UN Condemns Israeli's Killing Refugees on the West Bank," and "Romanian President meets with Arafat."

Third-World stories. This category includes Third-World coopera-tion and development.

South Africa.
United Nations.
Iran-Iraq War.

United States and the West Bloc. Stories about Japan, Australia, and New Zealand are included in this category. Stories dealing with the diplomatic relations between these countries and other countries are also included. Examples of such stories are "Japanese Foreign Minister Plans to Visit East-European Countries," "U.S. Announcement of Soviet Top Delegation's Visit to the U.S.," and "The U.S. Statement of its Support to ASEAN Stance towards Vietnam."

Soviet Union and the East Bloc. Apart from news about these countries and their interrelations, news about their relations with other countries is also included. Such stories include: "Soviet Leader's Statement on Disarmament," "Romanian Leader Meeting with West German Foreign Minister," "Polish Premier Visits India," and "Japanese Communist Party Delegation Visits Yugoslavia."

China's economic reform and achievements. Apart from positive stories, also included in this category are stories such as "Party Members Warned Not to Obstruct Reform," "Criticizing Unhealthy Tendencies."

Disasters.

China's culture, tourism, and stories of human interest.

Others. Included in this category are three stories: "Pakistani Protest on Violation of Air Space by Afghanistan Aircraft," "Iran Arrests 20 Terrorists," and "India Receives MiG Planes."

Percentages were calculated by the number of stories in each category.

Of the total number of 107 news stories, 12 deal with China's relations with foreign countries, which is 11.2 percent of the total. Twelve stories concerning China's economic reforms comprise another 11.2 percent, and 15 stories on Chinese culture, tourism, and human-interest topics comprise 14 percent of the total. Therefore, news relating to China in general comprises 36.4 percent, or a little more than one-third of the total stories.

Stories about conflict in Southeast Asia and West Asia (the Iran-Iraq War and the Middle-East conflict) and the situation in the Korean Peninsula comprise 32.5 percent, or a third of the total. It seems Radio Beijing is somewhat concerned with these "hot spots" in Asia.

News about the United States and the Western countries comprises 8.4 percent of the total, while news about the Soviet Union and the East-European countries constitutes 6.5 percent. Although the percentage of news in the Soviet Union category is lower than that of the United States category, these are relatively comparable percentages.

The sequence of the categories is intended to reflect the actual rank-order of the daily news program. This rank-order implies the degree of importance Radio Beijing attaches to the various countries. The general

TABLE 7.1. English-Language News Programs of Radio Beijing (11–17 February 1985)

Topic	11	12	13	14	15	16	17	Total
Foreign Relations	2	1	2	3	1	2	1	12
Southeast-Asian Conflict	1	1	2	1	1	1	2	9
Korean Situation	1	1			1			3
Middle-East Conflict	3	3	3	2	3	3	2	19
Third-World Stories	3			2			1	7
South Africa	1				2		1	4
United Nations		1			2		1	4
Iran-Iraq War	1			1				2
US and West	1	2	2	2	1	2		10
USSR and East	1	1		1	1	2	1	7
China's Economic Reforms	4	3	1	2	1	1		12
Disasters	1							1
Culture, Human Interest		1	2	1	2	5	3	14
Others		2		1				3
Total	19	15	14	15	14	16	14	107

pattern reflected by the rank-order shows that news about China's relations with other countries is more important than all other news. News about Asia and the Third World ranks next. News about the superpowers and the Second-World countries is third with news about the United States category slightly ahead of the Soviet Union category.

Problems and Efforts toward Improvement

In its early years the scripts Radio Beijing aired differed little in style and content from the releases of the Xinhua News Agency, its main source of information. They were for the most part merely translations of these releases or newspaper articles. In the mid-1950s, efforts to develop the radio's own style began. Rewriting, interviewing, and even experimenting with radio plays began. These efforts were interrupted by the Cultural Revolution, and they were not resumed until 1978. Since then, many changes have been made in the programming:

1. The news is more timely, much shorter, and covers a wider area.

The timeliness is due primarily to the expansion of news sources. Besides Xinhua and major newspapers and magazines, Radio Beijing receives information from its bureaus across the country and in several major cities abroad—Tokyo, Islamabad, Belgrade, Paris, Mexico City, and Washington. In addition, special correspondents are sent to cover the visits abroad by Chinese leaders, those of foreign dignitaries to China, and important international conferences and sports meets. Their voiced reports add much to the timeliness of the newscasts.

Rewriting in concise and simple radio language is now a must. Because the newscast (including international and domestic news) on a one-hour transmission is limited to 15 minutes, each item averages 1 minute only. The commentary or news analysis that follows usually lasts from 4 to 5 minutes. More voiced reports and shorter stories represent a big step forward from the newscast beamed 15 years ago. At that time, the program was 30 minutes of straight talk, which seemed to drag on forever.

2. More programs are geared to the interests, tastes, and styles of specific audiences.

Listeners in different areas vary in age, sex, race, and nationality, as well as in social, economic, and cultural background, and the levels of their understanding of China are not the same. No stereotyped program can satisfy their varied interests. Even programs on the same topic need different approaches for different audiences, and sometimes it is necessary to add explanations and background material to help people have a better grasp of the topic. Therefore, the language services know more about the target audiences and have been encouraged to display their creativity by producing programs better suited to their listeners. They have been doing so ever since the late seventies. Outstanding among these programs are "The Chinese Muslims" produced by the Arabic Service, "Friendship Square" by the Japanese Service, and "China and the Spanish World" by the Spanish Service. The program, "Listeners Letter Box," is aired regularly by more than 20 language services. Besides answering questions raised by listeners, the program quotes letters or plays tapes sent by them, which may consist of comments or suggestions on programming and announcing, and impressions of their visits to China. The English Service also devotes a biweekly program, "Listeners Calling," to such material. Sitting in their living rooms, some listeners have heard their own comments and those of others broadcast over Radio Beijing, and they like it. Mr. Ivan Grishin wrote from Canada: "I heard your 'Listeners Calling' show the other day and I loved it. It was great hearing the comments and views of other Radio Beijing listeners. It's great to know that other listeners also find your programs interesting."

3. More attention is being paid to presentation, and listeners have welcomed the new, relaxed, and friendly tone of the announcers, who regard them as their equals and friends.

In some language broadcasts, one or two hosts or hostesses preside over the programming. With their friendly tone, they give a warm, personal touch to the transmissions. On special occasions, such as Christmas or New Year's, they extend festive greetings to the listeners on behalf of the radio station. These changes, though still in the initial stage, have been acknowledged by some listeners' publications and organizations. *The Dx'ers Calling,* a monthly published in Australia, commented in its December 1983 issue:

> Those of you who have been able to compare the output of the English Service of RB over the past 20 years cannot help but have been struck by the enormous change in program content. Perhaps there would be some truth in this statement for any radio station but for RB it is more pronounced. RB is now responsive to listeners' letters and suggestions and provides a wide and varied program format.[25]

International Broadcasting, a magazine published by the Association of North America Radio Clubs, conducted a poll among its readers in 1979 and Radio Beijing was named the radio station that had made the "greatest improvement . . . in the previous year." In 1983 the Japanese journal *Shortwave* also conducted a poll on the best foreign radio station. Radio Beijing's Japanese Service was voted the second best among broadcasts in the same language of more than 30 radio stations. A year earlier in 1982, a poll jointly sponsored by a DX'ers Club in Saar, West Germany, and the Deutsche Welle showed that Radio Beijing's German Service was the fifth best-liked broadcast among similar services of 28 radio stations. Opinion polls in some developing countries, such as Bangladesh, also place Radio Beijing in a top spot.[26]

To supplement its regular broadcasts, since 1980 Radio Beijing has also been sending reports on China and recordings of its programs by airmail, telephone, or satellite to local stations in Pakistan, Colombia, Peru, Venezuela, Argentina, Barbados, Zimbabwe, Italy, Spain, Northern Ireland, Australia, and the United States. In June 1986 its English Service coproduced a phone-in show with an American local station, WOI in Ames, Iowa. A Chinese agricultural expert answered questions on Chinese agriculture that were first phoned in to WOI by local residents and then routed to Radio Beijing. For Radio Beijing, this is a new way of providing information on China to American listeners.

Despite its improvement in the last few years, Radio Beijing still faces many problems. The most pressing is its weak signal in some areas of the world. It also needs to further expand its news sources and overcome a shortage of qualified broadcast journalists. These problems have attracted the attention of all concerned and were taken up at the National Conference of Radio and Television in 1983. At present, steps are being taken to increase the transmitting power, including the construction of more shortwave transmitters.

There is still much room for improvement in Radio Beijing's programming, especially its newscasts. In order to have better programs and news that is even more timely, Radio Beijing needs more professionals, particularly those proficient in foreign languages. It also needs to have more bureaus abroad. Most of its staff members, however, have had little journalistic training. Some are Chinese who have returned from overseas, and some are graduates from foreign-language institutes in the country. As a remedy Radio Beijing has invited specialists from around the world to work with its staff members. At present some 40 specialists from more than 20 countries are working at Radio Beijing. They have contributed much to improving the programs.

Another remedy is sending its announcers, editors, and reporters abroad to study foreign languages or broadcast journalism. Many have already returned from such studies in countries like Japan, Pakistan, Sri Lanka, Egypt, Iraq, Syria, France, Germany, Italy, Britain, and the

United States. Their numbers are still too small, however, to meet the need for more professionals. Some universities in China, like the Shanghai International Studies University, are currently offering courses in English on print and broadcast journalism. This is a very practical way to train qualified workers for the media and it is sure to help to solve at least one of the problems Radio Beijing is now facing.

8 ▧ Television in China

History of China's Television

Chinese television didn't begin until 1958, and then with only a channel serving the capital, Beijing. In the 30 years since, Chinese television has gone through three tumultuous stages, as has the country itself.

China first began to experiment with television in 1956. The Soviet Union supplied most of the equipment and technical assistance. But the experimental broadcasts on 1 May 1958 marked the true beginning of China's television broadcasting. Regular schedules of television services were published for the first time in September 1958. The first station was established in Beijing and was called Beijing Television, with one channel only for the capital.[1]

By 1960 fewer than a dozen cities had stations that served the densest urban areas, which was far from being a network. There was only one link between Beijing and the nearby industrial city of Tianjin. More distant stations had to rely on films and tapes "bicycled" from one to another. Bicycling is a universal term for sending TV material by any means — planes, cars, and so on — other than direct electronic transmission.[2]

The break between China and the Soviet Union in the middle of 1960 greatly hampered the development of all aspects of the Chinese economy. Broadcasting was no exception. The Russian engineers were sorely missed; spare parts were virtually unobtainable. Only in the late sixties did local manufacturing and the development of technical institutes for training and research manage to get the program of expansion moving again.

By 1970, 30 urban stations had been developed, but only Beijing had 2 stations. And the stations in Beijing, Tianjin, Shanghai, and Guangzhou (Canton) were engineered for live broadcasting. These 4 stations, the country's largest, were also connected by microwave links. In 1971, however, with the installation of microwave trunk lines, trans-

212

mission of Beijing Television was extended to the entire nation. The station had assumed a role as headquarters of a national television network. In December 1972 there was at least one station in each of China's 29 provinces and autonomous regions except Tibet. By January 1975, 47 stations operated, serving every province and autonomous region except Tibet, which is apparently too remote and mountainous to be accessible to microwave and cable relays from the capital, Beijing.[3]

During the first few years of the Cultural Revolution, television was stopped entirely. Many broadcasters were dismissed, and equipment was again not maintained; policies were confused or absent. Recovery was slow (in *The Universal Eye,* Timothy Green recounts how in 1970 a visiting British broadcaster "computed up that 18 minutes out of a total of 26 minutes during the main evening news bulletin one night carried rolling captions of Mao's thoughts with background music of 'The East Is Red.' "). The staple fare, it seems, consisted of the news as just described, and the five model Peking operas approved and advocated by Jiang Qing, Mao's wife.

Programs remained fairly straightforward for some years (mainly live relays and news), but many technical advances were made. Beijing Television, ever in the vanguard, began to experiment with color in 1973. Indeed, as the regional stations began to develop and assert themselves, Beijing Television started to play a dual role: It provided regional stations with a national service, while also supplying the inhabitants of Beijing municipality with a local service. On 1 May 1978 (its 20th birthday), a major structural reform was instigated. Beijing Television changed its name to China Central Television (CCTV), which is responsible for a national service as well as a capital service. And a brand-new organization, called Beijing Television, was inaugurated with the job of providing a purely local service in the Beijing area.

Although China's television program services started as early as 1958, they did not become a way of life for the Chinese people until the late 1970s. The past few years have witnessed the rapid development of China's television. By the end of 1984, China added 53 program-originating TV stations to the number of 52 in 1983, reaching a total of 105. In addition, TV rebroadcasting stations and low-power TV frequency translators, which serve the county seats and some rural districts, had increased up to 7,475 according to the 1983 figures. And there were 411 microwave stations.[4]

Today both the central and regional stations are looking to other countries as a source not only of equipment, but also of programs, apart from their efforts to develop stations on their own. In the past China's exchanges with other countries have been erratic. The USSR, which supplied so much at the very beginning, ended its support abruptly in 1960. The few moves toward international agreements (such as an exchange agreement with VISNEWS of Britain in 1965) were sabotaged by the Cultural Revolution, when all contacts with foreign countries, especially in cultural matters, were prohibited. After 1969 foreign contacts were reestablished. China became a member of the Asian Pacific Broadcasting Union (ABU) in December 1973 and has taken a leading role in its affairs. In the last few years many foreign broadcasters have visited China, and numerous Chinese television delegations have visited Europe, Japan, and North America. The U.S. networks and most European broadcasters have signed agreements of collaboration.

In 1976 Chinese television began to broadcast world news with footage provided by counterparts abroad. With the development of China's TV and the increasing demand for international news in its domestic market, China, in early 1980, signed an agreement with VISNEWS of Britain and Universal Press International Television News (UPITN) of the United States to receive international news via communication satellite. On 1 April of that year, China's TV began to broadcast international news obtained through satellite, and that enabled the Chinese audience to view the events happening outside China on the same day, or one or two days later. Visits by top Chinese leaders to other countries also were shown to the Chinese audience through images instead of mere words.[5] One of the first entertainment programs to be made in China by a foreign company was a Bob Hope special, "The Road to China," which NBC transmitted in September 1979.

The flow of programs is two-way. China has regularly bought foreign programs, and recently its purchases have increased substantially. In late 1979 China Central Television made China's first-ever purchase of a U.S. series, "The Man from Atlantis" (Taft-HB Productions). CCTV bought the rights to show the series three times over the next four years, an unusually long-lived contract. In November 1979 CCTV bought two series from the British Broadcasting Corporation (BBC), "Anna Karenina" and "David Copperfield," and a play, "Robinson Crusoe." Purchases of this type have increased greatly and are not limited to the central TV station. Some regional stations also have gained the right to buy entertainment products from other countries. In early 1985 CCTV bought from CBS-TV several packages to be shown to millions of Chinese through the national network for one year. Various TV movies, "60 Minutes," and several National Basketball Association all-star and play-off games were among the purchases.[6]

Besides CCTV, all TV stations at the provincial and municipal levels originate their programs. The CCTV originates two channels. The Beijing municipal station has one channel; Shanghai, two channels; Tianjin, Guangzhou, and Chendu, two channels; the rest have one channel each. In addition, all program-originating stations retransmit CCTV national service; therefore, all audiences can receive the CCTV national service and their local service. In Beijing the audience can receive CCTV national service, CCTV's special capital service, and the local service provided by the Beijing Television Station.

All stations in China use the USSR-sponsored "D" standard of television. The system has 625 lines, a channel width of 8 megahertz (MHz) (relatively generous) and a vision bandwidth of 6 MHz (also generous). The sound signal is frequency modulated (FM).[7]

When China began to experiment with color television in 1973, it used both the Phase Alternation Line (PAL) system, developed by West Germany and used by the United Kingdom and others, and the Color Sequence with Memory (SECAM) system developed by France and used by the Soviet Union and throughout Eastern Europe. It finally chose the PAL system and has developed its own version. CCTV was the first station to switch to color. In 1973 CCTV inaugurated a second channel with a full-color service and broadcast specifically to the Beijing area. At the end of 1979 the national network followed suit and also began transmission in color, although black-and-white programs are still being produced.[8]

The bulk of studio equipment is made in China. Chinese factories are capable of producing cameras (both film and video), most sound equipment, lighting equipment, and some tape recorders. There is an interesting new range of color videotape recorders (VTRs) using one-inch tape (No. SCL-1) or half-inch tape (SD-292). The Shanghai Film Machinery factory also has developed a magnetic film-recording system; one model (2C 35-6) can record six channels on 600 meters of 33-millimeters (mm) stock. The film's footage and tension are controlled by photoelectric cells. In the same league is the Seagull series of flying-spot 35-mm color telecine. The telecine uses a cathode-ray tube imported from the United Kingdom; otherwise, all components are made in China. Sizes range from 8.75 mm to 35 mm.[9]

Chinese-made equipment is lacking most in the areas of optics and electronic editing. Most lenses are imported from Japan; Canon lenses are very popular. As for VTR editing, the choice in China, as outside, is often Ampex. In the small gauges of VTR and videocassette, Sony is equally prevalent.

Along with the modernization drive in the past few years, television in China has developed very rapidly. The Chinese government did not fail to recognize the importance of this modern propaganda tool and has provided a large sum of money to importing advanced technology and equipment in the field. Communication satellites have also been sent into orbit for better and faster transmission of telecommunication.

TV sets, especially color ones (which used to be considered a luxury), have entered more and more Chinese homes. According to a report by the Ministry of Radio and Television, by the end of 1984 more than 46 million TV sets were scattered around the country.[10] Television is still more popular in urban areas, but it also enjoys increasing popularity in rural areas due to the prosperity of the countryside and the fact that farmers can now afford to buy TV sets, even color ones. The number of TV sets in China has increased dramatically recently and is likely to increase even more rapidly in the next few years.

The Party and the government have paid great attention to the development of television in China. In 1983 the proposal for setting up a new central color television center was approved by the government, and the project is one of the 70 most important projects in the seventh five-year plan. On 31 May 1983 construction of the new television center, a 24-storied complex with a total floor space of 104,000 square meters in Beijing, was begun.

China's Television Industry

China founded its own television industry in 1958 by setting up its first television station in Beijing with a transmission power of one thousand watts, equipment designed and made in the country, and its first television camera. In the same year, China's first batch of black-and-white TV sets, two hundred in all, were produced. The annual output was 4,300 sets by the middle of the 1960s.[11] Then came the 10 catastrophic years that seriously hampered the development of the new industry.

Since the Cultural Revolution, the Party and the government have in recent years allocated large appropriations to the television industry. Investments in 1979 and 1980 exceeded the total investment for the previous eight years. Production has increased by leaps and bounds. Today the advanced status of China's relatively young television industry is indicated by the following facts:

The strongest television transmission power can be as high as 40 kilowatts.

Of the country's 29 provinces, municipalities, and autonomous regions, 25 had built their own television industries by the end of 1980.

Through 1982 more than 50 television production plants turned out all types of television sets (plus spare parts) for family use, for teaching medical treatment, and for industrial purposes, as well as equipment for transmission, receiving, and relaying.[12]

The nation's output of television sets, as one of the most desirable, welcomed durable goods, is going up every year. In quality, its main performance specifications are close to those made in other countries.

Production on a limited scale of UHF 48-channel television sets is under way.

Home-made picture tubes, as they were first made in the early 1970s, are enjoying an ever-growing popularity. Shanghai-made tubes have an average life span of four, five, and six thousand hours or more for 9-inch, 12-inch and 16-inch tubes respectively. The quality of picture tubes made in other parts of the country is also catching up with those made in Shanghai.

China's television industry has imported some advanced technology from developed countries. By 1982 three imported color-television assembly lines were in operation in Beijing, Shanghai, and Tianjin, and another eight TV-spare parts assembly lines were being installed.[13]

With the development of China's television industry, the country is capable of producing black-and-white and color television sets in all sizes. The Chinese government has announced that China will stop importing assembled TV sets to protect the nation's own television industry.[14]

China Central Television

China Central Television (CCTV) is a state television station under the direct administration of the Ministry of Radio and Television of China. This state organization is the center of the nationwide network. Theoretically, it is under the direct leadership and control of the Chinese Communist Party and the state, as is every other media organization in the country.

CCTV, when it was established in 1958, carried the name of Beijing Television. After a major structural reform, it received its present name — China Central Television — in May 1978. CCTV has been used by the Party and the state to popularize policies and decisions and motivate the masses in the construction of Communism. Its tasks are to transmit news, deliver government orders or decrees, provide education, and enrich the people's cultural life.[15] In the present historical era, the task of

CCTV, as indicated clearly by the Chinese Communist Party Central Committee, is to "agitate and educate the whole Party, the whole army, and the people of all nationalities in the country to contribute to the socialist construction and to build socialist spiritual and material civilizations."[16]

Administrative Structure of CCTV

Together with the Central People's Broadcasting Station (CPBS) and Radio Beijing, China Central Television is one of the three big broadcasting stations under the Ministry of Radio and Television. CCTV's administrative structure is also a miniature of the structural pattern of the national broadcasting system. The centralized power is vested in the hands of the director of CCTV, who is responsible for the Ministry of Radio and Television.

The horizontal structure of CCTV can be divided into four sections: the administrative section, the editorial and news gathering and distribution section, the technical section, and the logistics section (Fig. 8.1).

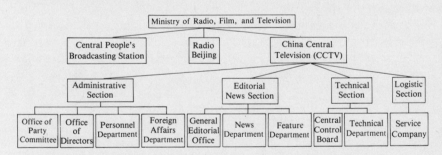

Fig. 8.1   Administrative structure of China Central Television.

The administrative section consists of the Office of the Party Committee, Office of Directors, Personnel Department, and Office of Foreign Affairs. The Office of the Party Committee and Office of Directors are responsible for setting the policy and tone of the broadcasting according to the directives of the Central Propaganda Department and the Ministry of Radio and Television (Fig. 8.2). But they have little direct impact on the program-production process of CCTV. However, the Personnel Department of the section has the power to appoint, promote, dismiss, and assign duties to professional people such as editors and reporters. According to orders from above, the department is also authorized to appoint heads of individual departments in other sections. The Office of

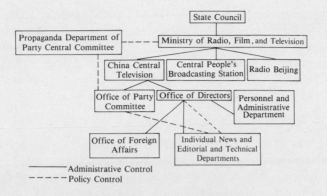

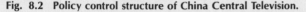

Fig. 8.2   Policy control structure of China Central Television.

Foreign Affairs is responsible for all exchange activities with other countries and represents CCTV in foreign affairs.[17]

The editorial and news gathering and distributing section includes the General Editorial Office and individual news and program departments. The highest body of the section is the General Editorial Office, which administrates and assumes responsibility for the seven news and program departments: the News Department, Special Features Department, Department of Literature and Art, Department of International Affairs, Department of TV Education, Department of Military Affairs, and the Office of TV Weekly.

The technical and production section is composed of departments responsible for CCTV's technical staff and program production, such as relaying, videotaping, film developing and printing, acoustics, and lighting. This section is closely connected with the editorial and news sections, and these two sections work together to broadcast CCTV's programs. Other departments not involved in either administration or editorial and news business naturally fall into the logistics section, the least important section of CCTV's structure.

CCTV currently has nearly one thousand workers. News and editorial staff and others engaging in program production amount to 35 percent of the total employees of CCTV. Technicians make up about 40 percent, general workers 15 percent, and administrative personnel 10 percent.[18]

Programming and Content of CCTV

China Central Television produces three services on the different channels, with a total of 131.5 hours of programs weekly. Viewers of

CCTV are not required to pay any license fee for reception of programs. The services are financed totally by the government. Channel 2 is regarded as the primary service and is distributed to all stations in the country. Channel 8 is distributed only within the municipality of Beijing. Both services are beamed out by the same 7.5-kilowatt transmitter. The third service is the educational service on CBTVU.

NATIONAL SERVICE OF GENERAL PROGRAMS (CHANNEL 2). This is the main service of general programs of CCTV covering information, education, and entertainment. Monday through Saturday, Channel 2 broadcasts 6½ hours daily, and on Sundays it provides service for 14½ hours. The following are the programs that it offers.

News. "Midday News," "Evening News," "News Special," "Look and Think."

Sports. "Sports Window," recorded and live sports broadcasts both domestic and international.

Features. "Across the Motherland," "People," "National Minorities," "People's Army," "Science and Life," "Health and Hygiene," "Cultural Life," "Around the World," "Animal Kingdom," "Spring Shoots."

Services. "At Your Service," "What's On," "Information on New Commodities."

Educational. Educational programs on science and technology, liberal arts, agriculture, economics, foreign languages.

Arts. "Television Theater," "Drama Appreciation," "For Music Amateurs," "Garden in Bloom," "Speak and Sing," "Highlights from the Theater," "Variety Show," "Melody of Friendship," TV plays, feature films.[19]

Transmission hours of the first service are Monday through Saturday, 12:00 to 1:00 P.M., 5:30 to 11:00 P.M.; Sunday, 8:30 to 11:00 P.M.

BEIJING LOCAL SERVICE OF GENERAL PROGRAMS (CHANNEL 8). This service offers to Beijing residents general programs in a wide variety of series as well as the following specific programs: "Land of Beauty," "Advice on Everyday Living," "Our Glorious History," "TV Plays," feature films, dramas, plays, song-and-dance performances, variety shows, documentaries, science films, cartoons, live sports broadcasts, rebroadcasts of the "Evening News" of the national network.[20]

Transmission hours of Channel 8 are Monday through Saturday,

9:00 A.M. to 12:00 P.M., 7:00 to 11:00 P.M.; Sunday, 7:00 to 11:00 P.M. This service is on the air 7 hours a day Monday through Saturday, broadcasting only 4 hours on Sunday because Channel 2 offers a 14½-hour broadcast on the same day.

EDUCATIONAL SERVICE ON CENTRAL BROADCASTING AND TELEVISION UNIVERSITY. Central Broadcasting and Television University (CBTVU) is coordinated by the Ministry of Radio and Television in conjunction with the State Education Commission (the former Ministry of Education). CBTVU was officially launched in February 1979, and offers a range of academic courses both on radio and television. According to statistics for 1983, about 600,000 people are currently following various courses on CBTVU, and of this figure, 420,000 are officially enrolled students. (More will be discussed about higher education on television later in this chapter.)[21]

Courses offered by CBTVU are mechanics, electronics, mathematics, physics, Chinese language and literature, and economics. Enrolled students take three hours of classes in the morning and another three hours in the afternoon. Because the CBTVU courses are broadcast nationwide, they are sent out on Channel 2 by CCTV, sharing the channel with the first service. Transmission hours for this educational service are Monday through Saturday, 8:30 A.M. to 12:00 P.M. and 1:30 to 4:10 P.M.

NEWS PROGRAMS. CCTV news plays quite an important role in all CCTV programs and accounts for about 15 percent of total program time. In 1983 CCTV broadcast more than 6,100 pieces of domestic news and over 5,000 items of international news, of which more than 3,200 was news footage received from foreign news agencies via satellite.[22] The rest of the international news was provided by the Xinhua News Agency and other sources. Domestic news is usually gathered by CCTV staff reporters or sent by local stations that are connected with CCTV through microwave trunk lines.

CCTV's "Evening News" is one of the programs with the highest viewing. An estimated 90 percent of television viewers watch the "Evening News."[23] This news program became more popular after April 1980 when CCTV began to broadcast a 10-minute satellite international news segment that enabled Chinese viewers to see what happened on the same day or the previous day outside China.

Important events within the country always receive extensive coverage. Viewers can see the news of the day, such as the meetings of the Communist Party Central Committee and the National People's Congress, in the evening. The trial of the Lin Biao and Jiang Qing cliques had the highest viewing rate in December 1980, and about 300 million people watched. In the past few years, news about the economic reforms in all fields in China's modernization drive has taken up the lion's share of news over CCTV. The current economic policy, which calls for self-improvement and for China to catch up to the more developed countries, has affected the news judgment of CCTV reporters and editors. As a result, CCTV officials say that they give a high priority to science and technology news.[24]

In the 30 years since the inauguration of CCTV, its news has gone through three difficult stages. In its first phase, Soviet technology and the news styles of China's socialist big brother dominated CCTV. Newscasts followed the Soviet format, with the news readers giving domestic stories, then foreign news. CCTV's 7:00 P.M. newscast still holds to this model. The anchor usually reads either from a teleprompter or from copy sheets and reporters are seldom seen or heard. Anchors do voice-overs for most pieces.

By the early 1960s the Sino-Soviet political split was reflected in Chinese TV news. Soviet influences, and pro-Soviet stories, disappeared. Between 1966 and 1976 the radical forces of Chairman Mao's Cultural Revolution took hold throughout China. Chinese journalists of the period refer to themselves as "a lost generation." Standards of reality and truth were trashed, just as surely as the revolution's youthful Red Guards assaulted Buddhist temples, museums, libraries, their teachers, professional people, and other "vestiges" of bourgeois influences. "We only carried good socialist news," a newswriter remembered. "You know, how happy people were, how quickly China was developing."[25] The other side of China's domestic good-news policy was to depict the West either fleetingly or in the worst terms possible. The United States appeared as a place of riots, crime, poverty, and other man-made and natural disasters.

By the early 1980s both Mao and doctrinaire Maoism were dead. Deng Xiaoping and the new leadership were firmly in control. China turned more and more to the West. The pragmatists reached out for Japanese technology, U.S. investments, West-European joint ventures. Today CCTV's editing rooms are equipped with numerous Sony machines (though not necessarily as elaborate as their American counterparts). What really gave CCTV its new look, however, was the ministry's decision to subscribe to two Western TV news sources — VISNEWS (operating out of London) and WTN (based in New York) —

and to cut back on Soviet news services. The official explanation is that Moscow news comes in "too late,"[26] but CCTV has no problem with a Soviet event that might affect China—the Gorbachev succession, for example, got big play.

FEATURE PROGRAMS. Apart from news programs, CCTV tries to enrich people's knowledge through other special-feature programs. There is a program entitled "Across the Motherland," which spotlights the scenic beauties and special features of various localities in China. A special weekly program "Around the World" provides viewers with a window through which they can view the world. This program has featured, among other things, the agroindustrial complexes in Yugoslavia, a new type of hospital in West Berlin, the music center in Sydney, offshore oil drilling in Mexico, and different cultural customs in the world.

Other programs of the same nature or with the same purpose include "Science and Technology," "Health and Hygiene," "Advice on Everyday Living," and "Cultural Life." The last deals with almost every field of literary and artistic endeavor, ranging from theater, literature, cinema, music, and dancing to art, calligraphy, and photography. Professionals and amateurs alike find them immensely absorbing.

Entertainment is a very significant part of CCTV programs. More than half of CCTV programs are recreational. In the early years, they were mostly feature films or live theatrical performances. In recent years, however, a problem emerged as TV sets found their way into many Chinese homes and the government began to insist on profitable enterprises. However, while TV audiences asked for more new films and theatrical performances, cinemas and theaters, out of box-office considerations, have protested. And TV stations have thus been forced to rely on their own ingenuity to meet the demand.[27] That is why TV shows are being developed at a fast tempo, and TV plays are enjoying the growing attention of Chinese audiences. In 1984 about 500 TV plays were produced by the central and local stations, and out of that number, CCTV turned out 81.[28]

TV plays in China are still in the developmental stage, and some are artistically immature and nondescript in style. However, those shows have touched on many facets of life—career, friendship, love, marriage. Many praise people and people's contributions to the country's modernization drive. Some recall the difficult years at war or the trauma wrought by the 10 years of turmoil; others deal with bureaucracy, conservatism, special-privilege mentality, social abuses, morality, and the legal system. Many programs are designed especially for children.

Up-and-coming TV plays have become the topic of the day, some trying to define what their salient features should be, others debating whether artistically they should be presented more like a modern play or like a film. The general public, however, simply asks for more and better TV shows, in addition to more and better TV entertainment in the form of local operas, songs and dances, musical programs, and other artistic forms.

Sports programs are always favorite programs on CCTV and have attracted millions of viewers all over China; CCTV does devote a lot of time to sports events. In recent years CCTV has broadcast live, or rebroadcast, more than 100 games or sports events each year. In 1983 alone, 121 games were carried on CCTV's channels.[29]

Educational programs are strongly emphasized by CCTV. As mentioned before, courses offered by CCTV include science, mechanical and electrical engineering, basic courses in technology, and many others. They are arranged by the CBTVU under the joint sponsorship of the Ministry of Radio and Television and the State Education Commission.

Students enrolled in a TV university live more or less like regular college students, attending TV classes together regularly in the morning as required. This method has proven better than attending classes separately at home. They receive tutoring in the afternoon. Tutors explain the main points and the difficult parts of the lectures to help students understand them better. Most TV-university graduates will be assigned jobs after completing their course requirements.

A 30-minute English lesson given every evening by CCTV is particularly popular. It began in 1978 as a course open to all with no registration or examination required. Anyone who attends regularly and does the required homework may master basic English grammar and about a thousand words in 20 months. The lessons, taught by well-known English professors and teachers from foreign-language institutes or English departments of universities, are supplemented by conversation drills and miniplays. Viewers are expected to reach the intermediate level in two years. Teaching materials have been compiled and published for this purpose. Although they have been reprinted dozens of times, the demand still outstrips the supply. The popularity of those English lessons of CCTV has led to the introduction of a new program known as "English on Sunday," showing imported movies and documentaries with English dialogues.

Advertisements are new in China's mass media, appearing only after the Cultural Revolution. CCTV first began to carry commercials in 1979. Ever since, domestic advertising has played an increasingly important part in Chinese television. CCTV's operation is primarily financed by the Ministry of Radio and Television, but relies nowadays on commercial advertising to supplement its budget. Groups of 5, 10, or more spots are routinely blocked together, and the pitches are direct and consumer oriented, with music and 1980 graphics plugging makeup, mattresses, folk medicine, Chinese Roto-Rooter, and just about anything else. Rates run about seven hundred dollars for a 30-second spot.[30] Advertisements are always inserted between programs, and they are prohibited from interrupting regular programs like those on U.S. television.

Commercials seem to have found a place in television. Advertising units and clients alike stress the need for TV commercials which, they say, are helpful in cementing ties between production and marketing and in activating the market. Commercials also play a useful role, some argue, in disseminating knowledge about various commodities and arousing the interest of potential consumers. However, it is very difficult to predict how far CCTV will go with advertising because it still receives some opposition from society.

CCTV always tries to get feedback from its viewers and improve its programs. A great deal of attention is paid to assessing audience size and program popularity. CCTV ensures contact with its viewers by sending personnel on investigations and organizing panels that invite viewers to give their opinions and suggestions. CCTV recruits staff members specifically to deal with viewers' correspondence.

CCTV maintains good relations with television organizations in various countries of the world and collaborates closely with them in many ways: exchanging, buying, selling, and coproducing programs; accepting foreign commercials; and exchanging news and live international sports broadcasts via satellite. In 1987 CCTV moved into a new, modernized television complex.

3 ❧ Education and Role Perception

9 ▨ Journalism Education in China

Introduction

Journalism education at Chinese universities and other higher-learning institutions is directed by the Number 1 Higher Education Department of the Education Commission. The department is responsible for enrolling journalism students, assigning jobs upon their graduation, training faculty members, compiling textbooks, and sharing experience in teaching among different universities. As an important part of the nation's media system, journalism education is also under the supervision of the Press Bureau of the Propaganda Department of the Communist Party Central Committee. Because journalism education is one of the weakest links in the entire educational system in China, this dual leadership has proved necessary to rally more support from government departments and the entire nation.

According to the latest statistics, China had 5,346 graduate and undergraduate students of journalism at 27 universities as of the fall semester of 1984. Master's degrees in journalism were conferred by the Graduate School of the Social Science Academy (Beijing), the People's University of China (Beijing), Beijing Broadcasting Institute, Fudan University (Shanghai), and Jinan University (Guangzhou). The People's University and Fudan University began enrolling doctoral candidates in journalism in 1984 for the first time in the history of the People's Republic.[1] In addition, in 1984 China had 13 journalism colleges that taught more than 2,000 students by correspondence. These innovative colleges were run either by regular higher-learning institutions such as the People's University, or by major newspapers, such as the *Guangming Daily* in Beijing.

This chapter was written with the assistance of Qin Xinmin of the Xinhua News Agency, and is based in part on his 1986 M.A. thesis, "Journalism Education in the People's Republic of China," University of Missouri, Columbia.

In general, the journalism departments at the 27 universities were fashioned after the Chinese-literature departments. The majority of the faculty members are former teachers of Chinese literature, and the rest are former journalists with years of experience in the media. Most of the journalism departments have only a small faculty with a small number of students. They mainly offer print journalism courses because of limited equipment and funds.

University students are usually assigned jobs by the government upon graduation. This practice, modeled after the Soviet Union, has been criticized in recent years for discouraging competition and making students lazy. However, it does solve the problem of unemployment and gives such important media as the Xinhua News Agency and the *People's Daily* priority in selecting journalism graduates. Virtually all journalism students who have graduated in the past few years have been assigned to newspapers, radio and television stations, magazines, and Communist Party propaganda departments. The job opportunities provided by the media have by far outnumbered the graduates, and the media have been satisfied with the students' competence.

Between 25 May and 1 June 1983, the Communist Party Central Committee's Propaganda Department and the Ministry of Education jointly sponsored a conference on journalism education in Beijing. The conference, the first of its kind ever held in China, discussed serious problems in journalism education and worked out an ambitious but realistic plan for future development. A survey submitted to the conference found an acute contradiction between the supply of, and the demand for, journalism students. It found that journalism education had developed too slowly and was unable to provide enough competent reporters and editors in spite of the rapid increase in enrollment figures in recent years.[2]

In 1983 China's undergraduates in journalism made up only 0.12 percent of the total number of undergraduate students nationwide.[3] Most of the 27 universities that offered a journalism curriculum during that year found themselves short of competent faculty members, books, equipment, and funds. In 1983 China had only three hundred full-time journalism instructors. At the People's University, Fudan University, and Jinan University, three major institutions that train journalists and journalism researchers, the average age of the journalism instructors was over 50.[4]

Between 1949 and 1983, China graduated 5,200 journalism students. In spite of the acute shortage of well-educated journalists, only 3,000 of the students were assigned to work in the mass media. The rest were assigned to work elsewhere.[5] These numbers are ridiculously small compared to the country's total population of one billion and to its total number of mass media employees. A large number of those graduates could not find work in the mass media because they were not qualified politically, judged by Mao's ultraleftist standard, to work in these important posts.

Due to growth of the media and retirement of senior journalists, the conference predicted that China's print media, wire services, and broadcast networks would need some 90,000 graduates of journalism between 1983 and 2000. To ensure a rapid and healthy development of the media, in other words, the country each year needs more than 5,000 journalism students, a number similar to the total of journalism graduates in the 34 years between 1949 and 1983. This will require a drastic increase in the enrollment of journalism students. Before the date of the conference, the largest annual enrollment figure had been 453 in 1982, which is equivalent to only 9 percent of the annual need set up by the conference.[6]

China has 55 minority ethnic groups with a total population of 70 million. The culture and education of most of these minority groups has historically been backward. In 1983 China had 50 newspapers printed in 12 minority languages such as Mongolian, Tibetan, and Korean. But among the 1,300 editors and reporters of these newspapers, only a dozen had a journalism education.[7]

The conference therefore decided to establish the following objectives:

Increase the annual enrollment figure of journalism students from hundreds to at least 2,500 in the 1990s.

Expand the Journalism Department of the People's University of China into a journalism school and turn it into the national journalism education center.

Open journalism curricula at all universities with sufficient conditions.

Run journalism specialties and classes for minority ethnic groups and give priority to minority students in journalism enrollment.

Improve on-the-job training of media employees.

Encourage various kinds of adult education, such as night schools and correspondence colleges, and support people in self-education.[8]

Historical Background

In every society and nation, journalism education begins only after the press flourishes. Dr. Sun Yat-sen's 1911 Bourgeois Revolution, which overthrew the Manchu rulers of the Qing Dynasty and founded the Republic of China, made it possible for newspapers and periodicals to develop in both quantity and quality. The press began to play an increasingly important role politically and culturally, thus laying a foundation for university journalism education.

The Beijing University Journalism Society, China's first journalism research and education organization, was founded on 14 October 1918. The chairman of the society was Cai Yuanpei (Tsai Yuan-pei), a well-known scholar and president of Beijing University. Xu Baohuang (Hsu Pao-huang), a Chinese graduate of journalism from the University of Michigan, was elected vice chairman.[9] Xu and Shao Piaoping, another outstanding journalist, gave lectures to some 50 members of the society for more than a year. Based on their lecture notes, Xu and Shao also compiled China's first journalism textbooks: *An Outline of Journalism* and *Practical Journalism*.[10]

The society members were all teachers and students of Beijing University. Among them was Mao Zedong, the late chairman of the Chinese Communist Party, who attended the journalism lectures for half a year and received a certificate for it.[11] Throughout his life, Mao wrote and edited many news stories, commentaries, and editorials for the wire service and newspapers of the Communist Party.

In addition to classroom lectures, the journalism society also sponsored on-the-job training and visits to newsrooms. *Journalism Weekly,* a publication edited by the society members, became the first journalism research periodical in China and also the first Chinese publication printed from left to right instead of the traditional vertical style.

The journalism society ceased its activities in 1920 because Cai, Xu, and Shao all left the university and some of the student members graduated. But the society has been recognized both in China's mainland and in Taiwan as the first journalism research organization and the first undergraduate journalism curriculum in China.[12]

In the late 19th and early 20th centuries, aggression from Western powers and corruption of the Manchu rulers together turned China into a semifeudal, semicolonial society, strongly influenced by foreign countries in the areas of politics, economy, culture, and education. It was only natural that journalism education in China in its initial stage depended heavily on the Western countries, particularly the United States.

Beginning in the 1920s, journalism education began to draw more attention in China and journalism departments were set up at St. John's University in Shanghai (1920), Pingmin University in Beijing (1923), Yenching University in Beijing (1924), and Fudan University in Shanghai (1929).[13] The journalism department at Pingmin University was short-lived, but the other three became the pillars of journalism education in

China with important contributions to Chinese newspapers. More journalism departments were added later at Beijing University, Jinan University in Guangzhou, and the Central Political Institute in Nanjing.[14] All of these were located in cities controlled at the time by the Kuomintang government.

Many faculty members were American professors of journalism and Chinese graduates from such American institutions as the University of Missouri School of Journalism and Columbia University of New York. The late American journalist Edgar Snow, known for his coverage of the Communist-controlled areas in China in the 1930s and his contribution to the normalization of relations between the United States and the People's Republic of China, taught journalism at Yenching University for a short period of time when he first came to China in 1929. D. D. Patterson, chief editor of *Millard's Review* in Shanghai, became the director of the Journalism Department of St. John's University when it was established in 1920.[15]

Journalism education in China in its initial stage ran into tremendous difficulties. Yenching University, a missionary school set up by Americans in Beijing, was a typical example. For lack of competent faculty and a regular source of funding, this program failed to develop according to its plan and even closed down for a period. It was restored and expanded in 1929 with donations that the University of Missouri School of Journalism had solicited in the United States. The donations, received as operational funds for a five-year experiment, enabled Yenching's Journalism Department to employ new faculty members and buy new equipment. After the experiment was over in 1934, the university authorities decided to recognize the Journalism Department as a regular part of Yenching and give it regular funding. Meanwhile, various newspapers also offered support to Yenching so that it could train qualified journalists to meet their urgent needs.[16]

But the good days did not last long at Yenching. More difficulties came with the Japanese occupation in Beijing in 1937. The Yenching Journalism Department continued to train journalism students until the Pacific War broke out in 1940. It then moved to Chongqing in Sichuan Province in Southwest China, where Chiang Kai-shek had set up his wartime headquarters. It moved back to Beijing after World War II in 1945. But the Kuomintang government was so deeply involved in the subsequent civil war against the Communists that it had no time or money to take care of journalism education. It was the Communist takeover of the mainland that gave the Yenching Journalism Department new impetus for development.[17]

The first Chinese graduate school of journalism was opened in 1943 in Chongqing, wartime capital of the Kuomintang government. Jointly run by the Ministry of Information and Columbia University of New York, it enrolled students who had finished undergraduate courses of journalism at other universities. Modeled after the Columbia Graduate School of Journalism, it offered certificates of proficiency instead of master's degrees to students on completion of a one-year program.[18] Before the Communists overthrew the Kuomintang government and founded the People's Republic in 1949, China had never conferred a master's degree in journalism. The few people who did have such degrees had received them from foreign universities.[19]

The Chinese Communists knew the importance of the press even before the founding of the Communist Party in 1921. Many early Communists, such as Li Dazhao, Chen Duxiu, and Mao Zedong, were editors and regular contributors to democratic magazines that helped lay the foundation for the Party. Between 1921 and 1949, the Communists set up a large number of newspapers in the so-called "liberation areas" under their jurisdiction.

In spite of the difficulties caused by the Kuomintang and Japanese troops, the Communists managed to open several short-term journalism courses to train urgently needed reporters and editors. Among them were a journalism class at the Chinese Women's University in Yan'an, where the Communists had their headquarters during World War II, the Central China Journalism School, the Journalism Department of Zhongyuan University, and Southern Jiangsu Journalism School. In 1948 the Communists offered a journalism course in the suburbs of Beijing to a number of college students, who later became leading officials of newspapers, radio stations, and magazines, as well as propaganda departments of the Communist Party. Two months after the Communists took over Shanghai, they set up the East China Journalism School to train new journalists and to educate the employees of the Kuomintang-run newspapers in Communist ideology. A similar school was set up in Beijing under the leadership of the Press Bureau of the Central People's Government.[20]

The Communists did not start their own regular university curricula in journalism until they took over the entire mainland and the universities that Kuomintang could not take to Taiwan. In October 1949 there were 460 journalism students at seven universities and colleges in Shanghai, Beijing, Suzhou, and Guangzhou.[21] The first step of the new People's Republic of China in the field of education was to carry out an overall plan to restructure the existing universities by modeling them after those in the Soviet Union.[22] The hostility of the Truman administration towards Mao's government left China with no other choice but to turn to Stalin's Soviet Union.

Missionary universities set up by Americans and Europeans were either incorporated into other universities or given new names. According to the Soviet structure, colleges under universities were turned into departments or became separate colleges, each specializing in one branch of science. Under the reorganization, the Journalism Department of Yenching University was incorporated into the Chinese Literature Department of Beijing University and later into the Journalism Department of the new People's University of China in Beijing. The Journalism Department of St. John's University became part of the Journalism Department of Fudan University in Shanghai.[23]

Behind the plan was a deep distrust by the Communists of the intellectuals who had received a Western-style education. The changes were expected to cut off relations with the Western universities and make those intellectuals forget the past and accept the new Communist ideology. The distrust by the Communists also affected the 460 journalism students who did not go to Taiwan with the fleeing Kuomintang troops but waited for the Communists instead. An official of the Press Bureau of the Propaganda Department of the Communist Party Central Committee recalls:

> Quite a number of these students were progressive ideologically and supportive for revolution, and some even participated in underground revolutionary activities before liberation. But what they had received was mainly bourgeois journalism education, and their journalism departments had aimed at training editors and reporters to serve the exploiting classes. When we took over the universities, therefore, we took active measures to help them reform themselves.[24]

Among the measures he cites are Marxist-Leninist theories that were added to the curricula and veteran Communist journalists who came to lecture and to organize the students and faculty to participate in various political movements. The Communists then sent a number of senior editors to lead the journalism schools and departments or to join the faculty. Faculty members were urged to adapt the Soviet experience in journalism education to China's practical conditions and accumulate their own experiences. The newspapers welcomed journalism students as interns.

In 1954 the Marxism-Leninism College of the Communist Party Central Committee opened an advanced journalism course for chief editors, editors, and reporters of Party newspapers at the provincial level.[25] The Central Committee in July 1954 adopted a resolution to improve newspapers, demanding an increase in enrollment of journalism students. In accordance with the resolution, the then Ministry of Higher Education decided in 1955 to open a journalism department at the People's University of China in Beijing. The university, which offered only liberal arts programs, was set up in the early 1950s, when China was busy eliminating the influence of the United States and other Western countries from its universities and following the Soviet Union in an educational revolution.[26]

The faculty members of the new journalism department were mainly senior editors from the *People's Daily* and some provincial Party newspapers, who were transferred by the Propaganda Department of the Communist Party Central Committee. The first group of students was admitted in September 1955 to a four-year program. All were editors and reporters from the media in Beijing and some provincial capitals. They had passed the annual national entrance examination. In the years that followed, the department gradually reduced enrollment of media employees and increased that of high school graduates. The program was extended to five years in 1959.

In 1958 the journalism faculty of the Chinese Literature Department at Beijing University was incorporated into the Journalism Department of the People's University. Part of the incorporated faculty had come from Yenching University's Journalism Department, which, as mentioned earlier, had been set up with the help of the University of Missouri School of Journalism in the 1920s. Yenching's Journalism Department had been incorporated into Beijing University in 1952. So, in fact, the Journalism Department of the People's University has kinship with the University of Missouri. Among the current faculty members of the Journalism Department, seven are alumni of Yenching University.[27]

Because the new People's Republic needed time to recover from the civil war and the subsequent Korean War, journalism education did not develop rapidly until the latter half of the 1950s. In addition to the People's University of China, which had eight hundred journalism students and faculty members, journalism departments had been added to a number of universities in Hangzhou, Nanjing, Xi'an, and Guangzhou. The Beijing Broadcasting Institute was founded in 1959 to train reporters, editors, announcers, anchormen, and cameramen for the country's rapidly growing radio and television networks. The All-China Journalists Association also set up a journalism school to improve the skills of its members.[28]

As previously mentioned, before 1949 all journalism departments in

China were modeled after American journalism schools. In the missionary universities such as Yenching and St. John's, many courses were taught in English so that students could work both in Chinese and English. American journalism concepts and practices were taught. After the People's Republic was founded, China took the Soviet Union as a model in virtually every field. Journalism education was no exception. The journalism departments, old and new alike, began learning the Soviet Union's journalistic principles and practices.

China neglected education at the graduate level, particularly in the social sciences, for almost three decades. For one thing, the country had no financial resources or personnel to develop graduate education. With the nationwide illiteracy rate as high as 80 percent in 1949, priority had to be given to primary education. Furthermore, many Communist leaders, without a college education themselves, believed graduate education to be too theoretical and too far removed from the nation's practical needs.[29] Between 1949 and 1978, China offered graduate journalism courses to only two students at Fudan University in Shanghai. These students finished their studies in 1965 with no degree. China did not have an academic degree system until 1979.[30]

China's journalism education came to a halt during the 1966–76 Cultural Revolution, as did the education system as a whole. Classrooms were closed and enrollment stopped. Students and faculty members were told to "make revolution" on and off campus, and later were sent to work in rural areas. Some universities closed down journalism departments. After the death of Mao and the subsequent arrest of his widow, Jiang Qing, in 1976—particularly after Deng Xiaoping consolidated his power in 1978—China's journalism education embarked on a road of development at an unprecedented speed.

Development since 1978

After 1978 journalism education in China underwent profound changes. Both the nature of journalism education itself, as well as the relationship between the general media and the schools, developed in ways that have led to a most favorable system today for growth and achievement.

The Third Plenary Session of the CPC

The year 1978 is a milestone in contemporary Chinese history. The Third Plenary Session of the Eleventh Central Committee of the Communist Party held in December of that year ended an old era and ushered in a new one. Discussion of any development in China over the past few years cannot be conducted without mentioning this session.

People outside China usually believe the nation's current economic reform and open-door policy started in 1976 with the death of Mao Zedong and the subsequent arrest of his widow Jiang Qing and other radical leaders. That belief is incorrect. During the two years of 1976-78, Mao's personally selected successor, Hua Guofeng, carried out Mao's ultraleftist policies in every field of work, refusing any policy changes and suggestions for reform. He declared, "We firmly uphold whatever policy decisions Chairman Mao made, and we unswervingly adhere to whatever instructions Chairman Mao gave."[31] His loyalty to Mao was thus known as "two-whatever policy" and some China experts in the West called Hua and his followers "whateverists."

It was a crucial moment for China. Without abandoning Mao's dogmatic, ultraleftist policies, the nation could never rid itself of endless political chaos or become powerful and prosperous. Deng Xiaoping, who had been driven out of power twice during the Cultural Revolution, managed to come back at the Party plenary session. Supported by the majority of the Communist Party members and ordinary citizens, he not only successfully consolidated his power and reduced that of Hua's, but also led the Central Committee in adopting a series of measures that ran counter to Mao's ultraleftist policies. Without openly criticizing Mao for fear of unfavorable reaction in China and abroad, the Central Committee started a systematic and comprehensive correction of Mao's policies, which had brought tremendous suffering to the nation.[32]

Industrial production increased rapidly, farmers yielded bumper harvests for several years running, the armed forces became stronger, and the people's livelihood improved greatly. China opened its doors to the outside world. An all-round reform started in virtually every field of work.[33] China's educational system, which had been severely damaged during the Cultural Revolution, also benefited by Deng's reform. When Deng first regained power in 1977, he volunteered to take charge of education, regarding it as a key to national development. He said at a forum on science and education in August 1977: "What should our country do first in order to catch up with the advanced nations in the world? I believe we should start with science and education.[34]

Graduate Programs

The People's Republic of China started graduate education in 1950 with priority given to science and engineering. This was understandable,

because the country needed scientists and technicians in national reconstruction. Thus, in the 1950s, only a small number of graduate students
were enrolled to study the liberal arts, mainly political science. Before
1979 the People's Republic did not have an academic degree system,
regarding this as part of bourgeois education, and, as mentioned earlier,
China enrolled only two graduate students in journalism between 1949
and 1978. But in October 1977, with Deng's impetus for reform, the
Chinese government decided to resume a graduate education system. It
was too late to take in new students that year, because China's only
enrollment is in the fall semester. In the following year, a total of 10,708
graduate students were enrolled nationwide, a 600 percent increase over
the 1965 enrollment.[35]

Meanwhile, the Xinhua News Agency and the *People's Daily* both
felt an urgent need for high-level reporters and editors, and explored the
possibility of journalism education at the graduate level. But they found
that the existing journalism departments at a few universities were far
from able to train the large number of reporters and editors that were
needed.

Hu Qiaomu, then president of the Chinese Social Science Academy
and now a member of the powerful Political Bureau of the Party Central
Committee, suggested that a journalism institute be added to his academy and a journalism department opened in the academy's new graduate
school.[36] The journalism department would be jointly run by the
journalism institute, Xinhua, and the *People's Daily*.

The department, located in the headquarters of the *People's Daily*
in the east suburbs of Beijing, took in 85 students in the fall of 1978. The
People's University of China in Beijing and Fudan University in
Shanghai admitted 12 graduate students of journalism at the same
time.[37]

In 1978–83 China enrolled 377 graduate students of journalism, 80
percent of whom entered the Graduate School of the Chinese Academy
of Social Sciences.[38] Table 9.1 shows how the Graduate School of the
Chinese Academy of Social Science is the major force in graduate education in journalism. It is also the first graduate school in the People's
Republic combining education, research, and application. Its journalism
department in many ways is modeled after American graduate schools of
journalism.

The traditional Chinese way of graduate education, which is still
practiced in most university journalism departments, requires one professor to teach three to five students individually. Some conservative
educators claim that this method guarantees the quality of education. If
a professor teaches too many students, they argue, he will be distracted.

TABLE 9.1. Enrollment of Graduate Students in Five Schools of Journalism

Year	Chinese Acad. of Social Science	People's Univ. of China	Fudan Univ.	Beijing Broadcast Institute	Xiamen Univ.	Total
1978	85	8	4	0	0	97
1979	77	6	5	2	0	90
1980	29	0	0	5	0	34
1981	32	2	5	5	0	44
1982	25	5	8	2	0	40
1983	56	9	1	3	3	72
Total	304	30	23	17	3	377
%	80.8	7.8	6.1	4.5	0.8	100

When the Graduate School of the Chinese Academy of Social Science was set up, those educators expressed doubt concerning its feasibility, arguing that it did not conform to the Chinese national conditions. Some classes at the graduate school have as many as 20 students each. But the years have shown that the graduate school has greatly promoted China's journalism education at the graduate level in both quantity and quality.

The school's journalism department has established its principles of education as follows:

1. Guarantee an all-round development of students in morality, intelligence, and health. This is a slogan put forward by Mao in the 1960s, meaning that students should be loyal to the Communist Party's leadership, show excellent academic performance, and enjoy good health.

2. Create a positive academic environment in which students are free to explore, in the spirit of academic democracy, previously "forbidden" areas. This is important because many older-generation journalists and educators were criticized in the antirightist struggle and Cultural Revolution for such ideas as reader interest, news value, and journalism free from politics. The department, however, also requires students to support the "four basic principles," namely, Communist leadership, proletarian dictatorship, socialist policy, and Marxism-Leninism-Mao Zedong thought. To what extent students are given academic freedom is decided by the authorities.

3. Place emphasis on studies of basic journalist theory and encourage students to develop their abilities to report, edit, and research individually.

4. Invite veteran journalists to be part-time instructors.

5. Teach each student individually according to his or her talent and interest.

6. Pay close attention to ideological and political work, and have a strict examination and management system. [39]

Candidates for the three-year journalism program of the graduate school must have a bachelor's degree and at least two years of work experience in the mass media or in journalism education. Competition for admission has been so fierce that very often only one out of three candidates is admitted. Applicants take the annual nationwide entrance examinations for graduate students with exam papers provided by a special committee composed of editors and researchers from Xinhua, the *People's Daily,* and the Journalism Institute of the Social Science Academy. At the end of the three-year program, students who pass strict written examinations and an oral defense of their theses are given master's degrees. [40]

The sequences of the Journalism department have varied from year to year, based on the requirements from Xinhua, the *People's Daily,* and the Journalism Institute. So far nine sequences have been opened: history of world journalism, history of Chinese journalism, history of the Chinese Communist press, news reporting in Chinese, newswriting in English, news reporting in English, international news reporting, radio and television, and theory of journalism.[41]

The journalism department has a full-time faculty of 38 people including instructors, political workers, and management personnel. Because the department has only a few full-time instructors, it has so far invited as part-time instructors more than 100 senior editors and researchers from Xinhua, the *People's Daily,* and the Journalism Institute.[42] Some of its courses have been taught by professors from foreign countries, mainly the United States. Among them are James Aronson from Hunter College of the City University of New York, Lawrence Pinkham from the University of Massachusetts at Amherst, Jerry Werthimer from San Francisco State University, and Rod Holmgren from Monterey Peninsula College in California.[43] The department has also invited foreign journalism instructors and researchers to give short-term lectures and speeches. Among those are the chairman of the British Royal Society of Journalism, a senior researcher from the Journalism Institute of Tokyo University, the dean of the University of Missouri School of Journalism, and an associate dean of the Stanford University School of Journalism.

In the first three semesters, students take required and optional courses with enough credit hours. The fourth semester is devoted to on-the-job training in the mass media such as Xinhua, the China News Service, the *People's Daily, China Daily, Beijing Daily,* and other national newspapers. Students are required to complete a thesis in their last two semesters. Each semester lasts 4½ months, with a month-long winter vacation and a two-month summer vacation. There is no summer school.

Although the students who have graduated from the department have been generally praised for their competence in the various mass media, there is criticism that the students actually waste time by spending their third academic year writing theses. The *People's Daily* is planning to cut their own students' program to two years and let them finish their theses after they are on the job.

A look at the courses offered by the courses offered by the journalism department may help one further understand the importance of politics in journalism education in China. The primary-required course has been political science with works by Karl Marx, Lenin, and Mao

Zedong as the textbooks. Students are required to read the Chinese-language editions of *On Capital, State and Revolution,* and *On the Correct Handling of the Contradictions among the People.* The texts also include new documents of the Communist Party Central Committee and speeches by current Chinese leaders such as Deng Xiaoping, Chen Yun, and Hu Yaobang.

Foreign journalism professors invited to lecture at the department and many Chinese instructors have expressed skepticism about the necessity of studying Marxist works throughout the three semesters. Even a *People's Daily* commentator has argued that the century-old Marxist theory may not be able to solve the current problems China faces today, so why should the students spend so many hours on those Marxist classics? But the Marxist theory is here to stay in the curriculum, and the authorities believe it guarantees a firm political orientation of the students.[44]

Another course required for all students is a foreign language. In most classes English is taught, but the students may choose Japanese or Russian instead. Foreign-language instructors are invited from the Xinhua News Agency, Beijing Number 1 Foreign Languages Institute, and some English-speaking countries.

Other required courses differ from sequence to sequence. Among them are basic journalism theory, history of the Chinese Communist press, history of Chinese press, history of foreign press, news reporting and writing, editing, commentary writing, studies of major Chinese and foreign newspapers, broadcasting, newswriting in English, feature writing in English, and editing of English-language newspapers. Some of these courses may be required in one sequence and optional in another.[45]

Optional courses include studies of famous Chinese and foreign journalists, Chinese and foreign bourgeois journalism theories, sociology, psychology, and classic Chinese language. Optional courses, in general, started in China only a few years ago when the credit-hour system was tried. Many faculty members and students at the journalism department have suggested more optional courses and fewer required ones.

Some of the courses are undergraduate-level courses that are not offered in undergraduate programs at many universities. With the gradual improvement and perfecting of journalism curricula at these universities, such courses will be dropped at the Journalism Department of the Graduate School of the Social Science Academy.[46]

Between 1981 and 1983, three groups of 218 graduate students of journalism completed their studies and began working in the mass media, university journalism departments, and research institutes. Among them 176, or 80.7 percent, were granted master's degrees. One-third of the graduates were given jobs as journalism instructors, researchers, and others, while two-thirds worked in the mass media as reporters and editors (Table 9.2).[47]

As Xinhua and the *People's Daily* provide faculty members, houses, equipment, books, and funds for the Journalism Department of the Graduate School of the Social Science Academy, most graduates of the department have been assigned to work in these two media organizations. At the journalism-education conference in Beijing in the summer of 1983, officials from both Xinhua and the *People's Daily* expressed satisfaction with the quality of the graduates from the journalism department, and promised continued support for running the department.[48]

A small portion of the graduates have been assigned to the Journalism Institute of the Social Science Academy to work as researchers in journalism. Over the years, these newcomers have added young blood to the institute, where researchers used to have an average age of over 50. A few students have been assigned jobs in the Press Bureau of the Party Central Committee's Propaganda Department. To provide better supervision of journalism education nationwide, the Press Bureau also needs staff members with professional knowledge in journalism.

According to a survey, the mass media and journalism education institutions in China will need 3,300 people with a journalism education at the graduate level between 1983 and 2000.[49] Obviously the current system of graduate journalism education will have to be expanded if that need is to be met. But because competition for graduate education in journalism has been fierce over the years, only those who show outstanding performance in strict entrance examinations, written and oral, can be admitted. Even after they are enrolled, some may still have to drop out when they fail to pass examinations or complete the required number of credit hours.

The following is a list of some graduation theses by students who graduated in 1982 from the Journalism Department of the Graduate School of the Social Science Academy. The themes, selected by the students themselves, indicate the broad range of interest that exists.

Relations between the United States mass media and government.
Sino-American relations and related policies in news reporting.
Reform of the current international news flow.
Japanese-Soviet relations in recent years and related reports in the *People's Daily*.

TABLE 9.2. Jobs of Graduate Students from Four Schools of Journalism

Jobs	Chinese Acad. of Social Science	People's Univ. of China	Fudan Univ.	Beijing Broadcast Institute	Total	%
Media	139	2	2	1	144	66
Education	11	10	5	5	31	14
Research	24	0	0	0	24	11
Other	16	2	1	0	19	9
Total	190	14	8	6	218	100

Relations between the United States mass media and intelligence services.

Ethics of Socialist journalism.

Editorial policy of the French newspaper *Le Monde*.

Media law and press freedom in Japan.

Freedom of the press in the United States.

Control over television by the United States ruling class.

Language of international news reporting.

Relations between international reporting and propaganda.

Syrian newspapers in the October war.

Characters and functions of China's sports coverage.

Nonevent news in overseas reporting in English.

Linguistics of newswriting in English.

Angles of overseas economic reporting in English.

Analysis of feature writing in English by American correspondents in Beijing.

English-language newspapers run by British and Americans in pre-liberation China.

Unexpected events and their coverage in English.[50]

China places emphasis on practice instead of theory in graduate journalism education. Theoretical research in journalism and mass communication is still in its initial stage of development. The nation's urgent need for qualified reporters and editors has caused the graduate school and university journalism departments to give priority to the training of journalists.

Only the People's University of China and Fudan University have started to enroll doctoral students in journalism. Doctoral programs in journalism in China, as in other countries, mainly train senior researchers and educators. Many people in China, particularly those in the media, still believe that journalism does not need doctoral programs. But with the rapid development of the mass media, China needs not only practical journalists but also researchers in journalism and mass communication.

Double Bachelor's Degree Programs

For many years, journalism education in China concentrated largely on the print media, because television and local radio stations were not popular until a few years ago. Furthermore, newswriting was the least expensive journalism course, requiring only writing pads and pens. With the rapid growth of broadcast media, the situation has changed over the years. Since the 1983 conference, which called for new courses of journalism education, some university journalism departments have added courses in radio, television, photography, media management, international news reporting, and advertising.[51]

Although the Chinese language boasts the largest number of speakers in the world and is one of the five working languages of the United Nations, its usage is confined to China and scattered Chinese communities overseas. To enable the Chinese to know more about the outside world and to enable the people abroad to know more about China, the mass media in this nation have resorted to foreign languages, particularly English. The Chinese media, though less advanced than those in Western countries, have one of the world's largest overseas reporting services. The Xinhua News Agency, with branch offices in more than 80 foreign countries, sends out news items in Chinese, English, French, Spanish, Russian, and Arabic every day.[52] Radio Beijing has become the third largest shortwave station (following Radio Moscow and the Voice of America), with daily broadcasts in more than 30 languages.

With the current open-door policy and increase in foreign trade and exchange, the Chinese government has decided to expand its overseas reporting services, which also includes the English-language *China Daily, China Reconstructs, Beijing Review,* and several other magazines.[53] Yet the nation's foreign-language journalism education is far from enough to cope with this demand.

Before 1983 the Newswriting in English Faculty of the Journalism Department of the Graduate School of Social Science Academy offered China's only journalism class in English. To meet the shortage of bilingual journalists, faculties of international journalism have been added to Beijing University, Fudan University in Shanghai, Jinan University in Guangzhou, Beijing Broadcasting Institute, Beijing Foreign Languages Institute, and Shanghai Foreign Languages Institute.[54] Students selected are graduates of other departments and are granted a second bachelor's degree. Upon graduation they are assigned jobs by the Xinhua News Agency and other mass media with overseas services.

This so-called "double bachelor's degree system" has been used for several years. It has become so popular that the Education Commission has decided to increase enrollment in this program. Those who have two bachelor's degree are given salaries equal to those who have master's degrees. Even for the domestic Chinese-language newspapers, the double-degree system has proved useful. Students majoring in natural science, engineering, medicine, art, and sports can now also pursue a journalism program and thus become specialized reporters and writers. Most reporters now are qualified only for general beats. They know something about everything but are experts in nothing. It is difficult, if not impossible, for a reporter to write about a scientific discovery that he himself does not understand.

Undergraduate program

While the Graduate School of the Social Science Academy boasts 80 percent of China's enrollment of graduate students in journalism, university journalism departments emphasize undergraduate education. The largest journalism programs are offered at the People's University of China, Beijing Broadcasting Institute, and Fudan University.

The Journalism Department of the People's University is considered the best in terms of faculty, teaching experience, books, and access to the national media for training students on the job. The national conference on journalism education in Beijing in 1983 decided to expand that department into a school of journalism and national center for undergraduate journalism education.[55] But this goal has not been realized yet, for lack of faculty members, housing, equipment, and operational funds.

So far the People's University has graduated more than 2,400 students of journalism, who are scattered in newspapers, radio stations, and television networks throughout the country. Some of them are editors in chief and senior editors now. Between its establishment in 1955 and the beginning of the Cultural Revolution in 1966, the department admitted 1,160 students from all parts of China and another 18 from the Soviet Union, North Korea, Vietnam, and Mongolia. It also offered training during the same period to 221 reporters and editors from country newspapers.[56]

During the Cultural Revolution, the People's University suffered more damage than most other Universities. Beijing University, where some faculty members put up the country's first "Marxist-Leninist big character poster" (in Mao's words), was favored more than the People's University by Mao and his wife, Jiang Qing. When most other Universities were still closed in 1970, Beijing University started to enroll students from among workers, peasants, and soldiers. One year later a journalism faculty was set up in the Chinese Literature Department of Beijing University, taking in all faculty members from the Journalism Department of the People's University. Between 1970 and 1976 Beijing University enrolled 304 students in its three-year journalism program and took in another 136 media employees for one-year advanced studies.[57]

When the People's University was reopened in the fall of 1978, its journalism department began enrolling undergraduates for a four-year program and graduates for three-year studies. The department now has 389 regular undergraduates, 39 candidates for master's degrees, and 5 doctoral candidates. In addition the department is teaching another 903 students through correspondence; the students are scattered in the cities of Beijing, Tianjin, and Xi'an, Shandong Province, and the remote Xinjiang region.

The department now has 51 teachers with 18 librarians, technicians, and administrative officials. Its two specialties, print journalism and broadcasting, have seven teaching-researching sections of journalism theory, press history, news reporting, editing and commentary, basic writing skills, broadcasting, and photography. There are also two laboratories of broadcasting and photography.[58]

The educational objective of the department is to train qualified reporters and editors for the mass media with an all-round development in politics, general knowledge, and health. With regard to politics, students are required to study the basic theory of Marxism, support the Communist Party, love socialism, possess patriotism and internationalism, abide by the law, and be willing to serve the people and national development. In addition, students should have the basic knowledge and skills of journalism, understand the history of the Chinese press, know the general situation of the foreign mass media, show a high literary level and ability to investigate, and be able to read foreign-language newspapers and other publications. They should also enjoy good health and be able to prepare themselves for a difficult, challenging journalism career.

Required courses for regular undergraduates of four years include 5 courses in political science history of the Chinese Communist Party, philosophy, political economy, scientific socialism, and current political situation; 11 courses in basic knowledge—classic Chinese language, modern Chinese language, classic Chinese literature, modern Chinese literature, foreign literature, logic, Chinese history, modern world history, contemporary world history, foreign language, and physical training; and 10 courses in journalism—journalism review, journalism theory, basic writing skills, news reporting, newswriting, newspaper editing, newspaper commentary writing, history of the Chinese press, foreign press, and black-and-white news photography. Optional courses for regular undergraduates of four years include literature review, fine arts review, policy and propaganda, journalism seminar, press history seminar, famous Chinese and foreign correspondents, radio and television, advertising, color photography, law seminar, and newswriting in English.

For correspondence students of three years, the following courses are offered: philosophy, political economy, logic, Chinese history, classic Chinese, modern Chinese, readings of Chinese literature (classic, modern, and contemporary), literature review, journalism theory, history of the Chinese press, news reporting, newswriting, and editing.

The People's University rules that optional courses should make up 15–20 percent of the total number of courses. Graduation requires a total of 157 credit hours.

Compared to American students, Chinese students have fewer choices in selecting courses. Chinese universities began offering optional courses and exercising a credit-hour system only a few years ago. The traditional oriental way of education, still found in some universities in China, gives instructors the right to decide courses and students the duty to take whatever is offered them.

Like other universities, the People's University emphasizes practical journalistic skills in undergraduate journalism education. Its general principle is to train students to be active in reporting and skillful in writing. Students take writing classes throughout their four years in the department. Freshmen study basic writing skills in classes similar to composition classes but closer to newswriting. The main purpose of these classes is to teach students how to describe and comment. Sophomores and juniors take newswriting courses. Seniors study commentary writing and complete their graduation theses for bachelor's degrees. They may also choose newswriting in English as an optional course.

Unlike graduate students who choose their master's-degree theses and doctoral dissertations themselves, undergraduates are often assigned topics by their instructors. The following is part of a list of bachelor's-degree thesis topics suggested to students enrolled in 1978 by the faculty of the Journalism Department of the People's University. It shows that undergraduates also have a broad range of interests.

> The art of newspaper criticism.
> Journalists as professional investigators and researchers.
> Readers' interest.
> Readers' psychology.
> News value and readers' psychology.
> The "Social Responsibility Theory" of bourgeois journalism.
> Forecast of broadcast programs and listener's psychology.
> Social news and morality.

Professional ethics of the socialist journalists.
Role of economic news in promoting national development.
An analysis of the causes of pseudonews.
One-sidedness in news reporting.
How mass communication promotes the progress of humanity.
Freedom of the press in the West.
American columnist Walter Lippmann.
Early newspapers in China.
Printing houses in the late Ming dynasty and *Jiang Bao* (*Capital Gazette*).
News pages of the *New York Times*.
Pagination of the *New York Times*.
Causes of the development of Japanese journalism.
Propaganda by *Pravda* on a specific issue.
News story leads.
The book *Red Star Over China*.
The book *Ten Days that Shook the World*.
Application of the classic poems in newswriting.
Social functions of news photography.

To get practical training, students help run the university's four-page tabloid that is published twice a month. The Journalism Student Union also offers a newsletter. These facilities, though, are shabby compared to journalism school and departments in the United States. The State Commission of Education has approved the department's request to publish a regular newspaper entitled *College Students,* which will be sold nationwide. Preparation is under way, but the major problem is financial. In this respect, broadcasting majors are better off than students of print journalism. In the fall semester of 1985 the department enrolled one hundred broadcasting students for the national television network and the Xinhua News Agency. These students have access to video recording facilities and closed-circuit television and are able to produce their own television news.

Students taking news reporting courses are sent to cover events in Beijing as their homework. Throughout their sixth semester they go to provincial and municipal newspapers for on-the-job training, and their instructors go with them. With help from veteran reporters and editors of the newspapers and from their instructors, students spend two-thirds of their time on reporting and writing and one-third on editing. During their four years in the department, students also must spend nine weeks doing manual work in factories or farms and in military training.

Another major institution offering undergraduate journalism programs is Beijing Broadcasting Institute, which was founded in 1959. It exists under the dual leadership of the Ministry of Radio, Television, and Film, and the Beijing municipal government. The institute is one of the few Chinese higher-education organizations that combine liberal arts and engineering. Its purpose is to train reporters, editors, radio announcers, television anchormen, directors, engineers, and technicians.

Since its founding, the institute has graduated nearly 4,000 students, who are now working in radio and television networks nationwide. Currently it has more than 1,000 undergraduates, and it employees total 700, including 280 full-time teachers. The institute has the following eight departments:

Journalism Department, which trains students to work as reporters and editors for the electronic media.

Art Editing Department, which prepares students to be art reporters and editors for radio and television stations.

Anchoring Department, which produces radio announcers and television anchormen who speak the standard Mandarin dialect.

Television Department, divided into three specialties to train television news reporters, television news program editors, and directors of television plays.

Foreign Languages Department, which provides teachers and translators for the broadcasting system and other departments.

Electronic Engineering Department, which teaches students to be engineers and technicians for the radio and television transmitting networks.

Television Broadcasting Engineering Department, which trains specialists for television broadcasting nationwide.

Microwave Engineering Department, which produces experts in microwave transmission of radio and television programs.[59]

Of all higher-learning institutions that offer journalism courses, the Beijing Broadcasting Institute is the best equipped. Its radio announcing room, television anchoring room, broadcast program production center, and laboratories have computers, FM transmitters, television transmitters, closed-circuit television systems, and audiovisual teaching facilities. Its library has more than three hundred thousand books and six hundred magazines.[60]

Media Cooperation

Obviously, the task to train enough qualified journalists for the country's rapidly growing mass media is a difficult one—a great gap exists between demand and supply. The efforts of journalism departments and schools alone are far from enough. China's policy of journalism education can be said to be "walking on two legs." One leg is regular education by journalism schools and departments at the college level. The other leg consists of part-time classes, night schools, correspondence courses, television and radio colleges, self education, and on-the-job training.[61]

Tremendous efforts have been made by the various mass media in China to develop journalism education through noncollege channels. The media urgently need journalism students, and they have the means to train students. A review of the measures taken by the Xinhua News Agency over the past ten years may help explain this situation.

On 29 January, 1983 Xinhua submitted a report to the Communist Party Central committee suggesting that Xinhua improve its work to become an advanced world wire service with "Chinese characteristics." Xinhua's ambition is to join the ranks of AP, UPI, Reuters, and AFP in the 1990s. Party General Secretary Hu Yaobang and the Committee immediately gave the proposal the go-ahead.[62]

By the term "advanced," Xinhua means the following:

The ability to provide timely and full reports of major events in China and worldwide.

A worldwide news-gathering system including reporters and information sources.

A worldwide communication network equipped with modern technology.

A number of well-known reporters, editors, and commentators, as well as qualified technicians and management personnel.

By the term "Chinese characteristics," Xinhua means:

Guidance of Marxism-Leninism Mao Zedong thought, support for the leadership of the Communist Party, and a unified channel through which the government can distribute major information.

Continued efforts to serve the people and regard them as the main object of news reporting.

Continued authenticity and objectivity of its news coverage and responsibility to its Chinese and overseas readers.

Being authoritative in reporting news in China, unique in opinions on international events, and reliable in coverage of the Third World.

Continued efforts to provide the Communist Party Central Committee with accurate and reliable investigative reports on Chinese and overseas events.[63]

What is the most important factor that decides the success or failure of Xinhua's strategic plan? Some people argue that it is the lack of up-to-date equipment and facilities. But this is not true: Xinhua photographers are now equipped with the most advanced and sophisticated Japanese cameras, even better than many foreign correspondents in Beijing. Yet Xinhua still lags behind its foreign counterparts such as AP, UPI, and Reuters in terms of quality and quantity of news photography. The key lies, instead, in the education of personnel.

Xinhua now has more than five thousand employees, but still finds itself short of competent editors and reporters, particularly foreign correspondents, to help achieve its ambitious goal of becoming a world news agency. In addition to the Graduate School of the Social Science Academy and Fudan University, which now train bilingual journalists for Xinhua, the news service has decided to sponsor its own journalism education programs.

As the first step, Xinhua in 1984 turned its training center into a college-level school of journalism which, once it is recognized by the State Commission of Education, will begin offering undergraduate courses with bachelor's degrees. The school now is offering a two-year training program, mainly to editors and reporters from Xinhua's general headquarters in Beijing and branch offices nationwide. Courses include writing, reporting, editing, creative news writing, basic journalism theory, general Chinese history, modern Chinese history, history of Chinese and foreign newspapers, political economy, philosophy, logic, English, classic Chinese, European and American literature, Russian literature, and contemporary Chinese literature.

The school also plans to have graduate programs and confer master's degrees in journalism, but what the school needs most now is a large number of competent faculty members. Currently Xinhua sends young middle-aged reporters, editors, and translators to the Journalism Class at the Central Communist Party School in Beijing.[64]

The *People's Daily* over the past decade has also paid close attention to the education of its personnel. The paper's former director, Hu Jiwei, has specified the four principal areas of such education: Marxist theory and understanding of the Communist Party's policies; basic knowledge of science, law, economy, education, and art; professional knowledge, including reporting, writing, and editing; and professional ethics.[65]

The *People's Daily* has spent a huge sum of money on the Journalism Department of the Graduate School of Social Science Academy, which is located inside its headquarters in Beijing. The Communist Party organ has decided to continue investment in the department, instead of running its own school of journalism as Xinhua plans to do. But the *People's Daily* also has a plan to rotate its editors and reporters in a graduate-level journalism class. The first of these classes began in 1983. Candidates under the age of 40 must have a college education and at least five years of experience in the media. They must pass a strict examination to be admitted to the two-year program. During the two years, they receive full pay while attending school.[66]

The *People's Daily* decided in this way to upgrade the education of its journalists under the age of 50 to the graduate level within five years. This graduate class is different from the previous classes run by the *People's Daily* in many ways. It is the longest class, a two-year program. Other classes ranging from two to six months were too short to achieve very remarkable results. In addition the newspaper leaders have decided within the next few years to compile a complete set of textbooks for the class so that students will have a systematic education. The texts are being written by veteran editors of the paper and faculty members of some universities.[67]

The class also differs from previous classes in that the students are given opportunities to practice. The paper originally intended to let the students edit letters from readers into a tabloid. The *People's Daily* each day receives about two thousand letters from its readers nationwide, providing rich sources for investigative reports and in-depth stories. However, this plan did not materialize because of the confidential nature of most letters. But the chief editors' second plan, to run an overseas edition of the *People's Daily,* was realized. Many of the stories in the eight-page full-size paper are written by the students of the rotating class. The overseas edition has been a success since it began publication in July 1985.

Finally, the new class does not require students to study a foreign language, unlike most other such classes. As most students will not be able to use foreign languages, they concentrate their energy in these two years on journalistic theory and practice. The current nationwide craze for foreign languages, mainly English, may turn out to be a waste of time for most learners who seldom, if ever, use a foreign language.

There are some other avenues of journalistic education not yet mentioned in this chapter. The All-China Journalists Association, for instance, has also founded a school of journalism with a three-year program for media employees in Beijing.[68] China also encourages self-education in journalism. *China Daily* and some other national media have hired a large number of reporters, editors, and translators through written and oral examinations. Many of them have not had a regular university journalism education, but have taught themselves journalism.

Conclusion

In China both Communist Party leaders and ordinary citizens like to use the phrase "Chinese characteristics" in discussing everything. Modernization of the country should have Chinese character. So should democracy and freedom. The list goes on and on to include the space industry, television programs, sports items, music, and even fast food.

What, then, are the Chinese characteristics of journalism education in China?

First of all, journalism education in China serves politics.

China, however, different from the Soviet Union, is after all a socialist country, or rather, a Communist country as Americans and other people in the West call it. China is one of the few countries openly declaring that the media should work according to government principles and act as propaganda tools of the ruling party. The authorities regard the mass media as important to consolidate their leadership, while success of failure of the media in the future largely depends on what kind of journalists the universities produce.

The policies of the Communist Party and the government have a strong influence upon the practices of the media and therefore upon journalism education. While it may be true that government policies have a bearing on the media in virtually every nation, this is particularly obvious in China in ways quite different from those in other countries.

Unlike the Soviet Union, China does not have systematic press censorship. Chinese reporters, editors, and media officials exercise voluntary self-censorship. Experienced reporters and editors know clearly what to do and what not to do in order to achieve the Communist Party's goals. Whether to publish a story or not and when to publish it requires a high level of political consciousness, mastery of the Marxist theory, and understanding of the policies of the Communist Party and government. To import such knowledge to students is a challenging, important task for journalism education in China.

Hu Yaobang's *On Our Party's Journalist Work* has become required reading for every Chinese journalist, journalism student, and faculty member. In a talk at a meeting of the Party Central Committee Secretariat, Hu Yaobang, who worked for a long time as a Party propagandist during World War II, explained clearly some important Communist principles in the mass media. These principles are also important to journalism education. Hu began in this manner:

> What is the nature of our Party's journalist work, after all? . . . Speaking of its most fundamental nature, the Party's journalist work is the Party's organ. This idea has solid ground and should never be suspected.[69]

Second, the purpose of journalism education in China is quite different from that in Western countries.

The American press is, at least in theory, a watchdog keeping an eye on the government through an adversarial role. Journalism education in the United States therefore encourages students to analyze the workings of government and government officials. They are taught to examine what the government does in relation to what it is expected to do under the United States Constitution.

Chinese media, however, are propaganda tools and a bridge between the government and the people, reporting complaints and criticisms from the citizens and explaining policies of the authorities. The media are government departments, owned and controlled by the Party. Journalism education in China trains students in Communism, patriotism, and collectivism. They are taught to be loyal to the Communist Party and to the government.

In his book *On Our Party's Journalist Work,* Hu says:

> The fundamental interest of our people is uniform, and the political orientation and basic policies of the Party Central Committee and the State Council represent the interest of the people. It is inevitable and natural for the masses to speak in one voice about these fundamental issues, while it is unnatural to make a "different" sound toward them.[70]

While many Americans believe the media in their country report too much "bad news," many Chinese think their media report too much "good news." What is the best proportion for journalists and journalism educators? Hu Yaobang has a ready answer:

> In our newspapers, about 80 percent of the space should be devoted to achievements, the positive side, and commendations, while 20 percent to shortcomings, the negative side, and criticisms.[71]

Third, Chinese and Western journalism educators have different views on news value.

China calls itself a developing, as well as a socialist, country. The prevailing Chinese views on news value are close to those shared by other socialist countries such as the Soviet Union and by other developing nations. While the privately owned media in the United States compete for such sensational news items as murder, rape, and robberies, the Chinese media seldom report such stories except for a few carefully selected ones that serve to educate the people and warn the would-be criminals. Most stories found in the Chinese media are "good news" items, such as construction of new factories, overfulfilled farm production quotas, and improvement in people's livelihood.

One of the generally agreed upon factors in deciding news value is timeliness. With some reservation, Chinese journalists and educators believe that news should be timely. Hu's idea is that

> journalist work should seek timeliness, but not unconditionally in all issues. . . . Our Party's prestige often suffers from hasty, premature reports of major news and events without necessary approval from the higher authorities. . . . Timeliness is not hastiness, and timeliness of major news is subsidiary to political tasks.[72]

The Chinese mass media are never willing to publish any news items that might embarrass the Communist Party and government. In the past few years, conflicts between Chinese and African students have frequently occurred at universities in Beijing, Shanghai, and Tianjin. Each time it was the foreign correspondents in China who reported the event first. The Chinese media kept silent until the problem was solved and then published stories to sum up the event and praise the friendship between the Chinese and African people.

Fourth, the nature of news also makes journalism education in China different from that in the West.

In a Western country, the mass media are usually private enterprises owned and controlled by big-monopoly capitalists. News is a commodity. Fierce competition forces the media to sensationalize news in order to attract readers and to earn profits. This obviously has a strong influence upon journalism education, which, among other things, teaches students how to beat rivals with scoops, how to get exclusive news and how to dramatize, if not sensationalize, events.

In China, however, all mass media are operated and controlled by the Communist Party and government. The media are the Party's organs, while journalists are government employees. The media do not sell news. At least in theory, this situation enables Chinese journalists to report news more completely and objectively. Chinese journalism students are taught to seek truth from facts and be responsible to the people. Chinese journalism education is the product of the unique political, social, and cultural structures of the People's Republic. It bears marks of the traditional Chinese culture, shows the influence of foreign countries with advanced mass media, and carries a strong socialist character.

Modern journalism education started late in China. War, famine, and government corruption hindered its development in the first half of this century, while ultraleftist policies discouraged its rapid growth in the first three decades of the People's Republic. The current period is the most favorable one for development in journalism education, which is encouraged by the policies of the Communist Party and government and helped by exchange with foreign media and universities.

American journalists and journalism instructors have tried hard in the past decade to help journalism education in China by introducing the American approach to journalism education. They have achieved varied results. Those who wanted technical changes have succeeded while those who sought fundamental changes in principle have failed. They should bear in mind what General Secretary Hu Yaobang says about learning from the mass media in the Western countries:

> Of course we should earnestly learn the advanced techniques of the mass media in capitalist countries in writing, editing, and communicating and their advanced management; but we should not learn the basic principles of their bourgeois journalist work because our social system is different from theirs.[73]

10 ▩ Role Perception: A Pragmatic Approach

![decorative border]

Introduction

Earlier chapters reviewed the history of China and traced the history of the mass media in an effort to provide an understanding of developments in the field of journalism since the end of the Cultural Revolution. Under the pragmatic leadership of Deng Xiaoping, China's modernization program has encompassed all aspects of life in the People's Republic, including journalism.

Former Premier Zhou encouraged a more pragmatic approach to journalism when he addressed Chinese journalists at the Beijing International Airport prior to President Nixon's arrival in China on 21 February 1972. That historical day not only marked a new beginning for Sino-U.S. political relations, but also predicted a new dawn for journalism — at least in regard to China's approach to international journalism — in a nation that had once slammed the door on the West. At that time, Premier Zhou's address on journalism was designed to encourage Chinese journalists who were writing for overseas audiences to reconsider their approach to writing.

As in all countries, the structure of the Chinese media is based on the country's social, economic, and political systems. Major changes in all three of these systems have resulted in Deng's rise to power. The news in late 1984 of a restructured economic system incorporating more free-market concepts in all aspects of Chinese society is but one of the latest

This chapter was written with the assistance of William A. Mulligan, associate professor of journalism, California State University at Long Beach, and is based in part on his dissertation (1986), "Journalism Revolution in China," University of Missouri, Columbia. This chapter is a summary of the Q-methodological aspect of the above dissertation. Those interested in the methodological explanation and detailed tables are encouraged to refer to the original dissertation.

signals to the world that China plans to continue its policy of pragmatism so that the world's most populated nation might be modernized by the end of this century or early next century.

Even though China is adopting what it considers to be the best of Western life for all aspects of the society, the nation wants all changes to be uniquely Chinese, reflecting the principles of Marxism-Leninism and Mao Zedong thought. For foreign readers, Chinese journalists will continue to reflect such principles of the Chinese Communist Party. But Chinese journalists recognize more than ever before the importance of utilizing news articles, as well as the content, structure, and organization of the Western news article if China wishes to tell the world its message effectively.

So Chinese journalists have a twofold responsibility in regard to the foreign press: (1) to utilize the Western concept for better informing other countries about the 55 nationalities that share the world's most populated country; and (2) to adhere to the principles of Marxism-Leninism and Mao Zedong thought. The first responsibility is based on pragmatism while the second is the call of the revolution.

Methodology

As a result of the Chinese commitment to improving journalistic communication with other nations, the Western press has continued to have increased confidence in the Xinhua News Agency. William A. Mulligan conducted a structured Q-Methodology study to ascertain the role of the Chinese journalists and to determine if they themselves perceive a change in attitudes of Chinese journalists toward Chinese journalism since the end of the Cultural Revolution in 1976. William Stephenson defines Q-Methodology as a method by which an individual can model for himself what his attitude is toward complicated topics, issues, or situations.[1] Keith Sanders says that this simply means that a person's attitude is his or her "Q-sort." To determine a person's attitude, a concourse of statements must be traversed to locate problems.[2] In William Stephenson's words:

> A concourse ["universe"] of statements of such opinion is the foundation upon which Q-methodology operates. There are two distinct modes of thinking in science, one concerned with "statements of fact," to establish the truth or falsity of the facts, . . . and the other with theory, that is with "statements of problems," to establish their range and the variety of facts to which they apply. The search, in Q, has always been to distinguish problems, not to develop truth or falsity of fact.[3]

Information, or statements, on Chinese journalism for the Q-study interviews were chosen from the following: personal interviews with three Xinhua News Agency leaders; a meeting with a fourth Xinhua News Agency leader; newspaper and magazine articles from the Chinese and Western press; the Xinhua News Agency's *News from Foreign Agencies and Press* and *Xinhua News Agency News Bulletin;* academic papers by Chinese journalists; and the writer's personal journal. To eliminate unnecessary statements and redundancies, the 200 statements were edited down to *n* of 53 opinion statements for the Q-study interviews with 10 Chinese journalists doing graduate work at the University of Missouri School of Journalism, and 18 journalists (including one Chinese) living in the United States who have either worked for news organizations in China or who have knowledge of the Chinese media as teachers, foreign editors, or news editors for metropolitan American newspapers.[4]

A structured Q-sample was chosen to mirror the theory Chinese socialism/communism versus capitalism. Along with theory, other components of the first level of the Q-Methodology design are as follows: *writing,* including objective reporting, propaganda, and art; *economics,* involving collective ownership, free market, industrialization, Third-World economic alliances, and modernization; and *emotion,* reflecting cultural identity, socialist fervor, and dissension. The second level of the design—*demand, identification,* and *expectation*—reflects the base of China's media structure: the social, economic, and political systems.[5] Referring to the power base of a society, Harold D. Lasswell has written:

> Symbols of identification, demand, and expectation reciprocally influence one another, and interplay with changes in the division of labor. Optimism and devotion may affect the work rate and the birth rate, modifying the value hierarchy. The development of power machinery may cheapen production and lead to the expansion of the market. Demands which are serviceable in extending the market may be redefined in terms of the master symbols of nation or state. Such dynamic interrelations between "material" and "ideological" continue to redefine areas of activity, sentiment, and organization.[6]

Demand refers to a determination for change or preference symbols; identification reflects the way things are in the society; and expectation predicts the way things will be in the future.

The 28 journalists involved in this study were chosen purposely rather than randomly; the results of this study are not intended to be applied to a larger population. The only requirement for the Chinese subjects was that they had studied journalism in the United States while the American subjects had to have working experience in China with a Western or Chinese news organization, or had to have knowledge of the Chinese media as teachers, foreign editors, or news editors for metropolitan American newspapers. As a result of such experiences, both sets of journalists had a better understanding and perspective of the two different political, economic, and social systems reviewed in this study. By studying and analyzing such small groups, Q-Methodology provides insight into human attitudes and behavior. Such understanding can provide an understanding of other political, economic, and social systems.

After completing the demographic questionnaire, each person involved in the study was asked to sort a deck of Q-cards containing the 53 statements (see Appendix). Subjects were asked to sort from right to left — from the most positive statements to the most negative statements in regard to their attitude toward journalism in the People's Republic of China. The classifications of the study provided for positive, negative, and neutral responses to the statements.

Demographic information was obtained from the demographic questionnaire, including nationality, age, education, area of study, length of professional career, political leaning, and attitude toward the Chinese press. Three of the American respondents and 2 of the Chinese respondents were female. Eleven respondents were Chinese nationals while 17 were Americans or American residents, including 1 ethnic Chinese and 1 respondent who listed his nationality as Lebanese-Syrian.

The average age of the respondents, who ranged from 24 to 59 years old, was 36. Most of the respondents listed at least four years of college, a bachelor's degree or the equivalent, as their highest educational level. However, one respondent was in the process of completing his dissertation for a doctoral degree in journalism while another respondent had already earned such a degree. One bachelor's-degree respondent said he had completed some graduate work, but not a graduate degree.

Thirteen of the respondents stated that their major area of study had been journalism, but one person who majored in journalism said that most of his courses had been in English, while another respondent reported that he had majored in communication arts. One respondent listed liberal arts along with journalism as his major area of study, and another said he had majored in English and history. Other major areas of study reported by the respondents included foreign language or English language, English language and literature, Chinese language and literature, international politics, and history.

The length of journalism service ranged from less than 2 years to 38 years. Most of the respondents, 9 people, or 32 percent, had between 11 and 20 years of journalism experience. One person did not respond to the question.

Eleven of the respondents, or 39 percent, listed their political leaning as liberal while 4 respondents, or 14 percent, stated they were conservative. Eight respondents, 29 percent, reported that they were neutral and 2 respondents, 7 percent, said they did not know their political leaning. Three people did not respond to the question. One respondent, a liberal, asked why the data form did not include categories for those "left" of liberal and "right" of conservative.

Of the 28 respondents, 11, or 39 percent, stated that they were positive toward the Chinese press. Of the remaining 17 respondents, 12, or 43 percent, reported holding a neutral attitude toward the Chinese press while 4, or 14 percent, stated that they had a negative attitude. One person said that she had a positive attitude toward some aspects of the Chinese press but a negative attitude toward other aspects of the press in the People's Republic, but that she was definitely not neutral.

Findings

The 28 subjects expressed their opinions and attitudes toward the press in the People's Republic of China by ranking the 53 statements on a scale of plus 5.00, "agree with the most," to minus 5.00, "agree with the least."

The Quanl program of analyzing the factors extracted three factors based on the responses. The following section is an analysis of these factors, or archetypical journalists, that emerged: "The American," "The Chinese," and "The American-Chinese."

Factor I: The American

Ten respondents clustered on factor I. Because they all reflected strong support for truth, justice, and the American way in socially responsible, objective journalism, this type has been named The American.

Factor I, The American, is a composite of all Americans, two females and eight males, ranging in age from 20 to 59 with an average age of 37. Eight have worked in journalism for 10 years or more while the remaining two have 7 and 4 years of experience. In regard to their political leanings, four are liberal, three are conservative, and three are neutral.

The American's complex nature emerged from the analysis. Foremost, The American is a strong advocate of objective American journalism. The two most-agreed-with items were the importance of fact and truth in news reporting. One respondent who considers himself neutral in political leaning and attitude toward the Chinese press stated that "as much objectivity as possible is the key to honest journalism." Other items with positive scores above plus 1.00 indicate The American feels that the press has a positive role to play in furthering a country's progress, there is a need for feature articles in the socialist newspapers, and all journalists need certain restrictions, either by law or by the limits of taste and good sense.

The American realizes that foreign correspondents' copy is not censored, but that reporters may face pressures. To a lesser degree, The American recognizes the important role of Premier Zhou in the development of a new China and during the Cultural Revolution, and slightly believes that the Cultural Revolution can be safely criticized. There is, too, the realization that there is a subtle difference between news and propaganda with the idea that news is not a commodity or enterprise for making profit.

The American has a general feeling that most of the national and international news in *Renmin Ribao* is from the Xinhua News Agency and that the agency will soon become an international news service with Chinese characteristics. However, The American thinks that the agency must provide timely material or people will not read the reports, and that television should have a greater role in the People's Republic.

The American's negative attitude, represented by the negative scores of minus 1.00 or lower, emphasizes allegiance to the social responsibility theory of the press. There is strong disagreement with the idea that the courts must clamp down on dissidents seeking freedom of opinion and that China needs to suppress speech freedom to avoid another Cultural Revolution. One journalist wrote in response to freedom of the press that "if China suppresses freedom of speech it will be engulfed by a people's revolution." Another stated that "it's not freedom but ignorance that leads to distorted reporting on the Third World."

The American disagrees with the theories of Marx and Lenin as the guiding principles of journalism and press freedom in the People's Republic: "Political philosophical theories should not be the only guide for journalists."

Other items reinforcing The American's distrust of the Chinese press are disagreement with a tax and other restrictions on foreign correspondents in Beijing and censorship; not believing that members of the All-China Journalists' Association should be required to support the Communist Party; and disagreeing that the policy of equal pay no matter the work should be changed for Chinese journalists.

The American slightly disagrees with the suggestion that America and its press should become open to outside influences and that more freedom for journalists will cause no harm even if they do find some dissidence. On the subject of dissidence, The American expresses moderate to slight disagreement with Chinese attitudes and policy on the negative end of the scale.

On the economic situation of the Chinese, The American tends to think that most urban residents are better off and that Beijing "pragmatists" want to establish cooperation with the United States and economic relations with capitalist countries. The American moderately disagrees that a campaign to curb foreign imports of consumer goods into China is being pushed by the *Renmin Ribao* and that the United States will not tolerate censorship of American art sent to Beijing. Slight apathy is expressed toward the idea that the Communist Party leadership is based on Mao Zedong thought.

In summary, The American thinks that a journalist should be responsible and base his or her work on facts and truth. The American believes the press can play a positive role in a nation's future, thinks that feature stories and advertisements have a place in the socialist press, and recognizes a need for certain restrictions on journalists.

Factor II: The Chinese

Seven people clustered on factor II. Because all seven are nationals from the People's Republic and because they strongly identify with a press that promotes China and the Communist Party, this type has been named The Chinese.

Factor II, The Chinese, is a composite of five males and two females, ranging in age from 26 to 48, with an average age of 37. One person has a master-of-arts degree in English and two have earned master-of-arts degrees in journalism. The remaining four Chinese are college graduates. They all hold a positive attitude toward the Chinese press and have from 2 to 25 years of experience in journalism. Two in the group reported their political leaning as liberal; two stated they did not know; and three left the question blank.

Based on the analysis, The Chinese emerged as a strong supporter of the Chinese Communist press system—agreeing that the All-China Journalists' Association should require members to support the Communist Party and that the main job of the media is to introduce China to the world and report the world to China. The Chinese also believes that the journalist is free as long as the truth, or a correct picture of China, is presented, and that stories should explain the policies of the party and government — the news is a tool of education and is not for profit.

The Chinese tends to believe that Chinese journalists should be guided by the theories of Marxism and Leninism. The three most popular items indicate that The Chinese believes in and recognizes both Mao Zedong and Zhou Enlai: Mao set a new direction for China while "Zhou was the pragmatist who kept things going."

The Chinese also believes that the press plays a positive role in promoting the country within, and as a world messenger will promote mutual understanding and friendship between the Chinese people and other peoples of the world. The Chinese believes that the Xinhua News Agency seeks objective and balanced writing and will become an international news agency with Chinese characteristics, but that news items must be timely or they will not be read. The Chinese thinks that TV needs a larger role in the People's Republic.

Some concepts reflect a negative attitude, represented by negative scores on the questionnaire. There is strong disagreement with the idea that "Beijing 'pragmatists' took a line at establishing cooperation with U.S. imperialism and at developing economic relations with capitalist countries." In regard to economic policies, The Chinese is in opposition to the *Renmin Ribao* leading a campaign for stiffer limits on foreign products that compete with domestic manufactures and a tax and other regulations on foreign correspondents. There are also slight reservations about the changing of the "Big Pot" or "Iron Rice Bowl" system of equal pay no matter the work. There is disagreement, however slight, that advertisements for foreign goods are aimed at only tourists and diplomats.

With regard to the foreign press, The Chinese says that correspondents' news copy is not censored but they may be subject to pressures. The Chinese believes that newspeople from other countries should not report on activities of dissidents in the People's Republic. However, The Chinese is slightly apathetic toward dissension and does not think that if journalists have more freedom and access to the people they will find more dissent. There is also disdain for countrymen who pass on state secrets to foreigners.

To summarize, The Chinese thinks the most important job for the Chinese press, as an educational instrument, is not to make a profit but to introduce China to the world and the world to China. The Chinese believes that Chairman Mao controlled new China's course while Premier Zhou ran the government, and that the press plays a positive role in the country's future. As a socialist journalist, The Chinese believes that press freedom depends on the presentation of news based on truth and facts, and that stories, which should support the Party and the people, should also explain government policies.

Factor III: The American-Chinese

Five male respondents clustered on factor III. Because three are Americans and two are Chinese, the group has been named The American-Chinese.

Factor III, The American-Chinese, is a composite of all males ranging in age 24 to 54 with an average age of 37½. Two respondents have worked in journalism for more than 25 years, one for more than 10 years, and two for 2 years or less. Of the five subjects, the 54-year-old journalist has the most experience, with 33 years. All have college degrees. Of the three Americans, one is a journalism doctoral candidate; one, with majors in English and history, received a fellowship after college; and one has a bachelor-of-arts degree in journalism. Of the Chinese, one earned a bachelor-of-arts degree in the English language while the other has a bachelor-of-arts degree in the English language and literature.

In reference to their political leanings, three of the respondents are liberal and two are conservative. Four subjects are neutral and one is positive in their attitudes toward the Chinese press.

Based on the analysis, The American-Chinese emerged as a believer that the press may play a positive role in a country's future and that introducing China to the world and the world to China is the job of the Chinese press. A liberal with a positive attitude toward the Chinese press, The American-Chinese also thinks that with more freedom journalists may find dissidence, but not enough to cause harm.

The American-Chinese believes that the Chinese press has an important role in national social development, and that in a socialist country "positive" reporting, as a part of the total reporting package, is more national than in the commercial/crisis/entertainment Western capitalist press. The American-Chinese believes an honest and conscientious journalist must base his news reports on the facts, no matter what his personal opinion is, and that the press does play a positive role in China's development but must have more independence. At the other end of the scale, the archetypical American-Chinese strongly disagrees that news should be a commodity for making profit, that courts need to clamp down on dissidents, and that China will have another period of chaos similar to the Cultural Revolution if it does not suppress speech freedom.

To summarize, The American-Chinese proposes a journalistic system with more freedom for the People's Republic that introduces China to the world and the world to China with stories based on truth and facts. This archetype thinks that the press plays a positive role in a country's future, believes events that people cannot control should be reported, and recognizes a need for human-interest stories in the socialist press. The American-Chinese is amused by what some foreign correspondents write about China and suggests that the United States open itself to outside influences.

Conclusion

A major change revealed in the study is the shift in Chinese journalists' perception of journalism in the People's Republic since the end of the Cultural Revolution. Even though politics remains both the force behind journalism as well as the number-one news topic in China, the focus is no longer on Marxism-Leninism and Mao Zedong thought, but on the practical applications of journalism first proposed by Liu Shaoqi and later emphasized by Zhou Enlai.

In 1956, then President Liu encouraged the Xinhua News Agency to be a civic agency, learning from both Tass and Western news agencies, publishing good and bad news, avoiding too much political news, and honoring reporters' writing styles and granting them bylines. Before President Nixon's arrival at the Beijing International Airport in 1972, Premier Zhou urged a more pragmatic approach for Chinese reporters by encouraging them to learn from their American counterparts. In the last few years, the learning of Western journalistic skills, as well as English, has brought benefits both to Chinese journalists and to the people as a whole.

Since the end of the Cultural Revolution, journalists in the People's Republic have more than ever before recognized some Western journalistic techniques, most evident in the transfer of news from the East to the West via the Xinhua News Agency's Department of Domestic News for Foreign Services, in the English language *China Daily,* and in the education of Chinese journalists—both in China and in the United States.

Some of Liu Shaoqi's suggestions are apparent in today's news reports from China. Xinhua, more of a civic agency than ever before and now recognizing a need to print both good and bad news, pays more attention to Western journalism techniques, which has resulted in an increased usage of its releases by Western news agencies. However, political reporting remains a top priority, but the emphasis is no longer on Marxism-Leninism and Mao Zedong thought as it is on political issues and the policies of Deng Xiaoping and Zhao Ziyang. Generally, reporters are not encouraged to develop their own styles; and, even though

Xinhua now gives a few bylines, as does the *China Daily,* bylines still remain few in number or are often pseudonyms, an old tradition in Chinese writing.

The second major news topic, economics, also reflects the emphasis on the practical in today's China. As an educational tool, the press plays an important role in furthering the development of the People's Republic through an ambitious national modernization program. Because of the tragic events of the Cultural Revolution, culture, ranking as the third most important news topic, has attracted renewed interest and appreciation among the people and the government.

Although China is adopting the best from the West not only in journalism but in many aspects of society, it continues to insist that all changes in society be uniquely Chinese. The focus may not be on Marxism-Leninism and Mao Zedong thought, but the principles of that philosophy will continue to be a cornerstone of Chinese journalism. In regard to the foreign press, the Chinese journalists still recognize a twofold responsibility: (1) the Western concept of better informing the world of China; and (2) the uniquely Chinese concept of the principles of Marxism-Leninism and Mao Zedong thought. Pragmatism is the basis for the first responsibility, while the call of the revolution, the cornerstone of new China, encourages modernization of an ancient nation.

The major significance of this study is the contribution of the study's participants to a better understanding of international journalism, especially the journalism of the People's Republic of China. The press may play a positive role in furthering the progress of the country, and many of the journalists have recognized an important role of responsibility for the press and have forecast a bright future for China.

While carrying out Zhou Enlai's ideas of practical journalism and Deng Xiaoping's modernization program in the People's Republic, the journalists of China are participating in a two-front revolution—the development of a world press system and the modernization of one of the world's most ancient countries.

In reporting about the happenings of the world's largest populated nation—where 51,000 people are born and 17,000 people die each day—The American, The Chinese, and The Chinese-American share one central attitude about news reporting—truth. All three types of journalists listed among their top choices of "agree with the most": "The best support—report the truth."

The journalism revolution in China continues.

Afterword

4 June 1989. This was the day the democratic reform movement was crushed by troops in Tiananmen Square in Beijing, and a slow but increasingly substantial improvement of the Chinese press freedom was totally stopped by the Chinese Communist Party.

The major part of my research for this book was completed quite sometime before this tragic day, and I am writing this unplanned afterword with the anguished wish that this horrible event is just another hurdle to overcome for the better future of Chinese people, mass media, and society.

Ever since the establishment of the People's Republic of China, Chinese media had long operated under strict ideological and political controls. But in the past decade it had become increasingly bold, with prominent newspapers and magazines publishing articles of dissident writers and openly criticizing sensitive political subjects.

Press freedom peaked in May with all major Chinese media enthusiastically covering the student movement for democratic reform. Chinese journalists actively participated with the student movement. Even after martial law was declared on 19 May 1989, a group of journalists from the official Xinhua News Agency, with banners denouncing censorship and demanding press freedom, joined students in the street.

Since government troops crushed the protesters in Beijing on 4 June 1989, the Chinese Communist Party has reclaimed strict control over the Chinese media. Chinese journalists have been forced to undergo intensive political education, and debate on freedom and other political issues has vanished from the media.

According to the *People's Daily* (*Renmin Ribao*) of 7 August 1989, Chinese news organizations were told to forget about press freedom and concentrate on "correct" Marxist ideas, signaling a further crackdown on liberal thinking. The *People's Daily* accused a "small group of thugs"

271

of using the ideal of freedom of the press to confuse their readers, "cook up rumors, and instigate attacks on the party and the people" during May-June pro-democracy protests. The paper said: "Freedom of the press, like other forms of democracy and liberties, is relative and not absolute. The press shoulders the important duty of the spreading of policies and guiding principles of the party and the people, and must take a clear-cut stand in supporting correct political directions."

Under the direction of the Chinese Communist Party, the media has been rewriting the history of the recent events. Chinese newspapers and magazines now devote much space to party propaganda and official accounts of events during the protests, fulfilling their role as tools for political education. CCTV and Radio Beijing repeatedly broadcast documentaries praising the military for crushing the protests to "protect the nation."

The future of the mass media system in China cannot be predicted without knowing what kind of political development might occur in that country. A nation's press or mass media system is closely related to its political system. The media is largely determined by its politico-social context, and in turn its functions are compatible with its national political ideology.

The current Chinese government under the leadership of Deng Xiaoping has said that for the moment what the country needs most is not political democracy but economic development to rebuild its economy, which was brought to the verge of destruction by the Cultural Revolution.

Deng sternly holds onto the "Four Cardinal Principles" lest any rashness in political reform should lead to unrest. Deng's four principles are: to firmly uphold Marxism-Leninism-Mao Zedong thought; firmly uphold the Party's leadership; firmly uphold the socialist system; and firmly uphold the proletarian dictatorship.

Even though Chinese news organizations are forced to function under the control of the Party once again, Chinese journalists and the people will fight for the freedom of the press that is so vital for the building of the democratic society. It is difficult to imagine the future of the mass media system in China. But it is certain that the future reformed media system will not be a replica of the American model, and that the reform process will be a long and slow one.

Appendix

Q-Sort Statements

1. Chinese journalists should take the theories of Marxism and Leninism as the guiding thought in every branch of their work. (Hu Qiaomu in address to journalists, *China Daily,* Beijing, 18 February 1983; demand, theory)

2. "It's interesting to see the things that the reporters say you can't do. They say — 'you can't go to eat in a Chinese restaurant unless you are fluent in Chinese,' 'you can't rent a bicycle' and 'you can't ride the subway without permission.' I think it would be helpful if some of these reporters left their apartments occasionally." (*Washington Post* article by Philip F. Zeidman quoting son John who died of disease in China, 3 March 1982 in *China Daily,* editorial page; demand, theory)

3. The United States will [would] not tolerate Chinese censorship of artistic materials sent to Beijing under U.S.-China cultural agreements. (Reuters quoting Charles Wick of U.S. International Communication, 5 September 1981; demand, writing)

4. Foreign friends are not allowed in the telex room![,] . . . It is [was] here the careful filtering of any contentious news items takes [took] place." (David Dodwell, *Financial Times* of London, in *South China Morning Post,* 9 January 1983, p. 6; demand, writing)

5. "Big Pot" system (equal pay no matter the work) will be changed. We have introduced a system already. Each reporter will have a quota. . . . People will get working points. (Chen Bojian, vice director, Xinhua News Agency, 23 April 1983; demand, economics)

The source of each statement and category is listed in parentheses at the end of the statement. Matter in brackets within statements reflects the original item before editing, from William A. Mulligan's dissertation, "Journalism Revolution in China," University of Missouri, Columbia (with permission).

6. News is not a commodity or enterprise for making profit, but an instrument for educating the people. (Interview 27 April 1983 with Chen Lung, former director, Department of Domestic News for Foreign Services, Xinhua News Agency; identification, theory)

7. All sound and video products coming into China must [will] be checked at Customs and officers have been authorized to confiscate those which are religious, pornographic, anti-Chinese, anticommunist or antisocialist. (China News Service, Beijing, report in *China Daily,* 8 January 1983; demand, emotion)

8. The foreign ministry: journalists should not report [warned journalists not to report] on illegal activities of Chinese dissidents. (Associated Press in Xinhua News Agency's *News from Foreign Agencies and Press,* Beijing, 21 September 1981; demand, emotion)

9. A couple of years ago, some newcomers to China were telling their readers that there was a strong wave of political dissidence in China — all because there appeared on a stretch of wall in Beijing (which they nicknamed "Democracy wall") a few dozen "big character" posters. These were merely the last vestiges of the "cultural revolution." (*China Daily,* editorial page column, 9 September 1982; identification, emotion)

10. Party leadership is the leadership of the Party's Central Committee led by the Chairman Mao, the leadership of Mao Zedong's thought and the leadership of the proletarian revolutionary line represented by Mao. (*Renmin Ribao* [*People's Daily*], Beijing; editorial, Mao's views on press, 19 January 1976, reprinted; *Beijing Review,* 27 January 1976, p. 13; identification, theory)

11. China — after several decades of isolation — opened itself to outside and Western influences (transnational media and others), a lead the U.S. should [could] follow. (From "International News: Looking Ahead" by Jim Richstad and Michael Anderson in *International News: Policies and Prospects,* Richstad and Anderson, eds. [New York: Columbia University Press, 1981], p. 407; demand, emotion)

12. Propaganda [I was told] is information useful to the state. [I submit that] The subtle difference between propaganda and news is that news is what the head of every state wants. Propaganda is what he or she passes onto the masses. (From "AP Covering the World" by Keith Fuller in *International News Wires: Policies and Prospects,* Richstad and Anderson, eds., p. 271; identification, theory)

13. *People's Daily* relies mainly on Xinhua (New China) News Agency for both domestic and international news. (*Renmin Ribao* informational sheet, 24 March 1981; identification, writing)

14. Since consumers in China can buy imported cigarettes, beverages and wine with foreign currency only at major hotels, international

airports, clubs and the Friendship Store, these ads are obviously aimed at tourists and diplomats rather than Chinese. (Chen Lung [Wang Pei] China Features, of Xinhua, manuscript for *Advertising World,* April 1981; identification, economics)

15. In China, where official policy is often spelled out in newspapers, peasants in one commune are arming themselves with news cuttings — in case anyone tries to tell them they are acting improperly. (Associated Press, 5 July 1981; identification, economics)

16. The Chinese government announced Friday it should impose [will begin imposing] income taxes on foreign journalists living in China and tighten other regulations concerning correspondents. (United Press International, 8 May 1981; demand, economics)

17. By the end of 1981, almost one in every three urban residents owned bicycles, more than 50 percent owned wrist watches, 13 percent owned sewing machines, and 5.6 percent owned TV sets. (*China Daily,* 30 June 1982, p. 5; identification, economics)

18. Our (New China News Agency) . . . [must not be late]. Without timely coverage, readers will not read the piece. (News briefing with Chen Bojian, vice director of Xinhua News Agency, 22 April 1983; identification, writing)

19. [The Chinese regime has threatened to use] The courts must [to] clamp down on dissidents seeking freedom of opinion. (AFP, Reuters in *South China Morning Post,* 8 April 1981, reporting on *Hongqi* [Red Flag], Beijing, article; demand, emotion)

20. Living in Beijing is like living in a black-and-white picture. Everything is gray. Grass was outlawed during the Cultural Revolution as being too bourgeois. (Black-and-white picture reference from an early 1981 United Press International news dispatch by Paul Loong noted in William Mulligan's journal, 13 March 1981; statement from letter, William Mulligan, 1981; identification, emotion)

21. Masked representatives from the Association for Solidarity with the Chinese Democratic movement yesterday petitioned the Chinese authorities, through the local (Hong Kong) New China News Agency branch office at Wancahi, for the release of more than 20 Chinese dissidents. (*South China Morning Post,* 14 June 1981; identification, emotion)

22. Mr. Zhou (Enlai), who died in January 1976, is seen as a symbol of opposition to the Gang of Four ultraleftists now blamed for a "decade of disaster" in the 1966–76 Cultural Revolution. (Associated Press, Reuters in *South China Morning Post,* 5 April 1981, reporting on a *Zhongguo Qingnian Bao* [*Chinese Youth News*], Beijing article; identification, emotion)

23. A Chinese journalist is free to report anything he or she wishes as long as the article presents a correct picture of China. (Interview 27 April 1983 with Chen Lung, former director of the Department of Domestic News for Foreign Services, Xinhua News Agency; expectation, theory)

24. If Mao was the navigator toward a new China, Zhou [Enlai] was the man who kept the engines going. (Headline on review of *Zhou Enlai,* by Dick Wilson, *Houston Chronicle,* 10 October 1984; identification, theory)

25. In covering the Western world, New China News Agency reporters should [New China News Agency endeavors to] report news events in a matter-of-fact, objective and balanced manner. (Fan Songjiu, class report, University of Missouri, Columbia, summer, 1983; demand, theory)

26. Stories should be chosen that explain to people the policies of party and government and the best ways to carry out these policies. (Interview 27 April 1983 with Chen Lung, former director, Department of Domestic News for Foreign Services, Xinhua News Agency; demand, theory)

27. Events that human beings cannot avoid — such disaster news as landslides, earthquakes, plane crashes and floods — should be reported. (Interview 27 April 1983 with Chen Lung, former director, Department of Domestic News for Foreign Services, Xinhua News Agency; demand, writing)

28. Press may play a positive role in furthering the progress of the country. (Interview 28 April 1983 with Wang Ren Lin, deputy director, Department of Domestic News for Foreign Services, Xinhua News Agency; demand, writing)

29. All fish-bone television antennae on rooftops in the southern Chinese city of Canton [Guangzhou] have been [should be] dismantled to try to stop people watching "bourgeois decadent programmes" from nearby Hong Kong. (Agence France Presse, 15 July 1982; demand, economics)

30. An honest journalist conscious of his responsibility must respect and base his work on the facts, whatever his point of view or attitude to them. (Agence France Presse quoting *Renmin Ribao* commentary, 5 March 1982; demand, writing)

31. Bigger role for television is urged. (*Renmin Ribao,* 11 April 1983, p. 1; demand, economics)

32. Foreign (outside of China) news agencies do not cover the Third World. (Interview 29 April 1983 with Huang Zumlin, deputy

director of Department of International News, Xinhua News Agency; identification, writing)

33. There is no censorship of (foreign) correspondents' copy, although this doesn't mean they are not subject to pressures. (Victoria Graham, Beijing bureau of The Associated Press, in report by M. L. Stein, *Editor and Publisher,* 3 September 1983; identification, writing)

34. China must suppress "unlimited freedom of speech" or else the nation will again be engulfed by an upheaval like the Cultural Revolution. (United Press International, 20 March 1981, reporting on *Beijing Ribao* [Beijing Daily] article; demand, emotion)

35. A campaign for stiffer limits on imports of cars, watches and other products that compete with Chinese manufactures is under way in China, spearheaded by the *People's Daily. (Far Eastern Economic Review,* 7 May 1982; identification, economics)

36. "Introducing China to the world and reporting on the world to China" means an important job for the Chinese press. (Wang Yi, of the All-China Journalists Association, *China Daily,* 9 April 1983; expectation, theory)

37. [I said to the Chinese that] if you give more freedom to journalists, they can have access to the people and they may find dissidence, but surely there isn't that much dissidence and it cannot do that much harm. (Lois Wheeler Snow quoted by the *South China Morning Post,* 22 March 1982, p. 14; expectation, theory)

38. All-China Journalists' Association requires its members "to support all correct ideas and actions which are in the interests of the (Communist) Party and the people and to combat all erroneous ideas and behaviors that are against these interest." (*Christian Science Monitor,* 14 November 1982; expectation, theory)

39. The best support—report the truth. (*Renmin Ribao,* 19 September 1984; expectation, writing)

40. The work of editing in China will [needs to] be reformed. (*Guangming Ribao,* Beijing, 11 August 1984; expectation, writing)

41. Future plans include making Xinhua into a world news agency—characteristic of China—in a very short time. (News briefing with Chen Bojian, vice director of Xinhua News Agency, 22 April 1983; expectation, economics)

42. All of us (journalists) need certain restrictions placed upon us by our respective laws and the limits of taste and good sense. (*China Daily,* editorial page, 9 September 1982; expectation, writing)

43. The great majority of patriotic Chinese view with disdain people like Wei Jingsheng who pass on state secrets to foreigners. (Chen

Hui, *China Daily,* editorial page, 11 April 1983; expectation, emotion)

44. With a population of 1 billion, the advertising potential of the Central Broadcasting Station is immeasurable. (Bernard Hooley, ad executive, *South China Morning Post,* 21 March 1982; expectation, economics)

45. After long years of separation from the outside world, the Chinese people naturally are interested in reading foreign ads. (Article by Chen Lung [Wang Pei] for *Advertising World* from China Features division of the Department of Domestic News for Foreign Services, Xinhua News Agency, April 1981; expectation, economics)

46. [Some delegates criticized] The so-called "press freedom" advocated by the Western-controlled international media[.] allows Western news agencies to inaccurately describe the Third World countries . . . as ridden with poverty, backwardness, chaos and violence while local news agencies do not have the capacity to make their voice heard outside the frontiers. (*China Daily* reporting on the formation of the Asia-Pacific News Network, 30 December 1981; expectation, economics)

47. [After coming to power] Peking [Beijing] "pragmatists" took a line at establishing cooperation with U.S. imperialism [which only recently they described as "the enemy No. 1"] and at developing economic relations with capitalist countries. (Tass, 1 August 1981; expectation, economics)

48. Human interest news stories are welcome by the readers and should have a place in socialist newspapers. (*China Daily* reporting 16 June 1982 on commentary in *Jiefang Ribao* [*Liberation Daily*] of Shanghai; expectation, writing)

49. Ed (Snow) was with the underground and the dissidents, but foreign journalists cannot do that now because China is doing its best to prevent it. (Lois Wheeler Snow quoted by the *South China Morning Post,* 22 March 1982, p. 14; expectation, emotion)

50. Most of his stories are exposes of unrighted wrongs dating back to that 1966–76 period of chaos, which now may be safely attacked. (Associated Press in *South China Morning Post,* 20 April 1982; expectation, emotion)

51. A resident Dutch journalist with extensive dissident contacts faces expulsion from China because he and his Taiwan resident wife allegedly "behaved inappropriately." (Associated Press, *South China Morning Post,* 19 May 1981; expectation, emotion)

52. Chinese Customs officials in Hangzhou have impounded a book by the *New York Times'* former correspondent, Mr. Fox Butterfield, because its map depicts Taiwan as a separate entity. (Associated

Press reporting on comments of a foreign businessman, 22 September 1982; expectation, emotion)

53. Some Chinese advertisements are using sex to attract attention, while certain foreign posters on display in Peking [Beijing] are unsuitably worded. (Letter in the *Guangming Ribao* reported by *South China Morning Post,* 25 March 1982; identification, economics)

Notes

1. Historical Development

1. *China Handbook Series: History* (Beijing: Foreign Languages Press, 1982), p. 120.

2. Qian Xinbo, "A General Situation of China's Journalism" (in Chinese), *News Coverage for Overseas Service* 16 (January 1982): 8.

3. Ibid.

4. Ibid.

5. Lin Yu-T'ang, *History of the Press and Public Opinion in China* (Shanghai: Kelly and Walsh, 1936), pp.12–29.

6. *The Chinese Repository* (Canton: Printed for the Proprietors, 1833), 1:506–7.

7. Ibid.

8. Mao Zedong, "The Chinese Revolution and the Chinese Communist Party," *Selected Works of Mao Zedong* (Beijing: Foreign Languages Press, 1965), 2:308.

9. Ibid.

10. *China Handbook Series: Culture* (Beijing: Foreign Languages Press, 1982), p. 5.

11. John C. Merrill, *Global Journalism* (New York: Longman, 1983), p. 186.

12. Qian, "General Situation," p. 8.

13. Qi Qizhang, "How the Chinese Sought Their Way of Saving the Nation after the Sino-Japanese War" (in Chinese), *Renmin Ribao,* 16 April 1984, p. 5.

14. *China Handbook Series: History,* p. 120.

15. Immanuel C.Y. Hsu, ed., *Readings in Modern Chinese History* (New York: Oxford University Press, 1971), pp. 311–12.

16. Notes in Mao, *Selected Works,* 2:191.

17. Hsu, *Readings,* p. 313.

18. Qi, "How the Chinese Sought Their Way," p. 5.

19. *China Handbook Series: Culture,* p. 5.

20. Song Peihua, "Zhang Binglin — Bourgeois Revolutionary Propagandist" (in Chinese), *Guangming Ribao,* 13 June 1984, p. 3.

21. Gao Xiaoli, "Chen Tianhua — Propagandist Who Sounded the Alarm of Patriotism against Imperialism" (in Chinese), *Guangming Ribao,* 14 March 1984, p. 3.

22. Qian, "General Situation," p. 8.

23. Shi Xuanyuan, "Qiu Jin — Pioneer of the Women's Liberation Movement" (in Chinese), *Guangming Ribao,* 1 August 1984, p. 3.

24. *China Handbook Series: History,* p. 137.

25. Ibid., p. 138.

26. Ibid., pp. 138–139.

27. Jiang Nanxiang, "Ren Bishi's Great Contribution to the Chinese Youth Movement" (in Chinese), *Zhongguo Qingnian Bao,* 3 May 1984, p. 2.

28. Hu Xiuchuan, "*Xianqu* and *Zhongguo Qingnian,*" *Zhongguo Qingnian Bao,* 28 April 1984, p. 3.

29. Li Lubo, "Shao's Words of Wisdom," *China Daily,* 12 November 1984, p. 6.

30. Ibid.

31. Ibid.

32. Ibid.

33. Ibid.

34. *China Handbook Series: History,* pp. 145–46.

35. Xiao Sheng, "The Reorganization of the Kuomintang with the Aid of Communists and the First Kuomintang-Communist Cooperation" (in Chinese), *Renmin Ribao,* 1 February 1985, p. 5.

36. Chen Song, "Mao Zedong and *Zhengzhi Zhoubao*" (in Chinese), *Renmin Ribao,* 25 September 1984, p. 5.

37. *China Handbook Series: History,* pp. 154–55.

38. Ibid., p. 160.

39. The left opportunist line, represented by Wang Ming, dominated the leadership of the CPC Central Committee from January 1931 to January 1934. The wrong line was characterized by doctrinairism — seizing big cities and staging strikes and demonstrations by workers and students there.

40. Mao's strategy was to establish and develop rural bases and then encircle and finally seize the cities from the countryside for the nationwide victory of the revolution.

41. *Renmin Ribao,* 22 December 1984, p. 5.

42. *Qianjin Bao,* 2 July 1984, p. 3.

43. Xue Muqiao and Qian Junrui, "A Ray of Light in the Long Darkness" (in Chinese), *Guangming Ribao,* 6 October 1984, p. 3.

44. Chu Tunan, "China Belongs to the World" (in Chinese), *Guangming Ribao,* 4 September 1984, p. 2.

45. Lin Mohan, "*Shijie Zhishi* and I" (in Chinese), *Renmin Ribao,* 27 March 1984, p. 4.

46. Lu Yi, "Yun Yiqun — Outstanding Journalist of the Proletariat" (in Chinese), *Renmin Ribao,* 21 March 1985, p. 4.

47. Ibid.

48. *Guangming Ribao,* 6 July 1984, p. 4.

49. *Renmin Ribao,* 7 April 1984, p. 4.

50. Yang Shangkun, "In Memory of Wu Yuzhang" (in Chinese), *Renmin Ribao,* 4 April 1984, p. 5.

51. Gan Cisen, "Reminiscences of *Zhongguo Xuesheng Daobao*" (in Chinese), *Zhongguo Qingnian Bao,* 15 December 1984, p. 3.

52. Gu Jiaxi, "Newspapers That Should Be Published as Soon as Possible" (in Chinese), *Renmin Ribao,* 17 January 1984, p. 8.

53. Gan, "Reminiscences," p. 3.

54. *Fifty Years of the Xinhua News Agency (1931–1981)* (in Chinese) (Beijing: Xinhua News Agency, 1981), p. 3.

55. John A. Lent, ed., *Broadcasting in Asia and the Pacific* (Philadelphia: Temple University Press, 1978), p. 25.

56. Dai Bang, "Xinhua's Traditional Style of Work" (in Chinese), in *Veteran Journalists on News Coverage* (Beijing: Xinhua Publishing House, 1983), p. 449.

57. *Renmin Ribao,* 12 December 1983, p. 3.

58. *Renmin Ribao,* 28 December 1983, p. 2.

59. Ibid.

60. Ibid.

61. Ibid.

62. Ibid.

63. Ibid.

64. Ibid.

65. Mao Zedong, "A Talk to the Editorial Staff of the *Shanxi-Suiyuan Daily,*" in *Selected Works of Mao Zedong* (Beijing: Foreign Languages Press, 1975), 4:241.

66. Ibid.

67. Liu Shaoqi, "A Talk to the North China Press Corps," *Selected Works of Liu Shaoqi* (Beijing: Foreign Languages Press, 1981), 1:393.

68. Dai, "Xinhua's Traditional Style," p. 457.

69. Mao Zedong, "Talks at the Yan'an Forum on Literature and Art," *Selected Works of Mao Zedong* (Beijing: Foreign Languages Press, 1967), p. 3:22.

70. Dai, "Xinhua's Traditional Style," p. 461.

71. Ibid., pp. 464–65.

72. Liu, "A Talk," p. 399.

73. Ibid., p. 400.

74. Ibid., p. 401.

75. Mao, "A Talk to the Editorial Staff," p. 242.

76. Dai, "Xinhua's Traditional Style," p. 467.

77. Mao Zedong, "Get Organized!" in *Selected Works of Mao Zedong* (Beijing: Foreign Languages Press, 1967), 3:158.

78. James W. Markham, *Voices of the Red Giants* (Ames, Iowa: Iowa State University Press, 1967), pp. 356–57.

79. Ibid., pp. 357–59.

80. Ibid., p. 354.

81. Ibid., p. 355.

82. Ibid., p. 356.

83. Ibid.

84. Ibid.

85. Godwin C. Chu and Francis L.K. Hsu, *Moving a Mountain* (Honolulu: University Press of Hawaii, 1979), p. 103.

86. Lent, *Broadcasting in Asia,* p. 26.

87. Ibid.

88. Ibid., p. 32.

89. Mao, "Talks at the Yan'an Forum," p. 90.

90. Zhou Enlai, "On the Question of Intellectuals," in *Communist China 1955–1959: Policy Documents with Analysis* (Cambridge, Mass.: Harvard University Press, 1971), p. 130.

91. Zhou Enlai, "On the Historical Experience of the Dictatorship of the Proletariat," in *Communist China 1955–1959: Policy Documents with Analysis* (Cambridge, Mass.: Harvard University Press, 1971), p. 149.

92. Ibid.

93. Lu Dingyi, "Let a Hundred Flowers Blossom, a Hundred Schools of Thought Contend!" in *Communist China 1955–1959: Policy Documents with Analysis* (Cambridge, Mass.: Harvard University Press, 1971), p. 152.

94. Ibid., p. 153.

95. *Resolution on CPC History (1949–1981)* (Beijing: Foreign Languages Press, 1981), p. 27.

96. Ibid.

97. Ibid.

98. Ibid., p. 28.

99. Ibid., p. 29.

100. Ibid.

101. Ibid., p. 30.

102. Ibid.

103. Jurgen Domes, *The Internal Politics of China 1949–1972,* trans. Rudiger Machetzki (New York: Praeger Publishers, 1973), p. 140.

104. Ibid., pp. 140–41.

105. Ibid., p. 141.

106. Ibid.

107. Ibid., p. 152.

108. Ibid., p. 157.

109. Tacques Guillermaz, *The Chinese Communist Party in Power, 1949–1976,* trans. Anne Destenay (Boulder, Colo.: Westview Press, 1976), pp. 366–67.

110. Xu Zhankun, "How to Reform Economic News Reporting?" in *Veteran Journalists on News Coverage* (in Chinese), p. 298.

111. Xu, "How to Reform," p. 301.

112. *Guangming Ribao,* 24 February 1984, p. 2.

113. *Guangming Ribao,* 21 July 1984, p. 1.

114. *Renmin Ribao,* 20 November 1984, p. 1.

115. *Renmin Ribao,* 22 December 1984, p. 4.

116. *Guangming Ribao,* 2 July 1984, p. 1.

117. Xu Zhankun, "On Laws Leading to Deep-Going Reporting," in *Veteran Journalists on News Coverage,* pp. 48–49.

118. Ibid.

119. Ibid.

120. *Renmin Ribao,* 22 October 1983, p.1.

121. *Renmin Ribao,* 9 August 1984, p. 3.

122. *China Daily,* 13 February 1985, p. 3.

123. Ibid.

124. *Renmin Ribao,* 28 February 1985, p.7.

125. Ibid.

126. *Renmin Ribao,* 26 March 1985, p. 5.

127. Ibid.

128. Ibid.

129. Ibid.

130. *Renmin Ribao,* 26 February 1984, p.1.

131. *Renmin Ribao,* 20 March 1984, p. 1.

132. *Renmin Ribao,* 5 April 1984, p. 1.

133. *Renmin Ribao,* 8 April 1984, p. 1.

134. *Renmin Ribao,* 25 April 1984, p. 1.

135. *Renmin Ribao,* 26 May 1984, p. 5.

136. *Renmin Ribao,* 11 August 1984, p. 5.

137. *Renmin Ribao,* 4 August 1984, p. 5.

138. Ibid.

139. Ibid.

140. *Renmin Ribao,* 26 April 1984, p. 4.

141. *Renmin Ribao,* 11 June 1984, p. 4.

142. Ibid.

143. *Renmin Ribao,* 4 January 1985, p. 4.

144. *Renmin Ribao,* 25 May 1984, p. 5.

145. Xiang Changfu, "The Importance and Role of Professional Radio Reporters," *Journal of Beijing Broadcasting College* (in Chinese), no. 1 (1985): 4.

146. Ibid.

147. *Radio and Television in the People's Republic of China* (Beijing: Ministry of Radio and Television, 1984), p. 5.

148. Ibid.

149. Ibid., p. 6.

150. Ibid.

151. Ibid., p. 7.

152. *China Daily,* 15 April 1985, p. 1.

153. Ibid.

154. Ibid.

155. Ibid.

156. *China Daily,* 1 December 1984, p. 1.

157. *Guangming Ribao,* 29 June 1984, p. 2.

158. *Guangming Ribao,* 1 December 1984, p. 1.

2. Xinhua News Agency

1. Interview with Chen Lung, 27 April 1983 in Beijing. Chen Lung, an overseas Chinese from Java Island, Indonesia, went to China in 1935 to study at Yenching University, now Beijing University. He joined the student movement against Japanese aggression against China. In 1937, when the Japanese occupied Beijing, he left the city for Yan'an, where he became one of the 15 members of the Xinhua News Agency. Chen Lung said he met Edgar Snow several times and pointed out that the American journalists interviewed Chairman Mao before Xinhua News Agency interviewed the Chinese leader. When Chen Lung, 52 years old, suffered a stroke on 14 December 1981, he was on his way to another session of the National People's Congress to supervise the Xinhua News Agency's coverage. He is paid about two hundred Chinese yuan (one hundred dollars in U.S. money) a month and lives with his family in Xinhua housing. Both his parents were primarily schoolteachers.

Fan Songjiu reported in "Edgar Snow and China" (thesis, University of Missouri, December 1984, p. 49), that journalism courses at Yenching University were first taught in the Political Science Department in 1918 by Hsu Pao-hua, a Chinese graduate of the University of Michigan and editor of Jen Pao. Roswell Britton, also a graduate of the University of Michigan, established a journalism department in 1924, but the program was discontinued in 1927 for financial reasons. In 1929, Vernon Nash of the University of Missouri responded the courses.

2. Chen Lung, 27 April 1983.

3. Interview with Wang Renlin, 28 April 1983, at Xinhua News Agency, Beijing. Wang Renlin, 56 years old, is from Shanghai. His father worked in a Shanghai bank and his mother was a housewife. He graduated from the Yenching University, where he majored in English and studied French. He started working for the Xinhua News Agency in 1949.

Wang Renlin said news work is too strenuous and if he had a chance to do some other type of work, he would. He receives about 136 yuan (68 dollars in U.S. money) a month, but reminds the interviewer: "Of course you know we have got this additional subsidy as a readjustment of commodities." He lives in an apartment at his wife's work unit, People's University.

4. Ibid.

5. Interview with Huang Zumin, 29 April 1983, at Xinhua News Agency, Beijing. Huang Zumin, age 52, is a graduate of Xinhua University, where he majored in English. His father was a teacher and his mother a housewife.

6. Chen Lung, 27 April 1983

7. Wang Renlin, 28 April 1983.

8. Huang Zumin, 29 April 1983.

9. Lu Dingyi, also a vice premier in charge of cultural and educational affairs, in a speech at Xinhua News Agency, 21 September 1957, cited by Ignatius Peng Yao, "The New China News Agency: How It Serves the Party," *Journalism Quarterly* 40 (Winter 1963):83. Lu Dingyi also mentioned at the time that Xinhua is a weapon of class struggle.

10. Franklin W. Houn, "The Press in Communist China: Its Structure and Operation," *Journalism Quarterly* 33 (Autumn 1956):503–6.

11. Wang Chia-yu, "Peiping's 'New China News Agency'," *Issues and Studies* (Taipei, December 1967), cited by Roger L. Dial, "The New China News Agency and Foreign Policy in China," *International Journal* 31, no. 2 (1967):316.

12. Chen Bojian, briefing on Xinhua News Agency reform, 23 April 1983, at Xinhua News Agency, Beijing.

13. Ibid.

14. Ibid.

15. "China's News Agency Aims for Third World Countries," *Dallas Morning News,* 23 December 1984, p. 42A.

16. Ibid.

17. During the period 2–14 December 1982, the National People's Congress was meeting in Beijing. A special group of polishers may have been used to copyedit the news services from the NPC and this group may have also received the Foreign Reaction File, which was usually delivered to Room 703 of the Department of Domestic News for Foreign Services. The *South China Morning Post* and *News from Foreign Agencies & Press* continued to be reviewed 12–18 April 1982, 13–20 August 1982, and 2–14 December 1982 to determine foreign-agency use of Xinhua News Agency dispatches.

18. *Xinhua News Agency News Bulletin* carries the same information issued by the Xinhua News Agency wire. One exception, though, was information on the reinstatement of People's Liberation Army ranks, which was released over the wire 21 August 1981, but not carried by the *Xinhua News Agency Bulletin* on 22 August 1981. However, the English-language *China Daily* in Beijing did carry the news that ranks would be reinstated after 16 years without them. The *South China Morning Post* reported the news and also the information puzzle (23 August 1981, p. 6, and 24 August 1981, p. 6). Apparently the ranks were not going to be reinstated and apparently Xinhua's Department of Domestic News for Foreign Services released the information by mistake.

19. "Oilseed Output Up," *South China Morning Post,* 6 May 1982, p. 5.

20. See "Economic Growth More Than Expected," *South China Morning Post,* 16 December 1982, p. 7, and "China-Economy" "Industry Growing 7 Percent — Bad Managers Face Removal," Associated Press dispatch, 19 December 1982.

21. The total of 1,928 includes duplications among agencies. For example, AFP and AP might both produce a story from the same Xinhua News Agency dispatch, which

would equal two foreign press stories that named Xinhua News Agency as the source. Updates and new leads on foreign press stories were not counted as news stories unless the stories were substantially changed.

3. People's Daily (Renmin Ribao)

1. For this chapter, the primary source of information on the historical development of *Peoples's Daily* was Zhang Qianxiang, former editor of *People's Daily*. Zhang responded to a questionnaire submitted to him by the author in August 1986.
2. Ibid.
3. Ibid.
4. Ibid.

4. China Daily

1. "Peking Paper for Outsiders finds a Niche," *New York Times,* 17 December 1981.
2. Ibid.
3. "News, Views—*China Daily* arrives in U.S.," *Christian Science Monitor,* 21 July 1983.
4. "China's Only Daily Printed in English Sets N.Y. Debut," *Wall Street Journal,* 1 June 1983.
5. "Peking Paper," *New York Times.*
6. "China's English-Language Daily Soothes Foreigners with Hometown News," *Christian Science Monitor,* 29 March 1983.
7. For this study, author interviewed Feng Xiliang at his office in Beijing on 6 June 1986.

5. World Economic Herald (Shijie Jingji Daobao)

1. "Economic Newspapers in Present day China," *Xinwen Zhanxian,* 6 January 1986, p. 5.
2. Ibid.
3. "For China's Modernization—Five years of the *World Economic Herald*" (in Chinese), *Jiefang Ribao,* 4 July 1985, p. 3.
4. *Contemporary Economic Newspapers in China* (in Chinese) (unpublished article by Fudan University), 1985, p. 36.
5. Ibid.
6. Ge Gongzheng, *History of Newspapers in China* (in Chinese) (Shanghai: Fudan University Press, 1965), pp. 5–6.
7. Franklin Houn, *A Short History of Chinese Communism* (Englewood Cliffs, N.J.: Prentice Hall, 1969), pp. 173–77.

8. James C. F. Wang, *Contemporary Chinese Politics* (Englewood Cliffs, N.J.: Prentice Hall, Inc. 1985), pp. 14–15, and pp. 17–18.

9. Houn, p. 35.

10. Wang, *The Cultural Revolution in China: An Annotated Bibliography* (New York and London: Garland, 1976), p. 115.

11. "Decision on the Reform of Economic Structure," *Beijing Review,* no. 44, 1984, p.7.

12. Ibid., pp. 7–8.

13. Ibid., p. 8.

14. Xun Zhankun, "How to Reform Economic News Reporting," *Veteran Journalists on News Coverage* (in Chinese), p. 298.

15. Wilbur Schramm and Daniel Lerner, *Communication and Changes* (Honolulu: The University Press of Hawaii, 1976), p. 119.

16. "On Journalism under the Party" (in Chinese), *People's Daily,* 4 April 1985, p. 1.

17. "For China's Modernization—Five Years of the World Economic Herald" (in Chinese), *Jiefang Ribao,* 4 July 1985, p. 3.

18. "A Message from *Renmin Ribao*" (in Chinese), *World Economic Herald,* 20 June 1985, p. 1.

19. "A Message to Readers" (in Chinese), *World Economic Herald* 20 June 1980, p. 1.

20. *1984 Bulletin of the Shanghai Statistical Bureau* (in Chinese) (unpublished document), p. 3.

21. *Economic Newspapers in Today's China* (in Chinese) (Shanghai: Shanghai People's Press, 1985), p. 45.

22. *Jiefang Ribao,* 4 July 1985, p. 1.

23. *Bulletin of the Journalism Department of Fudan University* (in Chinese), 1985, p. 1.

24. Ibid., p.6.

25. *Jiefang Ribao,* 4 July 1985, p.3.

26. "Congratulations and Hopes" (in Chinese), *World Economic Herald,* 20 June 1985, p. 2.

27. Qian Junrei, *To Explore Newspaper Work in the New Era by Looking at the Operation of the "World Economic Herald"* (in Chinese) (Shanghai: Fudan University Press, 1983), p. 5.

28. Ibid., p. 14.

29. "A Successful Economic Newspaper—*World Economic Herald*" (in Chinese), *Business Journalism Research,* September 1984, p. 11.

30. Junrei, *To Explore Newspaper Work,* p. 8.

31. "The Experiment of the *World Economic Herald*" (in Chinese), *Jiefang Ribao,* 20 May 1985, p. 3.

32. "Congratulations and Hopes" (in Chinese), *World Economic Herald,* 20 June 1985, p. 2.

6. China Public Broadcasting System

1. John A. Lent, ed., *Broadcasting in Asia and the Pacific* (Philadelphia: Temple University Press, 1978), p. 24.

2. "China's Central People's Broadcasting Station," *Beijing Review,* 22 February 1982, p. 20.

3. "China People's Broadcasting Undertaking" (in Chinese), unpublished document, 1985.

4. Ibid.

5. Yi Mei, "People's Broadcasting in China" (in Chinese), *People's Daily,* 25 April 1950.

6. Ibid.

7. Wen Ji-zhe, "A Survey of the People's Broadcasting Affairs in China" (in Chinese), *People's Daily,* 1 February 1950.

8. *China Journalism Yearbook 1982* (in Chinese) (Beijing: China Social Science Publishing House, 1982), p. 317.

9. Yi, "People's Broadcasting in China."

10. Alan P. L. Liu, *Communications and National Integration in Communist China* (Berkeley: University of California Press, 1971), p. 187.

11. Zhou Xinwu, "China's Broadcast Affairs during the Great Leap Forward" (in Chinese), *Xinwen Zhanxian (News Front),* 24 September 1959, p. 5.

12. Lent, *Broadcasting in Asia,* p. 26.

13. "Chinese People's Broadcasting Undertaking."

14. *UNESCO, Statistical Yearbook 1972* (Paris: UNESCO, 1972), p. 838.

15. "Chinese People's Broadcasting Undertaking."

16. Kang Ying, "History of the New Chinese People's Broadcasting Undertaking," *China Journalism Yearbook 1982* (in Chinese) (Beijing: China Social Science Publishing House, 1982), p. 19.

17. Liu, *Radio Broadcasting in Communist China,* p. 10.

18. *Xinhua News Agency Dispatch,* 24 December 1956.

19. "Reliance on the Masses," *Guang Min Daily,* 27 March 1956.

20. Ibid.

21. Ibid.

22. Ibid.

23. Editorial, *The People's Daily,* 12 December 1955.

24. "The Bureau of Broadcasting Affairs Convened the Sixth National Conference of Broadcasting," *Xihwen Zhanxian (News Front),* no. 6, 1959, p. 2.

25. *Xinhua News Agency Dispatch,* 21 September 1971.

26. Lent, *Broadcasting in Asia,* p. 29.

27. "Broadcasting West Serve the Continuing Leap Forward of the Industrial and Agriculture Production," *Xinwen Zhanxian (News Front),* no. 22, 1959. p. 10.

28. Lent, *Broadcasting in Asia,* p. 29.

29. *Xinhua News Agency Dispatch,* 27 October, 1969.

30. Su Tung-geng, "Development of the China Communist Wired Broadcasting Networks" *China Communist Affairs Monthly* (in Chinese), 12 June 1969, p. 54.

31. Shen Yung, "Development of the China Communist Wired Broadcasting System in Rural Areas," *Studies in Chinese Communism* (in Chinese), 6 (June 1969):78.

32. "Wire Communication in the Countryside," *Beijing Review,* 22 February 1982, p. 22.

33. Kang, "History," p. 19.

34. "Wire Communication," p. 22.

35. *China Journalism Yearbook 1982,* p. 319.

36. "Party Control of Communication Media," *People's Daily,* 11 June 1960.

37. Mao Zedong, *Selected Works of Mao Zedong* (Beijing: Foreign Language Press, 1967), p. 241.

38. "New Development in Running the Press by the Whole Party" (in Chinese), *People's Daily,* 11 June 1960.

39. Wen Jinshe, Zhao Yunuing and Xie Jun, "An Outline of the Development of Journalism Research in China," *China Journalism Yearbook 1983* (in Chinese) (Beijing: China Social Science Publishing House, 1983), p. 13.

40. Gan Xifen, *Journalism Theory* (in Chinese) (Beijing: People's University Press, 1982), p. 221.

41. Ibid., pp. 218–20.

42. Yang Zhaolin, "On Radio Broadcasting," *China Journalism Yearbook 1983* (in Chinese) (Beijing: China Social Science Publishing House, 1983), p. 116.

43. Ibid.

44. Ibid., p. 118.

45. John Howkins, *The Media in China.*

46. "The Central People's Broadcasting Station," *China Journalism Yearbook 1982* (in Chinese), p. 318.

47. Ibid.

48. Ibid.

49. Li Honggi, "The Basic Skills of an Editor," *Journalism as a Profession: A Monthly Publication by Xinhua News Agency,* April 1982, p. 12.

50. Lu Xichu, *The Theory of Broadcasting Edition* (in Chinese) (Beijing: Broadcasting Press, 1982), p. 570.

51. Ibid.

52. *Broadcasting Editors' Daily,* 19 February 1985, p. 2. (A publication limited within the Ministry of Radio and Television.)

53. Ibid., 26 February 1985, p.2.

54. Ibid., 19 February 1985, p.2.

55. Ibid., p.3.

56. *The Work of Ministry Radio and Television in 1984 and the Propaganda Work Requirement in 1985,* p. 13. (A document published within the Ministry of Radio and Television.)

57. Yang Zhaolin, "On Broadcasting Propaganda," *China Journalism Yearbook 1983* (in Chinese) (Beijing: China Social Science Publishing House, 1983), p. 116.

58. *China Journalism Yearbook 1982,* pp. 317–18.

59. Ibid., 317.

60. Ibid.

61. Ibid.

62. *The Work of Radio and Television Ministry in 1984 and Propaganda Guidelines in 1985.*

63. Yang, "On Radio Broadcasting," p. 118.

64. Michael Yahuda, *Toward the End of Isolation: China's Foreign Policy After Mao* (New York: St Martin's Press, 1983), p. 181.

65. *Beijing Review,* 6 January 1986, p. 14.

66. Ibid. China's vice foreign minister Qian Qichen, in a *Beijing Review* exclusive interview, states that the "two superpowers — the United States and the Soviet Union — threaten world peace with the arms race and contests in some of the 'hot spots' of the world."

67. Yahuda, *Toward the end of Isolation,* p. 234.

68. Ibid., p. 236.

69. Samuel S. Kim, *China and the World* (Boulder, Colo.: Westview Press, 1984), p. 129.

70. *Beijing Review,* 6 January 1986, p. 15.

71. Ibid.

7. Radio Beijing

1. Ling Yang, "Broadcasting Serves the People," *Beijing Review,* 28 February 1982, p. 26.

2. Wu Lengxi, Speech at the tea party commemorating the 35th Anniversary of Radio Beijing in Beijing, 18 September, 1982.

3. Wen Jizhe, Zhao Yuming and Xie Jun, "An Outline of the Development of Journalism Research in China," *China Journalism YearBook 1983* (in Chinese) (Beijing: China Social Science Publishing House, 1983), p. 13.

4. Ibid. p. 12.

5. Burton, Paulu, *Radio and Television Broadcasting in Eastern Europe* (Minneapolis: University of Minnesota Press, 1974), p. 8.

6. Alex Inkeles, *Public Opinion in Soviet Russia* (Boston: Harvard University Press, 1958), p. 161.

7. Wu Lengxi, Speech at the tea party commemorating the 36th Anniversary of Radio Beijing, 18 September 1983.

8. Wu Lengxi, Speech at the tea party commemorating the 35th Anniversary of Radio Beijing.

9. *Radio and Television in the People's Republic of China* (Beijing: Ministry of Radio and Television, 1984), p. 6.

10. Li, *Basic Skills,* p. 12.

11. Ibid.

12. Ibid.

13. Lu Xichu, *The Basic Theory of Broadcasting Editing,* p. 570.

14. Ibid.

15. Ibid.

16. Ibid.

17. Ibid.

18. Ibid.

19. Ibid., p. 573.

20. Ibid., p. 610.

21. Ibid., p. 611

22. Ibid., p. 612

23. Ibid., p. 613.

24. Ibid.

25. *Overseas Broadcast Daily* (in Chinese), 12 February 1985, p. 3. (A publication limited within Radio Beijing).

26. Ibid.

8. Television in China

1. *China Central Television.* (A pamphlet distributed by the Ministry of Radio and Television of the People's Republic of China.)

2. Howkins, *Media in China,* p. 27.

3. John A. Lent, ed., *Broadcasting in Asia and the Pacific* (Philadelphia: Temple University Press, 1978), p. 36.

4. *Summary of the Work of the Ministry of Radio and Television in 1984.* (A document published within the ministry.)

5. Shang Huashan, "The Uprising China Television," *China Journalism Yearbook 1982* (in Chinese) (Beijing: China Social Science Publishing House, 1982), p. 23.

6. "China Buys New TV Package from CBS," *Advertising Age,* 16 December 1985, p.66.

7. Howkins, *Media in China,* p.39.

8. Zhang Huasha, "The Uprising Chinese Television," *China Journalism Yearbook 1982* (in Chinese) (Beijing: China Social Science Publishing House, 1982), p. 22.

9. Howkins, *Media in China,* p. 40.

10. *Summary of the Work of the Ministry of Radio and Television in 1984.*

11. Ling Yang, "China's Burgeoning TV," *Beijing Review,* 9 March 1981, p. 26.

12. Situ Zheng, "China's Radio and Television," *China News Press* (in Chinese), 6 March 1983.

13. Ibid.

14. Ibid.

15. *China Journalism Yearbook 1982,* p. 366

16. Ibid.

17. Ibid.

18. Ibid.

19. *China Central Television.*

20. Ibid.

21. Ibid.

22. *China Journalism Yearbook 1984,* p. 9.

23. *China Journalism Yearbook 1982,* p. 23.

24. Edwin Diamond, "Television in China," *TV Guide,* 7 September 1985, p. 40.

25. Ibid., p. 38.

26. Ibid.

27. Ling, "China's Burgeoning TV," p. 23.

28. *Summary of the Work of the Ministry of Radio and Television in 1984.*

29. *China Journalism Yearbook 1984,* p. 9.

30. Jonathan Kolatch, "Chinese Television: Where New Values Mix with Old," *TV Guide,* 6 April 1985, p. 37.

9. Journalism Education in China

1. *China Yearbook of Journalism 1984* (in Chinese) (Beijing: China's Social Science Publishing House, 1984), p. 50.

2. Ibid., p. 59.

3. Ibid., p. 26.

4. Ibid., p. 59.

5. Author's notes, National Conference on Journalism Education in Beijing, 25 May–1 June 1983.

6. *China Yearbook of Journalism 1984* (in Chinese), p. 59.

7. Census Office of the Chinese State Council and the Population Department of

the State Statistics Bureau, *Main Statistics of the Third National Census of China* (Beijing: China Statistics Publishing House, 1982), p. 2.

8. *China Yearbook of Journalism 1984* (in Chinese), p. 60.

9. Ibid., p. 51.

10. Hsing-ti Cheng, "Improvement of Chinese Journalism Education Based on Missouri Practice," (M.A. thesis, University of Missouri-Columbia, 1969), p. 6.

11. *China Yearbook of Journalism 1984* (in Chinese), p. 51.

12. Ibid.

13. Zhang Jingming and Peng Jianan, "Chinese Journalism Education: Slow Progress Since 1918," *Journalism Educator,* 41 (Spring 1986): 11.

14. *Cheng,* "Improvement," p. 10.

15. Zhang and Peng, "Chinese Journalism," p. 12.

16. "A Brief Introduction to the Journalism Department of Yenching University" (in Chinese) (Beijing: Library of Yenching University, 1950, Mimeographed), p. 1.

17. Ibid., pp. 1–2.

18. Cheng, "Improvement," p. 10.

19. *China Yearbook of Journalism, 1984* (in Chinese), p. 48.

20. Ibid., pp. 56–57.

21. Ibid.

22. Zhang and Peng, "Chinese Journalism," p. 13.

23. Ibid.

24. *China Yearbook of Journalism 1984* (in Chinese), p. 57.

25. Ibid., pp. 57–58.

26. Ibid., p. 393.

27. Interview with Professor Cheng May, Journalism Department, People's University of China, Beijing, October 1985.

28. *China Yearbook of Journalism 1984* (in Chinese), p. 58.

29. Ibid., p. 77.

30. Ibid., p. 48.

31. *Resolution on CPC History (1949–81)* (Beijing: Foreign Languages Press, 1981), p. 49.

32. Ibid., pp. 49–50.

33. Ibid., pp. 51–56.

34. Deng Xiaoping, "Some Views on Science and Education" (in Chinese), *Selected Works of Deng Xiaoping (1975–82)* (Beijing: People's Publishing House, 1983), p. 45.

35. *China Yearbook of Journalism 1984* (in Chinese), p. 48.

36. Ibid., p. 49.

37. Ibid., p. 48.

38. Ibid.

39. *China Yearbook of Journalism 1982* (in Chinese) (Beijing: China's Social Science Publishing House, 1982), p. 391.

40. Ibid., p. 390.

41. Ibid., p. 391.

42. Ibid.

43. Florence C. Reynolds, "Chinese Learn Western J-Skills from U.S. Teacher," *Journalism Educator* 40 (Summer, 1985): 7.

44. *China Yearbook of Journalism 1984* (in Chinese), p. 63.

45. Ibid., p. 50.

46. Author's notes, National Conference on Journalism Education in Beijing, 25 May–1 June 1983.

47. *China Yearbook of Journalism 1984* (in Chinese), p. 50.
48. Ibid., p. 65.
49. Ibid., p. 62.
50. Ibid., pp. 713–15.
51. Ibid., p. 27.
52. Ibid., p. 106.
53. Ibid., p. 13.
54. Ibid., p. 27.
55. Ibid., p. 62.
56. *China Yearbook of Journalism 1982* (in Chinese), p. 394.
57. Ibid.
58. Ibid.
59. Ibid., p. 392.
60. Ibid.
61. Ibid., p. 28.
62. *China Yearbook of Journalism 1984* (in Chinese), p. 13.
63. Ibid., p. 106.
64. Ibid., p. 15.
65. Ibid., p. 66.
66. Ibid.
67. Ibid.
68. Ibid., p. 28.
69. Hu Yaobang, *On Our Party's Journalist Work* (in Chinese) (Beijing: People's Publishing House, 1985), pp. 1–2.
70. Ibid., p. 8.
71. Ibid., p. 18.
72. Ibid., p. 20.
73. Ibid., pp. 7–8.

10. Role Perception: A Pragmatic Approach

1. William Stephenson, *The Play Theory of Mass Communication* (Chicago: University of Chicago Press, 1967), chap. 1. For more on Q-Methodology, see Stephenson, *The Study of Behavior* (Chicago: University of Chicago Press, 1953).

2. Stephenson uses the word *concourse* to refer to the universe of statements developed for a Q-study.

3. William Stephenson, "Sir Geoffrey Vickers and the Art of Judgment" (manuscript accepted for publication in *American Psychologist,* March 1984), p. 4. In regard to "statements of facts," Stephenson cites Karl R. Popper, *The Logic of Scientific Discovery* (New York: Basic Books, 1959) and in reference to "statements of problems," he refers to Richard McKeon, "Scientific and Philosophic Revolutions," in *Science and Contemporary Society,* ed. F. J. Crosson (Notre Dame-London: University of Notre Dame Press, 1967), p. 23–56.

4. In-person Q-study interviews were conducted with 10 of 11 Chinese journalists and 1 American journalist doing graduate work at the University of Missouri School of Journalism. Interviews by mail were properly completed by 18 of the 20 journalists who returned the forms. Approximately 65 journalists — including selected foreign editors, news

editors, and journalists who have worked in China—living in the United States were mailed the Q-study interviews.

5. Methodology block design based on Doran Jay Levy, "A Q-Methodology Investigation of the Propaganda Effectiveness of *Soviet Life* Magazine" (master's thesis, University of Missouri School of Journalism, 1967), p. 36, who also refers to Stephenson's *The Play Theory*.

6. Harold D. Lasswell, "World Politics and Personal Insecurity" in *A Study of Power* (Glencoe, Ill.: The Free Press 1950), p. 46.

Bibliography

Books

Anhui Ribao. China Yearbook of Journalism 1982 (in Chinese). Beijing: China's Social Sciences Press, 1982.

Avedon, John F. *In Exile from the Land of Snows.* New York: Alfred A. Knopf, 1984.

Barnett, A. Doak. *China on the Eve of Communist Takeover.* New York: Praeger Publishers, 1963.

Bennett, Adrian Arthur III. *Missionary Journalist in China: Young J. Allen and His Magazines, 1860–1883.* Athens: University of Georgia Press, 1983.

Britton, Roswell S. *The Chinese Periodical Press, 1800–1912.* Shanghai: Kelly and Walsh, 1933.

———. *The Chinese Periodical Press, 1800–1912.* Shanghai: Kelly and Walsh, 1933; Taipei reprint: Chengwen Publishing, 1966.

Brown, Stephen R. *Political Subjectivity.* New Haven: Yale University Press, 1980.

Buck, Pearl. *China as I See It.* Compiled and edited by Theodore F. Harris. New York: John Day, 1970.

Butterfield, Fox. *China: Alive in the Bitter Sea.* Times Books, n.d.

Chen, Theodore H.E. *Thought Reform of the Chinese Intellectuals.* Hong Kong: Hong Kong University Press, 1960.

Cheng, Peter. *A Chronology of the People's Republic of China.* Totowa, N.J.: Littlefield, Adams and Co., 1972.

Chesneaux, Jean. *China: The People's Republic, 1949–1976.* Translated by Paul Auster and Lydia Davis. New York: Random House, 1979.

Chesneaux, Jean; Le Barbier, Francoise; and Bergere, Marie-Claire. *China from the 1911 Revolution to Liberation.* Translated by Paul Auster, Lydia Davis, and Anne Destenay. New York: Pantheon Books, 1977.

Chiang, Kuelin. *Twelve Years with the New China News Agency.* Taipei: Cheng Sheng Broadcasting Corp., 1962.

China Handbook Series: Culture. Beijing: Foreign Languages Press, 1982.

China Handbook Series: History. Beijing: Foreign Languages Press, 1982.

Chinese Newspaper Manual. New Haven, Conn.: The Institute of Far Eastern Languages, Yale University, 1952.

The Chinese Repository, Vol. 1. Canton: Printed for the Proprietors, 1833.

Communist China 1955–1959: Policy Documents with Analysis. Cambridge, Mass.: Harvard University Press, 1971.

Das, Nranarayan. *China's Hundred Weeds.* Calcutta: K. P. Bagchi, 1979.

Deng Xiaoping. *Selected Works of Deng Xiaoping* (in Chinese). Beijing: People's Publishing House, 1983.

Domes, Jurgen. *The Internal Politics of China 1949–1972.* Translated by Rudiger Machetzki. New York: Praeger Publishers, 1973.

_____. *China after the Cultural Revolution.* Translated by Annette Berg and David Goodman. Berkeley and Los Angeles: University of California Press, 1977.

Dutt, Gargi, and Dutt, V.P. *China's Cultural Revolution.* New York: Asia Publishing House, 1970.

Emery, Edwin. *The Press and America.* Englewood Cliffs, N.J.: Prentice-Hall, 1972.

Fifty Years of the Xinhua News Agency (1931–1981). Beijing: Xinhua News Agency, 1981.

Foreign Languages Press, ed. *China Facts and Figures: Ethnic Minorities.* Beijing: Foreign Languages Press, 1982.

_____. *China Facts and Figures: Four Great Inventions.* Beijing: Foreign Languages Press, 1982.

_____. *China Facts and Figures: Mass Media.* Beijing: Foreign Languages Press, 1982.

Guillermaz, Jacques. *A History of the Chinese Communist Party 1921–1949.* Translated by Anne Destenay. New York: Random House, 1972.

_____. *The Chinese Communist Party in Power 1949–1976.* Translated by Anne Destenay. Boulder, Colo.: Westview Press, 1976.

Harrison, James Pinckney. *The Long March to Power.* New York: Praeger Publishers, 1972.

Houn, Franklin W. *To Change a Nation.* East Lansing, Mich.: Michigan State University, 1961.

Howkins, John. *Mass Communication in China.* New York: Longman, 1982.

Hsu, Immanuel C.Y., ed. *Readings in Modern Chinese History.* New York: Oxford University Press, 1971.

Hu Yaobang. *On Our Party's Journalist Work* (in Chinese). Beijing: People's Publishing House, 1985.

Inkeles, Alex. *Public Opinion in Soviet Russia.* Boston: Harvard University Press, 1958.

Kim, Samuel S. *China and the World.* Boulder, Colo.: Westview Press, 1984.

King, Frank H., and Clarke, Prescott. *A Research Guide to China-Coast Newspapers 1822–1911.* Cambridge, Mass.: Harvard University Press, 1965.

Lasswell, Harold D. *World Politics and Personal Insecurity in a Study of Power.* Glencoe, Ill.: Free Press, 1950.

Lee, Hong Yung. *Politics of the Chinese Cultural Revolution.* Berkeley: University of California Press, 1978.

Lent, John. A., ed. *The Asian Newspapers' Reluctant Revolution.* Ames, Iowa: Iowa State University Press, 1971.

_____. ed. *Broadcasting in Asia and the Pacific.* Philadelphia: Temple University Press, 1978.

Lerner, Daniel. *The Passing of Traditional Society.* New York: Free Press, 1958.

Letter. *Liaoning Ribao* (Shenyang), 19 July 1973. Reprinted in *Renmin Ribao* (Beijing), 10 August 1973.

Lin Yu-T'ang. *A History of the Press and Public Opinion in China.* Shanghai: Kelly and Walsh, 1936.

Liu Shaoqi. *Selected Works of Liu Shaoqi.* Vol. 1. Beijing: Foreign Languages Press, 1984.

Lu Dingyi. *Let All Flowers Blossom, Let All Scholars Compete* (in Chinese), Beijing: Xinhua News Agency, 1956.

Lu Xichu. *The Theory of Broadcasting Edition* (in Chinese). Beijing: Broadcasting Press, 1982.

MacFarquhar, Roderick. *The Origins of the Cultural Revolution.* Vol. 1. New York: Columbia University Press, 1974.

_____. ed. *China Under Mao: Politics Takes Command, Selections from "China Quarterly."* Cambridge, Mass.: MIT Press, 1966.

Mao's China: Party Reform Document, 1942–44. Translated by Boyd Comton. Seattle: University of Washington Press, 1952.

Mao Zedong. *Mao Zedong Xuanji* [Selected Works of Mao Zedong ("Little Red Book")]. 3d ed. Beijing: People's Press, 1969.

_____. *Selected Works of Mao Zedong.* Vol. 2–5. Beijing: Foreign Languages Press, 1967–77.

Markham, James W. *Voices of the Red Giants.* Ames: Iowa State University Press, 1967.

Mathews, Jay and Mathews, Linda. *One Billion: A China Chronicle.* Random House, n.d.

Merrill, John C. *Global Journalism.* New York: Longman, 1983.

Merrill, John C.; Bryan, Carter R.; and Alisky, Marvin. *The Foreign Press: A Survey of the World's Press.* Baton Rouge: Louisiana State University Press, 1970.

Nagel's Encyclopedia-Guide: China. English version by Anne L. Destenay. S.v. "Neolithic Era." Geneva: Nagel Publishers, 1968.

1980 Zhongguo Baike Nianjian [1980 China's Encyclopedia Yearbook]. S.v. "Xinwen" [News]. Beijing, Shanghai: China's Encyclopedia Publisher, 1980.

Nixon, Richard M. *Memoirs of Richard Nixon.* New York: Grosset and Dunlap, 1978.

Paulu, Burton. *Radio and Television Broadcasting in Eastern Europe.* Minneapolis: University of Minnesota Press, 1974.

Popper, K. R. *The Logic of Scientific Discovery.* New York: Basic Books, 1959.

Radio and Television in the People's Republic of China. Beijing: Ministry of Radio and Television, 1984.

Resolution on CPC History (1949–1981). Beijing: Foreign Languages Press, 1981.

Richstad, Jim, and Anderson, Michael H. *Crisis in International News: Policies and Prospects.* New York: Columbia University Press, 1981.

Roots, John McCook. *Chou.* Garden City, N.Y.: Doubleday and Co., 1978.

Salisbury, Harrison E. *The Long March, the Untold Story.* New York: Harper and Row, 1985.

Schramm, Wilbur, ed. *One Day in the World's Press.* Stanford, Calif.: Stanford University Press, 1959.

Schramm, Wilbur, and Lerner, Daniel., eds. *Communication and Change: The Last Years—and the Next.* Honolulu: University Press of Hawaii, 1976.

Schulthess, Emil; Hamm, Harry; Snow, Edgar; and Egli, Emil. *In China.* New York: Viking Press, 1966.

Schurmann, Franz, and Schramm, Wilbur. *The China Reader: Imperial China: The Decline of the Last Dynasty and the Origins of Modern China.* New York: Random House, Vintage Books, 1967.

_____. *The China Reader: Republican China: Nationalism, War, and the Rise of Communism 1911–1949.* Edited by Franz Schurmann and Orville Schell. New York: Random House, Vintage Books, 1967.

Sheridan, James E. *China in Disintegration: The Republican Era in Chinese History, 1912–1949.* New York: Free Press, 1975.

Snow, Edgar. *Red Star over China.* Revised edition. New York: Grove Press, 1978.

_____. *Sinuo Wenji* [Collected Works of Snow]. Translated by [Fan] Songjiu, Kenan, Kexiong (personal names). Beijing: Xinhua Press, 1984.

Snow, Lois Wheeler. *Edgar Snow's China.* New York: Random House, 1981.

Spence, Jonathan. *To Change China: Western Advisers in China 1620–1960.* New York: Penguin Books, 1980.

Teixeira, Manuel. *A Imprensa Periodica Portuguesa no Extremo-Oriente.* Macao (Macau): Noticias de Macau, 1965.

Terrill, Ross. *Eight Hundred Million: The Real China.* New York: Deli Publishing, Delta Book, 1972.

Thirty-Five Years of Radio Beijing (1947–1982). Beijing: Radio Beijing, 1982.

Ting Wang, ed. *Chung-kuo Ta-lu Hsin-wen-chieh Wenhua Takeming Tau-lia Hui-Pien* [A Compilation of Press Articles on Peking's News Policy during the Cultural Revolution]. Hong Kong: 1973.

Townsend, James R. *Political Participation in Communist China.* Berkeley and Los Angeles: University of California Press, 1967.

Tseng, H. P. *History of Chinese Journalism.* 2d ed. Taipei: Graduate School of Journalism, National Chengchi University, 1966.

Twelfth National Conference of CPC. Beijing: Foreign Languages Press, 1982.

Wang, James C. F. *The Cultural Revolution in China: An Annotated Bibliography.* New York and London: Garland Publishing, 1976.

_____. *Contemporary Chinese Politics.* Englewood Cliffs, N.J.: Prentice Hall, 1985.

Wang Hsueh-wen. *Chung-kung Wen-tzu Kai-ke Yu Han-tzu Ch'ien-t'u* [The Chinese Communists' Reform of Written Chinese and the Future of Chinese Character]. 2d ed. Taipei: Institute of International Relations, 1970.

Wheelwright, E.L., and McFarlane, Bruce. *The Chinese Road to Socialism: Economics of the Cultural Revolution.* New York: Monthly Review Press, 1970.

White, Theodore H. *In Search of History: A Personal Adventure.* New York: Harper and Row, 1978.

Wilson, Dick. *The Long March 1935: The Epic of Chinese Communism's Survival.* New York: Penguin Books, 1971.

_____. *Zhou Enlai.* New York: Viking Press, 1984.

Xinhua Tongxunshe Wushi Zhounian Jinian 1931–1981 [In Memory of the Fiftieth Anniversary of Xinhua News Agency]. Beijing: Xinhua News Agency, November 1981.

Yahuda, Michael. *Toward the End of Isolation: China's Foreign Policy After Mao.* New York: St. Martin's Press, 1983.

Yao Ming-le [pseud.] *The Conspiracy and Death of Lin Biao.* New York: Alfred A. Knopf, 1983.

Yu, Frederick T.C. *Mass Persuasion in Communist China.* New York: Praeger Publishers, 1964.

China Yearbook of Journalism 1982 (in Chinese). Beijing: China's Social Sciences Press, 1982.

China Yearbook of Journalism 1983 (in Chinese). Beijing: China's Social Sciences Press, 1982.

China Yearbook of Journalism 1984 (in Chinese). Beijing: China's Social Sciences Press, 1982.

Index